Viewing the Islamic Orient

Viewing the Islamic Orient

British Travel Writers of the Nineteenth Century

Pallavi Pandit Laisram

Routledge
Taylor & Francis Group

LONDON   NEW YORK   NEW DELHI

First published 2006
by Routledge
512 Mercantile House, 15 Kasturba Gandhi Marg, New Delhi 110001

Simultaneously published in UK
by Routledge
2 Park Square, Milton Park, Abingdon, Oxfordshire, OX14 4RN

First issued in paperback 2015

Routledge is an imprint of the Taylor and Francis Group, an informa business

© Pallavi Pandit Laisram 2006

Typeset by
Astricks
New Delhi, www.astricks.com

British Library Cataloguing in Publication Data
A catalogue record for this book is available from the British Library

ISBN-13: 978-1-138-66233-9 (pbk)
ISBN-13: 978-0-415-40115-9 (hbk)

For my professors and my family

Preface

L ife in the nineteenth century appears so backward and remote when compared to the growth of technology and explosion of knowledge in the twentieth century that we are tempted to think we have actually advanced and progressed, and become citizens of the world. While it is true that the world is far better connected than it ever was and we have access to almost anything we want from anywhere in the world (as long as we have the money and the education to acquire it), our progress as human beings has proceeded at a snail's pace. The political ambitions and cultural perceptions that determined and dominated a nineteenth century Western traveler's view of the Islamic Orient have remained largely unchanged in the twenty-first century.

The troubled relationship between the countries of the West and the Islamic Orient in the late twentieth and early twenty-first centuries echoes, sadly, the tensions that existed in the British relationship with the Orient in the nineteenth century. For the British empire, the Middle East was politically and economically very important as it formed the land route to India, "the jewel in the crown." Consequently, the empire used whatever means it could to maintain its influence over the region. Since the latter half of the twentieth century, the U.S. has, for a number of economic and political reasons, sought to gain control or influence over these countries. The players have changed, but the power games remain the same.

The similarities are so great that the events of the nineteenth and early twentieth centuries read like news items of our current times. The creation of Iraq in the early twentieth century in an attempt to create a friendly state in the region and the ethnic, religious, and territorial disputes that arose in the process are eerily similar to the re-creation of Iraq and the attempt to create another "friendly" Iraqi government. The "white man's burden," a popular notion in the nineteenth century, is echoed time and again in speeches and TV images: the world is being freed of dictators and being made safe for democracy by the white man; the "axis of evil" is being destroyed and the Western world is coming to liberate the Orient and the Oriental. Until the Abu Ghraib exposé, the world was provided images of kindly soldiers distributing sweets to children and saving Iraqis from themselves. The de-humanizing of the "other" as something dangerous and irrational that must be contained at all costs gives rise to a depressing sense of déjà vu. It seems as though ancient fears of Islam and war-like Turks have been resurrected. In fact, the term "crusade" has sometimes been used to describe the invasion of Iraq. The ethnic strife and communalism engendered by stirring up such fears has encouraged people to gravitate toward what they regard as their "own" place, their sense of culture and community, and to make distinctions of "us" and "them".

Constrained by the historical, cultural, and political environment of nineteenth century England, British travelers also, naturally, viewed the Islamic Orient in a binary and essentialist manner. However, the nature of long distance travel in that century created a sense of physical and social displacement, which, combined with their personal encounter with the "other", led them to question their culture's conceptions of the Islamic Orient even as they subscribed to the dominant Western view of the Orient. Their sense of cultural and moral superiority, awareness of their imperial power, imaginative domination of the Orient, and their arrogant desire to "improve" the East was undercut by their doubts about their own culture and the human relationships they formed during their travels. While they reflected their culture's biases, the experience of travel enabled them to challenge and question traditional distinctions of "us" and "them".

In the twenty-first century, where the "other" lives just around the corner or sits next to us in the subway, we have become like travelers within our own countries. Reaching beyond ourselves and trying to understand "them" (the "other" community or ethnic group we meet at work or in our neighborhood) as human beings and individuals, not as types, has become a necessity in our rainbow society. Nineteenth century travelers to the Orient could physically distance themselves from their homeland, but modern city dwellers have to undertake the daunting task of imaginatively experiencing displacement, both physical and social, to transcend their culture, and travel creatively into another culture. Like the earlier travelers, they may not always succeed, but at least they would have had an honest look at "us" and "them". Ultimately, only such mental journeys will help people avoid conflict, and allow a meaningful, non-hegemonic, cross-cultural dialogue to take place.

Acknowledgments

It has been my good fortune to have had professors and friends who have constantly challenged me and given me thought-provoking feedback. I am deeply indebted to them for their patience, guidance, and interest in my work. I am grateful to the librarians of Pattee Library who obtained the books and journals I required, and helped me research material for the book.

The anonymous reviewer of the book gave insightful feedback that helped me clarify my ideas, and Sayantani Dasgupta smoothed the process of preparing the manuscript for publication by her careful and thorough editing.

Throughout the process, my husband gave me endless cups of tea and my daughters thoughtfully tiptoed around because "Mummy is studying". They gave me the space I needed to focus on my work.

I would like to take this opportunity to thank all the authors — whom I have referred to in this study — for the wealth of knowledge I gained from their works.

Contents

Chapter 1

Viewing the Islamic Orient

In the nineteenth century the Western world viewed the Orient through a complex set of stereotypes. The Orient was seen as an exotic, erotic, frightening place, and also as an inferior, unprogressive place, forever trapped in time, simultaneously attractive and repulsive. Underlying these varied attitudes was the Western world's binary vision of East and West. While the West regarded events, incidents, and inhabitants of the East as stereotypically "Oriental" — in a static manner — without reference to social, economic, and historical forces, it viewed itself contextually as a living, developing force. That is to say, it perceived the Orient as a place essentially different from the West and judged it by a standard it never applied to itself. This perception of the Orient, according to Edward Said can be defined as "a style of thought based upon the ontological and epistemological distinction between 'the Orient' and . . . 'the Occident' " (Said 1978, reprinted 1979: 2).

Edward Said, the first major critic to pursue an extended study of this style of thought and representation, further defines Orientalism as "a system of knowledge about the Orient, an accepted grid for filtering through the Orient into Western consciousness" (ibid., 6). The West did not try to understand the Orient; instead, it perceived the Orient in a way that suited its emotional needs and its political aims. Orientalism thus constitutes an imaginative

"Western style for dominating . . . the Orient" (ibid., 3). In spite of Said's harshness toward Orientalism, we should keep in mind the fact that this discourse is the natural outcome of contact between technologically superior nations and alien cultures which are technologically inferior, and toward which it has colonial intentions. Since Britain remained a world power throughout the nineteenth century, this attitude ("latent Orientalism" as Said calls it) did not change in spite of a growing body of knowledge ("manifest Orientalism") about the Orient and its people.

Numerous political statements and literary works bear testimony to this binary view of East and West. But to generalize that all westerners shared this view of the Orient or to argue that westerners did not question this stereotypical view of the Islamic Orient would be to "Occidentalize" the West. In other words, by dismissing all nineteenth century Western works about the East as Orientalist, one would be making the same mistake as the Orientalists.

Did Western travelers to the Orient completely buy in to the traditional, culturally acceptable view of the East? To claim that they simply voiced Orientalist notions of the East would be to deny their individuality and to deny the impact that travel and separation from their homeland had on them. Close study of four popular and influential nineteenth century British travel writers — James Morier, Alexander Kinglake, Richard Burton, and Gertrude Bell — reveals that while they echoed the traditional, culturally defined view of the Islamic Orient, the space they occupied as travelers enabled them to imaginatively step out of their culture and to question its assumptions about the Orient. Their works reveal that though Orientalist discourse had an extremely strong influence on Englishmen, this discourse reflected a value system that was capable of being shaken and questioned. Therefore, to make generalizations about the Western perception of the Orient would be an oversimplification and an Occidentalization of Western cultures.

The social and political milieu of nineteenth century British travelers to the Orient can be best understood through a survey of the centuries' old fear, hatred, and rivalry that the West felt toward the Islamic Orient. And to understand the unique position of

British travelers to the Orient, it is necessary to examine French and British involvement with the Islamic Orient and to observe how their attitudes toward the Orient were based on their country's political and economic needs.

Europe and the Islamic Orient

The Orientalist attitude as it manifested itself in the relationship between Europe and the Islamic Orient is very interesting because of the long history shared by these two worlds. The Islamic Orient was the West's first point of contact with the East, and as the European empire expanded, the Islamic Orient also became a political lifeline to the Eastern colonies since it was the only land route to that part of the empire. At the same time, however, from the time of the rise and spread of Islam, Europeans have been aware of the threat the Islamic world posed psychologically and physically.

By its very definition Islam challenged Christian hegemony since it considered itself to be a completion and fulfillment of the message of Jesus, while the Christian world, not surprisingly, branded Islam a heresy, and proceeded to denigrate it. Muslims regard Christ as the forerunner of Prophet Mohammad, and, according to them, Christ had foretold the coming of the Prophet in the parable of the vineyard (Matthew 21: 33–44). The parable is about a householder whose son and servants were destroyed by the husbandmen to whom he let out his vineyard. When the householder sent his servant to collect the fruits, the husbandmen killed him, and one by one they murdered all the servants he sent, and, finally, even the son of the householder. The parable concludes that the householder will now "miserably destroy those wicked men, and will let out his vineyard unto other husbandmen, which shall render him the fruits in their season . . . the stone which the builders rejected, the same is become the head of the corner." These words are regarded as a reference to Ishmael, from whom the Muslims trace their descent. Ishmael is the "rejected" one, and the tribe of Ishmael constitutes the other "husbandmen" to whom the "vineyard" will be let out.

In addition, Muslims as rigid monotheists deny the Christian trinity and view Christ only as a prophet of God, not the son of God. They do not recognize his death and resurrection because, according to them, Christ was carried up to the heavens and someone else was crucified in his place; instead they regard Mohammad as the last prophet, and believe that to him alone did the Angel Gabriel fully reveal the word of God. And, to add insult to injury, they also believe that at the second coming Christ will come again to lead the faithful — Muslims — into heaven and will consign the rest to hell.

This psychological usurpation of the Christian covenant with God combined with the expansion of Islam through "forced" conversions as a result of the growing physical power of the Arab and the Ottoman empires in Europe (respectively) naturally created a sense of fear and endangerment in the Christian West.[1] Probably because of this sense of threat the West proceeded to caricature Islam and the Islamic Orient. Sixteenth century Europe, reeling under the might of Sultan Sulyman's (1520–1566) armies, attributed everything vile and despicable to the Turkish national character. The English dramas of the sixteenth and early seventeenth centuries, which are representative of the European vision of the Orient, provide ample proof of this attitude. Shakespeare's plays, for example, associate lust, cruelty, and deceit with the Turks. In *The Merchant of Venice* the Duke begs Shylock to have mercy on Antonio because the losses "That have of late so huddled on his back [Antonio's], / Enow to press a royal merchant down, / And pluck commiseration of [his state] / From brassy bosoms and rough hearts of flints, / From stubborn Turks, and Tartars never trained / To offices of tender courtesy" (IV. i. 28–33). The hard-hearted Turk is also considered deceitful in *Much Ado About Nothing* where Beatrice has "turn'd Turk" because she has broken her vow never to fall in love with a man. A more serious kind of treachery is associated with the Turks in *Richard III* when Hastings, justifying the assassination of Richard, says, "What? Think you we are Turks or infidels? / Or that we would against the form of law, / Proceed thus rashly in the villains death" (III. v. 41–43). Disorder and lawlessness, as can be seen from these words, are considered aspects of the Turkish character. Sexual lawlessness, or excess, too was commonly attributed to the Turks. In *King Lear* "poor Tom" (Edgar) claims that he "in woman out-paramour'd the Turk" (III. iv. 91–92).

The Orient was the "other" world — different, strange, frightening, and morally inferior to sixteenth and seventeenth century Europe; a world that constituted a threat to the Western Christian way of life. In *Dekker His Dreame*, 1620, Thomas Dekker fearfully describes

> The Turkish Halfe-moone on her silver Hornes
> Tosses the Christian Diadem, and adornes
> The Sphaere of Ottoman with Starry light,
> Stolne even from Those, under the Crosse who fight.

In this vision of the Armageddon, Dekker associates the religion and the martial aptitude of the Turks with the forces of evil. This fear of the "other" was dismissed, or at least contained, by the West through denigration of the enemy. The Orient, it appears, existed for Europe only in its imagination while the real Orient was disregarded. In a sense, as Said argues, even before the Orient was colonized it was dominated imaginatively (Said 1979: 49–72 passim).

Even the militarily superior and relatively secular nineteenth century West felt sufficiently uneasy about Islam to denigrate it and to indulge in character assassination of Prophet Mohammad. In his 1845 article (republished in an 1897 anthology), "The Mohammedan Controversy", well-known Arabic scholar and historian of Islam, Sir William Muir, identifies the sense of threat that the Christian world continued to feel.

> Mohammedanism is perhaps the only undisguised and formidable antagonist of Christianity. From all the varieties of heathen religions Christianity has nothing to fear, for they are but the passive exhibitions of gross darkness which must vanish before the light of the Gospel. But in Islam we have an active and powerful enemy; — a subtle usurper who has climbed into the throne under pretence of legitimate succession. . . . It is just because Mohammedanism acknowledges the divine original, and has borrowed so many of the weapons of Christianity, that it is so dangerous an

adversary. The length, too, of its reign, the rapidity of its early conquests, and the iron grasp with which it has retained and extended them, the wonderful tenacity and permanent character of its creed, — all combine to add strength to its claims and authority to its arguments.

When the first tide of Mohammedan invasion set in towards the West, its irresistible flood seemed about to overwhelm the whole of Europe and extinguish every trace of Christianity, . . . ; but though Europe, as a whole, successfully resisted the attack, yet Mohammedan settlements continued for centuries in various quarters to exist upon it. Again, during the twelfth and thirteenth centuries, when Europe poured forth her millions into the East, the Crusaders established for a length of time in Syria and the Holy Land, a succession of posts which in the end were gradually swept away by Moslem arms. And finally in the fifteenth century, the closing conquest of Constantinople and establishment of the Turkish empire with its extended frontier towards Hungary and Italy, confirmed and perpetuated the last and most intimate relations which have taken place between Europe and Islam (Muir 1897: 2).

Although safe from any further Islamic invasions it seems that the memory of earlier conquests still lingers on in the West and survives in its perception of Islam as a conceptual opponent to the Christian religion. Islam, it appears, is still regarded as a living and dangerous corruption within Christianity, capable of quoting scripture like the devil to support its claims. An important aspect to observe in Muir's argument is his association of Christianity with Europe; for instead of discussing how Christianity withstood Islam he analyzes how Europe resisted and fought against it. The world is thus divided not only along East–West lines but also Islamic–Christian in the sense that Christianity is regarded as Western and not Eastern. We will see James Justinian Morier making these same distinctions in *The Adventures of Hajji Baba of Ispahan* where he conveniently forgets that both the manners and the morals of Christianity arose in the Orient. Even the atheist Gertrude Bell once wrote in a letter home to her mother (in 1902) that she thought Christianity was beyond the Oriental mind.

The internal threat to Christianity from Islam is made visible in the way Mohammedans could and did question and challenge the Christian scriptures. Not only did the Muslims reinterpret the parable of the vineyard, they also identified discrepancies in the Christian faith as can be seen from Muir's summary of some arguments from a seventeenth century Muslim tract in which a "learned Mohammedan, Ahmed Ibn Zain-al-abidin" challenged the validity of Christianity:

> The fact that Christ did not punish the woman taken in adultery, *is assumed as conclusive evidence* that Christianity abrogated the Mosaical law. . . . Ahmed also gives the Catholics a sly hit about the Reformation: 'It appears that you Christians oppose all prophets. You need not, therefore, reproach and reprobate the English as you do. . . . You say that when some cursed persons came who endeavoured to corrupt the Holy Scriptures, they were unable to succeed; but corrupted only those books, which their own reprobate doctors had written out; and these are the English, some of whom are now at Isfahan' (emphasis mine ibid., 9).

Although, as a Christian, Muir should not be disturbed by the claim that Christianity abrogated the Mosaic law, the very presence of such criticism has clearly put him on the defensive. Such attacks also aggravated the difference between the Christian sects as can be seen from Ahmed Ibn Zain-al-abidin's comment which suggests that the English cannot be regarded as Christians. Such controversies continued well into the nineteenth century as can be seen from Muir's list of various published tracts: *Controversial tracts on Christianity and Mohammedanism etc.*, 1824; *Mizan-ul-Haqq; or, a Resolution of the Controversy between Christians and Mohammedans* (in Persian), 1835; *Controversial Epistles between the Rev. C.G. Pfander and Syad Rehmat Ali and Mohammed Kazim Ali* (Urdu manuscript); *Controversy between the Rev. C.G. Pfander and Moulavi Syad Ali Hassan* (in Urdu), 1845; *Khulasa-i-Saulat-uz-Zaigham: An Urdoo Tract in Refutation of Christianity*, 1258 Hegiri; Answer to the above, 1845. Considering the currency of such debates it is not surprising that in Morier's popular novel on Persia *The Adventures of Hajji Baba of Ispahan*, 1824, we are informed of the "Frank dervish" who engaged in discussion with the ulema (Muslim religious leaders, expounders of the Muslim law) to explain and defend the Christian faith.

Almost in a childish tit-for-tat manner Muir reduces the Prophet to a Machiavellian character rather than a spiritually inspired human being in his *Life of Mohammad*, 1858–61. Muir argues that Mohammad deliberately borrowed from, and was not just influenced by, different religions to appeal to all Arabs: "Had Mohammad, stern to his early convictions, followed the leading of Jewish and Christian truth, and inculcated upon his fellows their simple doctrine, there might have been a "SAINT MOHAMMAD" — more likely a "MOHAMMAD THE MARTYR" — laying the foundation stone of the Arabian Church. . . . Instead of all this, he, with consummate skill, devised a machinery [Islam]. . . . To the Christian, he was as a Christian; to the Jew he became as a Jew; to the idolator of Mecca, as a reformed worshipper of the Ka'ba. And thus by unparalleled art and a rare supremacy of mind, he persuaded the whole of Arabia, Pagan, Jew, and Christian, to follow his steps with docile submission" (Muir 1912: xcviii). If Islam is a subtle enemy, Muir is an equally subtle aggressor! Under the guise of admiration of Mohammad's superior skill he has reduced the Prophet to a self-aggrandizing, scheming politician.[2]

Knowledge, Power, and Orientalism

In the eighteenth and nineteenth centuries European knowledge of and exposure to the Islamic Orient increased and to some extent this created a restlessness with the inherited notions of the Oriental "other." At the same time, however, Western advances in technology led to a shift in power from East to West serving only to heighten its prejudiced sense of superiority toward the Orient (as it definitely did in Muir's case).

European awareness of the Islamic Orient during this period developed along both intellectual and diplomatic lines. In 1704 Antoine Galland translated the *Arabian Nights* into French and popularized it on the continent and in Britain. Religion and history were studied in detail by George Sale, translator of the Koran (1734), and the Arabic scholar Simon Ockley took the unusual step of using Arab sources to write his *History of the Saracens* in 1708–18. Diplomatic ties too were established between Europe and the Ottoman empire. In James Morier's *The Adventures of Hajji Baba of Ispahan* we are informed that "numerous ambassadors . . . flock here [Turkey] to rub their foreheads against the threshold of the Imperial Gate. So many of these dogs are here, that it is necessary to put one's trust in the mercies of Allah, such is the pollution they create" (Morier 1897: 547).

The general reading populace and the scholars of the West received one more source of information about the works of travelers and adventurers. Many Europeans learned Arabic and even undertook explorations in the Arabian peninsula, often financed by scholarly institutions or governments, and ultimately recounted their adventures in popular form. Carsten Neibuhr, who explored the southern part of the peninsula (now Yemen) in 1762, was a member of an expedition sponsored by King Frederick V of Denmark. His book, *Travels in Arabia*, 1772, became a source book for Edward Gibbon's chapters on the Arabs in *The Decline and Fall of the Roman Empire* (vol. V, 1788). Another famous explorer, John Lewis Burkhardt (a Swiss), successfully traveled to Mecca and Medina in 1814, masquerading as a Muslim convert. He was partially sponsored in that the Association for Promoting the Discovery of Africa (a British organization) gave him a grant to study at Cambridge in preparation for his travels. His account of his journey, *Travels in Arabia*, was posthumously published in 1829.

Lack of official backing did not deter explorers and scholars. Lieutenant Richard Francis Burton, scholar, explorer, espionage agent, took leave from the Indian army and traveled to Mecca and Medina in 1853, passing himself off as a Pathan. The itch for travel, and serious exploration, could not be contained and even Victorian women undertook long journeys in the Orient. The most famous of these is Gertrude Lowthian Bell who crossed the Syrian desert on camelback in 1905, accompanied only by Arabs.

Naturally, this close contact with the Islamic Orient led to a tension in the traditional attitude toward it. The Orientals were now no longer regarded only as a barbaric, inferior people, but instead were also perceived, by some, as intelligent, generous, human beings. In his *History of the Saracens* (1708–18), Ockley writes:

> in Al Mamoun's reign [AD 813] . . . learning began to be cultivated to a very great degree. . . . And this love of learning was not confined to the eastern part, but was diffused throughout the whole dominions of the Saracens . . . into Spain; so that when learning was quite lost in these western parts, it was restored by the Moors, to whom was owing whatever of philosophy was understood by the Christians of these times (Ockley 1848: xviii).

This was a very daring statement to make since it not only shows appreciation of Arab civilization, but also claims that the Western world is indebted to it.

However, such statements were rare, for the Western attitude of superiority, previously engendered by fear, was now being reinforced by changes in technology and by increase in political power. In the eighteenth and nineteenth centuries, Europe made great advances in technology, and, as a result the centre of power shifted from the East to the West. Such advances, as Philip Curtin has argued in *Imperialism* (1971), could only heighten feelings of superiority and arrogance: "superiority feeling[s which] had once rested on little more than religious arrogance and ordinary xenophobia, . . . could now be buttressed by demonstrable superiority in power and knowledge. The result for Western thought was a wave of unquestioning cultural arrogance that rose steadily until well into the twentieth century" (Curtin 1971: xv).

Even the new-found sciences of the Western world which were now brought to the study of Eastern culture were clearly unscientifically biased by the traditional Western attitude toward the East. The famous Swiss anatomist, Georges Cuvier, considered to be the founder of paleontology, too, was not free from ethnocentric biases in his study of comparative anatomy. In *The Animal Kingdom* (published 1817, English translation 1872) he stated that there were "intrinsic causes which seem to arrest the progress of particular races," and that of all races the Caucasian race is the most beautiful and the most intelligent. All civilized nations are, according to him, indebted to the Caucasian race for their origin whereas from the Arabian branch of races (Cuvier believes) has sprung religion, and sometimes also arts and sciences, "but always enveloped in a strange and figurative style." The Arabs are therefore not only non-Caucasian, and hence inferior and uncivilized, their culture is also totally alien and mysterious to the Caucasians. Cuvier's so-called scientific and "objective" analysis is simply reinforcing, and being reinforced by, the traditional binary distinctions of East and West.

Not only did the West consider itself superior, it also regarded itself duty-bound to rule and "improve" the inferior Eastern countries and thus early feelings of superiority now began to take the form of imperialism. Lord Curzon, Viceroy of India from 1898 to 1905, and Foreign Secretary from 1919 to 1924, was a strong advocate of this avuncular notion as is evident from a 1907 speech of his published as "The True Imperialism" in *The Nineteenth Century*:

> Wherever this Empire has extended its borders — and I am far from confining the claim to the British Empire, though I think it is on the whole more true of Anglo Saxon expansion than of other races — there misery and oppression, anarchy and destitution, superstition and bigotry have tended to disappear, and have been replaced by peace, justice and prosperity (Curzon 1908: 154).

The world was, for Curzon, divided into the Anglo-Saxon races and the "other" races. Other races may, according to him, create an empire, but only the Anglo-Saxons, a superior breed, do something worthwhile to justify it.

It appears that Orientalism, the imaginative domination of the Orient, not only supported the European colonial attitude, it was also in turn reinforced by the colonialists: while scholars supported colonialists and used their knowledge to help the expansion of the empire, the very triumph of the colonialists justified the scholar's attitude of superiority toward the Orient. For example, Napoleon Bonaparte's conquest of Egypt in 1798 was, according to Said's study, accompanied by a team of Orientalists whose specialized knowledge of Egypt enabled him to conquer that country. Although Napoleon's military force was limited, his scholars' knowledge of Egypt's political structure made it possible for him to

exploit the enmity between the Egyptians and the ruling Mamelukes (Tartar aristocrats) to his advantage (Said 1979: 82). Even
the adventurer Richard Burton, who journeyed to Mecca and
Medina in 1853 to demonstrate his abilities, collected information
specifically for the use of the Royal Geographical Society. Half a
century later, this dangerous and powerful alliance between Orientalists and politicians still continued as the British sought to use
the Arabs against the Turks in the First World War. Even the
financially independent explorer Gertrude Bell ultimately joined
the Arab Bureau in Basra in 1916 to do military intelligence work.

The interesting change that took place in Orientalist attitudes
during the eighteenth century was that in addition to the psychological necessity to define the Orient as some alien and inferior
world, the West also needed the Orient to fill an emotional need.
In other words, a new form of possession and colonization now
emerged in Orientalist discourse. The Orient was now not only
considered backward, it was also regarded as exotic and erotic, a
place of freedom and abandon in which the Europeans' repressed
objects of desire took material form. The Orient was regarded as
one long Arabian Night, sensuous and luxurious, a land where
dreams came true.

Lady Mary Wortley Montagu, who accompanied her husband,
the British ambassador, to Turkey in 1716, gives a romantic account
of that country in her *Letters*. The women she meets at a bath, all
of whom are naked, "walked and moved with the same majestic
grace which Milton describes of our general mother. There were
many amongst them as exactly proportioned as ever any goddess
was drawn by the pencil of Guido or Titian — and most of their
skins shiningly white, only adorned by their beautiful hair" (Montagu 1893: 258). The picture grows progressively more sensuous
as we see "so many fine women naked, in different postures . . .
and many negligently lying on their cushions, while their slaves
(generally pretty girls of seventeen or eighteen) were employed in
braiding their hair in pretty fancies" (ibid., 286).

Lady Montagu has her "pretty fancies" as can be seen from her
description of a harem where "jessamines and honeysuckles . . .
twisted round . . . [tree] trunks, shedding a soft perfume, increased

by a white marble fountain playing sweet water in the lower part of the room, which fell … with a pleasing sound" (ibid., 317). This poetical description is full of images of a languishing, feminine, luxurious East, an East which she labels a few pages later as "Mahomet's paradise." The early religious attacks on Islam as lascivious took a new form in the eighteenth and nineteenth centuries: "Mahomet's paradise" now became an object of desire.

Alexander William Kinglake (1809–1891), author of the popular travel narrative *Eothen* (1844), observes this romantic attitude toward the Orient in the behavior of his friend Henry Stuart Burton (called Carrigaholt in *Eothen*). Carrigaholt roams the East collecting "(not only the scenery) but also the many dramatis personae belonging to his dreams" (Kinglake 1845: 39). These dreams were of course very fanciful: Carrigaholt "would imagine that he had a martial aptitude, and his fancies would sketch a graceful picture, in which he appeared reclining on a divan, with a beautiful Greek woman fondly couched at his feet, and soothing him with the witchery of her guitar" (ibid., 39).

For Kinglake himself, his travel in the East was a journey into the self. In *Eothen* he writes of "a time for loathing the wearisome ways of society. … And the moody longing for Eastern travel … " (ibid., 97–98). The East grants him liberation: it is an escape for "one who is dying from very weariness of that . . . pains-taking governess Europe" (ibid., 98). Ultimately, however, he leaves the East because he feels that it is the "birthless past", a "decrepid [*sic*] World," whereas the West is "the future that has no end" (ibid., 223). So although the East may be considered attractive, and a necessary alter ego to the European conciousness, it was still regarded as inferior to the West. The Orient could be only what the Europeans wanted it to be; they "Orientalized" the Orient, as Edward Said observes.

So pervasive and powerful was Orientalist discourse in the European conception of the Islamic Orient that, according to Said, no one writing or thinking about the Orient — scientifically, politically or imaginatively — could ignore the large mass of Western works available on the Orient. The writer was conditioned by Orientalism and by the Orientalist archive, that is, the large mass of written and unwritten cultural attitudes toward the Orient.[3] As a result the subject, the Orient, disappeared, and all that remained were works by Orientalists that fed on their own preconceived notions of the Orient. Orientals were never consulted; instead, Orientalists cited only each other to corroborate or challenge the work of other Orientalists.

A twentieth century demonstration of this attitude can be seen in the Orientalist Bernard Lewis' review of *Orientalism* in the *New York Review of Books*, 1982. Lewis attacks Said mainly on two counts. In the first place, he disagrees with Said's definition of "Orientalism" and "Orientalist". According to Lewis, Orientalism is purely the unbiased, scholarly study of another culture. He legitimately claims that the study of another culture is not in itself an act of domination or exploitation. But, on the other hand, Lewis also criticizes Said, and defends Orientalism, by suggesting that Said should have appreciated the value of Western scholarly research instead of exploring its intentions and attitudes toward the Orient. Commenting sarcastically on Said's approach toward Western writings on the Orient, he argues that "[s]cholarly criticism of Orientalist scholarship is a legitimate and indeed a necessary, inherent part of the process. Fortunately, it is going on all the time — not a criticism of Orientalism, which would be meaningless, but a criticism of the research and results of individual scholars or schools of scholars" (Lewis 1982: 56).

In the process of justifying scholarly Orientalism, Lewis is obviously evading some of the major points Said makes. He fails to recognize that Said's purpose is to study the symbolic aspects of Orientalism. Said makes it clear that he is not concerning himself with the study of Orientalism as a "veridic discourse" about the Orient, but, instead, is interested in observing it as a symbol of Western dominance over the Orient. Lewis also refuses to observe that even scholarly studies can be unconsciously biased by historical and cultural circumstances. He sums up his argument by claiming that "the most rigourous and penetrating critique of Orientalist scholarship has always been and will always remain that of the Orientalists themselves" (ibid.). This statement implies that only westerners can critique other westerners, even when the "Oriental" is the topic of discussion. Unfortunately for Lewis, such an attitude actually strengthens Said's thesis that Orientalism is a symbol of Western dominance.

Britain and France in the Islamic Orient in the Nineteenth Century

The nineteenth century witnessed the rise of two major, but very different, colonial powers, France and Britain. Although these nations shared a common Orientalist discourse, they also had some specific differences in their attitude toward the Orient, differences born of their unique historical and political circumstances. It is because of these dissimilarities that this book limits itself to a study of British literature alone.

A brief survey of historical and political attitudes as they manifested themselves in influential politicians, writers, and important diplomats of Britain will serve to demonstrate the complex nature of their perception of the Orient. The British approach to the Orient in the nineteenth century reveals itself to be a complex set of attitudes that see-sawed between a traditional religious and cultural view and a perception conditioned by the political and economic exigencies of the existing situation. Their paradoxical and conflicting representations of the Orient emerge sharply in their struggle over Persia and in the three major crises they were involved with in the Ottoman territory: the Greek rebellion, the Crimean War, and the Russo–Turkish War.

The case of the British envoy to Persia, Harford Jones Brydges (henceforth referred to as Jones), is a striking example of the way attitudes toward the Orient are shaped by tradition and the flux of politics and personal experience. While Jones was in the powerful position of the factor of the East India Company in Basra in 1792 he behaved arrogantly and outrageously; but when his country sent him to Persia to salvage their relationship with that country he not only behaved more cordially toward the Orientals but also began to change his opinion of them and rejected the Western perception of Orientals. As the East India Company's representative in Basra, Jones occupied a powerful position since the company's agent there also possessed consular powers. His arrogance, and that of Samuel Manesty (the other agent), is evident in the way they chose to protect an inhabitant of Basra who was under British consular protection even though he had murdered another citizen (a Jew). Governor Suleiman Pasha's letter to the British ambassador reveals their overbearing behavior: according to the letter Jones and Manesty asked to have "14 Jews . . . bastondoed [*sic*], imprisoned, and condemned to pay 25000 Piastres." The Pasha regarded such behavior as "cruel" and "inhumane", and asked the ambassador to remove Manesty and Jones, such "overbearing treatment not being of a nature to be tolerated" (entire letter reproduced in Daniel 1966: 155–56). Like many Englishmen, Manesty and Jones behaved, or tried to behave, like self- appointed kings.

However, long residence in the East, and the changing political climate could, and did, lead to great changes in Harford Jones. The Jones we see in Persia (1809–1811) is very different from the young Jones at Basra. Jones was sent as His Majesty's Envoy to Tehran because the British were afraid that French or Afghan influence there would ultimately jeopardize their Indian empire. The historical circumstances that led the British to send an envoy to Persia and the problems that Jones had to face there in that position are well-analyzed by Denis Wright, a twentieth century British ambassador to Persia, in his 1977 study, *The English Amongst the Persians During the Qajar Period, 1787–1921*. According to Wright, the first threat to British interest in Persia by a European power took shape in the form of Napoleon's invasion of Egypt in 1798. It seemed possible that Napoleon might invade India through Persia and so, as a result, the Government of India sent a young officer, Captain John Malcolm, to Persia in 1800 to negotiate a treaty with the Shah, Fath Ali, that would nullify any such threat. Under this treaty it was agreed that the Shah would attack Afghan territory if that country invaded India, and would also prevent the French from residing in Persia. In return the British promised to provide Persia with arms and men in the event that the Afghans or the French attacked it. The treaty did not mention anything about Russian invasions, so when the Shah asked for help against the Russian attacks, he received no response from the British. In 1807, disappointed with this alliance, the Shah leaned toward the French and agreed to declare war on Britain and allow French troops to travel through Persia to India. Realizing the danger this situation posed to British India, the English government sent Jones to Persia to persuade the Shah to ally himself with the British again.

Since the English were now in the position of beggars, Jones adjusted his personality accordingly, won over the Persians and drove out the French. In his book, *An Account of the Transactions of His Majesty's Mission to the Court of Persia in the Years 1807–11* (published in 1834), Jones refers to himself with pride as "His Majesty's Envoy," and often refers to the Persians merely as "Orientals". But his book also reveals that he has learned to regard the Persians as people with intelligence and with feelings. Jones in fact consciously disassociates himself from supercilious, arrogant behavior. In his preface he states "[t]hat which I am most anxious to prove to you is that if the Persians, as a nation, are accused of being addicted to some heavy vices, they nevertheless possess many and great virtues. One may allow oneself to smile at some of the pages of Hajee [*sic*] Baba, but it would [not] be . . . wise to estimate the national character of the Persians from the adventures of that fictitious character" (Jones 1834: vol. 1, viii).

Harford Jones was also a strong critic of Captain Malcolm who sailed to Bushire (in Persia) on April 17, 1808, while Jones was still at sea *en route* to Persia, with a force of 500 marines and soldiers in an attempt to force the Shah to accede to the demands of the English. In his account of his mission to Persia, Jones called Malcolm's style of diplomacy the "Indian style". Arrogance, contempt, and lack of sensitivity toward the "Orientals" characterized this style of diplomacy. It was called the "Indian style" because the absolute power of the British in India had bred this attitude in Englishmen toward "Orientals". The possession of such an empire made English men and women extremely arrogant; Kinglake, Burton, Bell, all demonstrate this imperialistic behavior in their works. In fact, in the *Desert and the Sown* (1908) Bell goes so far as to express her conviction that the Arabs *want* to be ruled by the British.

However, living in the Islamic Orient, the English had to learn to moderate this type of behavior, particularly since the Persians clearly expressed their dislike of the Indian-trained English officer. Even as late as 1919 we find the Persian foreign minister in London requesting that none of the British experts to be sent to Persia "should be Indian officers or Indian officials . . . because there was a popular impression in this country that they did not treat Persians as equals" (Wright 1977: 20).

Britain's relationship with the other major power in the Islamic Orient, Turkey, was of a similar nature in that it fluctuated between arrogance and alliance. Ever since Napoleon's invasion of Egypt (1798) and Russia's expansion toward the Black Sea in 1774 the British were forced to take an active interest in Turkey to protect their own empire. On the one hand, the British wanted to protect Turkey so that she could act as a buffer between Europe and their Indian empire, but on the other hand, they also continued to despise the Turks as they had done for centuries. Britain's political relationship with Turkey clearly demonstrates how the English attitude see-sawed from arrogance to alliance.

The Greek rebellion of 1821 brought this paradoxical attitude toward Turkey to the forefront. According to Sir Llewellyn Woodward's study, *The Age of Reform 1815–1870*, the British foreign secretary George Canning (1822–1827, later prime minister from April 1827 to August 1827) refused to go to war with Turkey, but at the same time could not overlook the public interest in Greece, particularly since Lord Byron's death at Missolonghi in 1824, where he died fighting for Greek independence (Woodward 1962: vol. 13, 217). Ultimately, of course, the British government had to get involved: public pressure and fear of Russian expansion forced their hand. But even when they signed a settlement in February 1830 with Russia and France for the creation of an independent Greece, they made the new nation as small as possible, leaving thousands of Greeks under Turkish rule, because they feared Russian influence in that country (ibid., 221).

The decision to create a small Greece was not an easy one for the British Parliament. In his speech to the House of Lords on February 12, 1830, the Earl of Aberdeen, a cabinet member from 1828 to 1830, vehemently criticized a motion to vote on the creation of a large Greek nation and called it "an act of wanton spoliation on a friendly nation" [Turkey]. Aberdeen himself was torn between hatred for Turkey and the political necessity to be friendly toward Turkey for he states in this same speech that he and the Prime Minister, the Duke of Wellington (1828 to 1830), believe in "the importance of preserving the Turkish Empire. . . . I do not regret it [the weakening of the Turkish Empire] from any love of the Turks . . . God forbid! I have seen and known the effect of the barbarous rule existing there . . . " Aberdeen obviously cannot ignore either the traditional opinion toward Turkey, or the current political situation that necessitated the preservation of that nation.

Britain's foreign policy had become a domestic issue for her people in the nineteenth century, perhaps because the British economy was so closely tied to its Indian colony. As far as the activities in the Islamic Orient were concerned, it was an issue over which the Britons were clearly divided and about which they expressed their attitudes during the Crimean War and the pre-Russo–Turkish War tensions. In 1853, the English faced a political crisis that forced them to ally themselves with Turkey in spite of their uncordial relationship. When the Crimean War broke out between Russia and Turkey in 1853 — the British ambassador to Turkey, Lord Stratford de Redcliffe, was suspected in his own time for having engineered the War — Britain took military action in support of Turkey since it perceived Russia to be a great threat to its position in Asia. Defending Turkey of course meant that Turkish rule over the Balkan Christians would be prolonged. However, political expediency forced the British to desert the cause of fellow Christians.

When the Russo–Turkish War broke out in 1877, Britain again had to ally herself with Turkey. This time the British population was clearly divided into pro-Turkish and anti-Turkish supporters, and deciding which side to support became a very sensitive issue for Britons. According to the historian George Trevlyan's study, *British History in the Nineteenth Century (1782–1901)*, this event aroused "passions as hot as any that Englishmen had felt about the doings of foreigners since the days of Burke and the French Revolution" (Trevlyan 1922: 373). The Turkish suppression of their Bulgarian subjects during the 1876 Bulgarian uprising had inflamed British passions. This event, which came to be known as the "Bulgarian Atrocities," was used by William Ewart Gladstone (Prime Minister of England from 1869 to 1874, then 1880 to 1885, and again from 1892 to 1894, and then a member of the opposition party) to inflame the passions of the working class and the clergy against the Turks: "Five millions of Bulgarians, cowed and beaten to the ground, hardly venturing to look upwards, even to their Father in heaven, have extended their hands to you" he declared. Gladstone was clearly dividing the world in the age-old Christian versus Muslim pattern. He evidently had his finger on the pulse of public sentiment since his statement that the Turks should carry themselves "bag and baggage" out of Bulgaria, and hence virtually out of Europe, became very popular. (It should be noted that the Bulgarians were not merely a pathetic, oppressed people. According to Frederick William von Herbert in the *Defence of Plevna, 1877*, their behavior toward wounded Turkish soldiers in the battle of Plevna was inhumane, and "the departure of the Turkish army [from Plevna] handed the town over to the Christians — that is to murder, outrage, rape, robbery, plunder, sacrilege, all of which throve exceedingly well under the Bulgarian interim *regime*" [von Herbert 1895: 350].)

However, Benjamin Disraeli (Prime Minister of England, 1874 to 1880) did not want to attack Turkey for he was well aware that Russia had invaded Turkey not only to free the "oppressed" Christians but also to extend her political ambitions. Disraeli was not alone in fearing that if Russia gained a foothold in the Mediterranean, Britain's Indian possessions would be threatened. According to Trevlyan, he carried the "majority of the middle class . . . and, at the critical later stages of the affair, the mass of ordinary citizens whose instinct is to support their country" (Trevlyan 1922: 375).

Disraeli intervened finally in 1878 when Russia had crushed Turkey by forcing the two nations to abrogate their previous treaty and to accede to his proposals and sign the new Treaty of Berlin (1878). By this treaty he both exerted his power over Turkey and yet protected her dominions; while it provided for the creation of a small Bulgaria carved out of Turkey (instead of a large one as the Russians had hoped) it still, at the same time, restored territories lost by them to the Russians. By doing so Disraeli planned to keep Russia out of the Mediterranean and reduce her threat to India.

Britain's imperial interests thus always forced her to support the countries of the Islamic Orient while, on the other hand, she still retained a traditional sense of arrogance and contempt toward the very people their nation supported. Like Harford Jones Brydges, the English residing or traveling in the Islamic Orient must have felt a similar sense of tension and uneasiness in their relationship with the people of the Orient. The "Orientals" would have seemed to them as simultaneously friends and equals and also enemies who were beneath contempt. Perhaps that is why even though people like Burton, Kinglake, and Bell behaved like "uncrowned kings" of the Orient, they were also often critical of the English attitude toward the Orient. In his *Personal Narrative of a Pilgrimage to Al-Madinah and Meccah*, 1855, Burton goes so far as to mock the Western definition of Oriental slave trade as barbaric by arguing that the coquettish husband-hunting women of the West are also like slaves, selling themselves for a price. He could, and often did, judge East and West by the same standards, not always making the typical Orientalist binary division between East and West.

The French, unlike the British, did not possess great influence in the Islamic Orient. As a result of Harford Jones' successful mission to Persia in 1807 the French lost political influence over the Shah, and with the fall of Napoleon in 1815 France lost her influence in Turkey. According to Norman Daniel's study, Turkey had leaned toward France during Napoleon's reign partly because it feared his power, and partly because alliance with France would result in protection from Russia. But with the fall of Napoleon, Turkey became dependent on the goodwill of other European nations, particularly Britain (Daniel 1966: 160–76). Perhaps as the result of these circumstances French travel accounts of the Orient tend to be detached from imperial concerns and are instead intensely personal and private in nature.

Egypt was the only part of the Ottoman empire in which the French retained considerable power. In 1801 British troops had crushed the French army in Egypt, but Napoleon's popularity in that country ensured the continuing influence of the French.

According to Francis Steegmuller, editor and translator of *Flaubert in Egypt*, it was French influence that persuaded the Turkish sultan (nominal ruler of Egypt) to confer hereditary sovereignty on his viceroy Mohammad Ali in 1841. Mohammad Ali took many Frenchmen into his service, thus greatly increasing French influence in Egypt (Steegmuller 1972: 27). Even after the British occupation of Egypt in 1882 France retained considerable power in Egypt, and, according to Trevlyan, "remained until the end of the century, hostile to our [British] work and influence . . . " (Trevlyan 1922: 387).

The French lack of power in the Islamic Orient was probably one of the reasons that led to the difference between the French and the British attitudes toward it. The French attitude of superiority was one of racial arrogance; the British approach was not only racial, it was also imperialistic. Take for example Gustave Flaubert, and Richard Burton's behavior in a similar context.

In his account of his travels in Egypt (*Flaubert in Egypt*), 1849–1850, Gustave Flaubert explains why he and his friend, Maxine Du Camp, are only partially dressed like the natives:

> We look quite the pair of orientals — Max is especially marvellous when he smokes his *narghile* and fingers his beads. Considerations of safety limit our sartorial splurges: in Egypt the European is accorded greater respect than the native, so we won't dress up completely until we reach Syria (Steegmuller 1972: 42).

As can be seen, Flaubert's observations about the different treatment accorded to Europeans and natives is stated in a very matter-of-fact manner. It is merely a fact that he has to be aware of for "considerations of safety." His tone is light-hearted and playful and does not display an arrogant awareness of his racial superiority, or the power it extends to him, even though he was acting as a representative of his government in Egypt. Richard Burton's reaction in a similar situation while on his long trek to Mecca and Medina, in 1852, is quite different. While traveling from Alexandria to Cairo by steamboat, disguised as a dervish, he accidentally bumped into an Englishman who

> half publicly, half privily, as though communing with himself,

condemned my organs of vision because I happened to touch his elbow. He was a man in my service [that is, the Indian Army]; I pardoned him in consideration of the compliment paid to my disguise (Isabel Burton 1893: 34).

Burton is, in effect, implying that an Englishman may not be treated rudely, but that bullying of Orientals by an Englishman is appropriate. He not only condones British arrogance, he approves of it and expresses a sense of brotherhood with the Indian officer as "a man in my service."

The difference between Flaubert and Burton is clearly evident. Flaubert merely sees difference in treatment of Europeans and natives as a necessary fact to be aware of; he does not participate in this difference by using or approving the power it grants him. Moreover, Flaubert is not conscious of the status of being a Frenchman in Egypt. He calls himself a European, even though it was specifically the French who were powerful in Egypt. Burton, on the other hand, indirectly supports the arrogant behavior of the officer by approving it. His attitude reveals not only racial, but also imperialistic overtones in that he does not simply distinguish between the "Oriental" and the "European," but, more specifically, between the "Englishman" and the "Oriental".

Flaubert revealed racial superiority very often and reduced the Orient to no more than an object of curiosity, but he did not display this imperialistic arrogance. Referring to his exploits with the Egyptian prostitute Kuchuk Hanem in one of his letters in *Flaubert in Egypt*, he says:

> The oriental woman is no more than a machine: she makes no distinction between one man and another. Smoking, going to the baths, painting her eyelids and drinking coffee — such is the circle of her occupations within which her existence is confined (Steegmuller 1972: 220).

Flaubert not only reduces a human being to an object in this description, he reduces all Oriental women to a specific type. He speaks as though his experience with one woman, and that too a prostitute, gives him the insight to comment on all Oriental women.

The Orient evidently exists for Flaubert only in his imagination. One could say that he dominated the Orient by shaping it in the way most conducive to him.

The attitude of other French travelers to the Islamic Orient too reveals this imaginative, rather than imperialistic, domination. Perhaps it was the lack of popular interest in the happenings in the Ottoman empire that contributed to this style of thought. The French were not only less powerful than the British in the Islamic Orient, they also had less reason to be involved in its affairs. France had no great Indian empire to protect, and hence the preservation of the Ottoman empire was not as vital to its economic interests as it was to Britain. The only reason why the French wanted to preserve Turkey was to prevent Russia from becoming too powerful, an aim that they could achieve without involvement in the Ottoman empire.

Alphonse de Lamartine (1790–1863), poet, philosopher, orator, rabble-rouser, and leader of the Provisional Government that was established after the fall of King Louise Phillipe in 1848, presents a succinct description of the nature of French interest in Turkey. In his account of his travels, *A Pilgrimage to the Holy Land*, 1835, he argues that supporting the Ottoman empire would be sound policy only "if there were still Turks capable of creating and organizing, not an army only, but a government which might observe the rear of the Russian Empire, and give her serious disquiet, while southern Europe engaged her in front . . ." (Lamartine 1978: 486). However, he fears that Turkey will fall and in consequence

> Russia will occupy the coasts of the Black Sea and Constantinople, Austria will spread herself over Servia, Bulgaria, and Macedonia to keep pace with Russia; France, England, and Greece, after disputing the road for some time, will respectively take possession of Egypt, Syria, Cyprus, and the Islands. . . . But, meanwhile torrents of blood will have flowed by sea and by land. . . . You will find more extensive deserts than ever the Turks had left (ibid., 487–88).

Fear of Russian expansion, and fear of a European war were the only reasons that motivated French interest in the Ottoman empire. And, as Lamartine argues, this was a matter that could be settled even without involvement in the politics of Turkey. All that the European nations have to do, he says, is to determine beforehand how the Turkish empire was to be divided and sign a treaty on that issue, thus ensuring its peaceful and equitable takeover!

Clearly only a politician, only someone who understands the intricacies of the relationships between the different European nations, would be capable of analyzing the situation the way Lamartine did. French popular opinion could not be expected to, and did not, perceive the situation in this light. According to Lynn Case's study, *French Opinion on War and Diplomacy During the Second Empire*, the French populace did not want to have any part of the Crimean War: they did not want to go to war, and they did not want to ally themselves with their traditional enemy, England. They finally became enthusiastic about the war when they realized that French interests in the Mediterranean would be affected by Russian expansion; but this interest was short-lived. As the war dragged on "war was neither accepted nor waged with enthusiasm" (Case 1954: 50). The moment the war was over, in 1856, the French government turned its back on England and proceeded to improve its relationship with Russia. The French were definitely more concerned with their European than their Eastern interests.

The French attitude during the Russo–Turkish War of 1877 was clear cut: they did not want to get involved for peace was, above all, most important to them. According to E. Malcolm Carroll in his study *French Public Opinion and Foreign Affairs 1870–1914*, "[t]he few in France who had shown any interest in the Near Eastern crisis and the Russo–Turkish War were agreed that the country must not be involved. The Serbs as disturbers of the peace, received little sympathy, and Russia was given no encouragement" (Carroll 1931: 76). Obviously, the French did not want to ally themselves with anybody; they preferred to remain neutral.

Not surprisingly, French literature on the Orient was of a personal, philosophical, nature. Even Lamartine's narrative of his trip to the East is concerned more with private meditations than with expressions of political power. In his *A Pilgrimage to the Holy Land* Lamartine is on a journey of religious regeneration, on a voyage in which his "imagination was enamoured of the sea, the mountains, the manners, and the traces of the Deity in the East. All my life the East had been the waking dream of my darksome days, in the autumnal and winter fogs of my natal valley" (Lamartine 1978: 16). The East is a private, poetical world for Lamartine. The English title of his book is metaphorically far more appropriate than the literally correct French title, *Voyage en Orient*.

Only at the very end of his account does he add a few pages called "Political Reflections." Neither physically, on the page, nor psychologically, do his political reflections on the crumbling Ottoman empire mix or intertwine with his view of the East as a place of spiritual regeneration. We do not see that tension of personal and political feelings that we find in the British perspective of the Orient, and which we shall see in their travel accounts.

To the French writer Gerard de Nerval (1808–1855) the journey to the East (in 1843) is a quest for meaning. His *Journey to the Orient* is a set of stories within stories, each one narrated either by his persona or a character within the story, with each story exploring questions of, among others, justice, art, wisdom, reality, womanhood. The people of the Orient cease to matter to Nerval and the Orient itself is regarded as merely a place where his imagination can have free rein. Had he remained in Paris, he would have been in a "hotel room, crammed with such knobby furniture that my imagination, like an imprisoned fly, will collide against one window after the other" (Nerval 1972: 23).

The nineteenth century French response to the Orient is undoubtedly one of domination for they viewed the Orient not as a living place but as an object, subject to their needs as Kuchuk Hanem was to Flaubert. But their perception of the Orient is of a relatively uncomplicated kind in that the personal response to the Orient was not distracted by an imperialistic attitude (if any) as the British approach was. The British response is more interesting because the private feeling for the Orient was often at variance with, and conscious of, the traditional attitude of superiority. The constant tension in the British political view of the Ottoman empire must have, to some extent, created the enviroment for such conflicting attitudes within individuals.

Studies on Orientalism

In the twentieth century, for the first time, the "Orientals" began to speak out against Orientalism. Even Western writers expressed their dissatisfaction with the Orientalist perception of the East. Edward Said's groundbreaking study *Orientalism*, 1978, not only created a considerable stir because of its militancy, it also analyzed the issue in a new light. While historical works like Norman Daniel's *Islam, Europe and Empire*, 1966, and V.G. Kiernan's *The Lords of Human Kind*, 1969, demonstrate only the development and changes in Western cultural attitudes toward the Orient, Said's study enables us to see these various perceptions of the Orient (as described earlier) as a discourse of power. *Orientalism* triggered considerable debate, both positive and negative, and was soon followed by other works examining the many facets of the Western representations of the Orient. The following selection surveys only the major issues relevant to this study.

The Western attitude toward the Orient, Said argues, was based on the premise that the Orient and the Occident are essentially different, and that "we", the Occidentals, are superior to "them", the Orientals. Thus an imaginative domination of the Orient exists at the root of all Western perceptions of it. Whether the Orient was regarded as an exotic or backward place by the West, this vision, according to Said, was a European invention. As already demonstrated in the historical survey, the West "Orientalized" the East: it claimed the right to define the Orient in the most convenient way. Orientalism, as Said defines it, is precisely this act of domination and manipulation of the Orient. Said's major point is that this need to define, and thus dominate, the Orient grew out of geographical, political, and historical circumstances. These circumstances in the West subjected its "knowledge" of the Orient — imaginative and scientific — to a will-to-power as can be seen in the historical survey presented earlier in this chapter. The Western colonial domination of the East in the nineteenth century is merely the culmination of an older, imaginative domination.

Knowledge of the Orient, even the so-called academic, objective knowledge, is permeated by this imaginative distinction of "us" versus "them". All knowledge of the Orient by an Occidental, Said argues, is therefore an act of imaginative domination. Said is not concerned with the validity of the observations made about the Orient, but with the symbolic act of observation: according to him "Orientalism is more particularly valuable as a sign of European–Atlantic power over the Orient than it is as a veridic discourse about the Orient (which is what, in its academic or scholarly form it claims to be)" (Said 1979: 6).

Said's attitude toward "knowledge" is open to question. On the one hand, there is considerable truth in his approach for the act of structuring and defining the Orient, the act of claiming to "know" the Orient, can be, and often is a symbolic act of appropriation and domination. Take for example the work of the nineteenth century historian Sir William Muir. His account of *The Life of Mohammad* (1912) is derived from various Arabic sources, but all that scholarly research ultimately only seems to be saying that "Islam and its followers, the Arabs, are inferior because I know they are inferior." The thrust of the entire book is to explain why Islam succeeded and thus to explain away this frightening phenomenon. According to Muir, Mohammad would not have succeeded if he had not received help from some perverted Jews and Christians, thus reducing Islam to a heresy, an offshoot of Christianity. Muir's "objective" study is therefore really a "subjective" study in that it merely echoed the traditional Western attitude toward the Islamic Orient.

On the other hand, this concept of knowledge as a form of power is very restrictive since it implies that no one can study another culture without in some way dominating it, without reflecting the power structure of that particular day and age. Said has failed to take into account the humanistic desire for knowledge. He makes only a passing reference to the great Persian scholar Edward Granville Browne (1862–1926) who translated a great deal of Persian works, and also did considerable research on Persian literature. Browne studied this area because he loved and admired the Persians, and the Persians, if not Said, showed their appreciation of him through speeches, gifts, and finally by conferring on him the royal Order of the Lion and the Sun.

"Knowledge" should therefore not be regarded as intrinsically a source of power, except when it is used as such, as it was, for example, by Napoleon Bonaparte. Said is correct in arguing that political-historical circumstances condition knowledge — Sir Muir's study is a good example of this thesis — but to argue that all knowledge by itself is a form of power is very limiting since it does not take into account an individual's imaginative opposition to his own culture's norms. As we will see, for very different personal reasons neither Gertrude Bell nor Richard Burton felt completely at home in British society and expressed their unease in their resistance to Orientalist perceptions of the East.

Said seems to realize that individuals did struggle against the dominant Western concept of the Orient. He defines three categories of writers who lived in the Orient:

> One: the writer who intends to use his residence for the specific task of providing professional Orientalism with scientific material, who considers his residence a form of scientific observation. Two: the writer who intends the same purpose but is less willing to sacrifice the eccentricity and style of his individual consciousness to impersonal Orientalist definitions. . . . Three: the writer for whom a real or metaphorical trip to the Orient is the fulfillment of some deeply felt and urgent project. . . . In categories two and three there is considerable more space than in one for the play of a personal — or at least non-Orientalist — consciousness (Said 1979: 157–58).

Category two is by far the most interesting one. In this category there is bound to be a tension between the Orientalist and the non-Orientalist perceptions of the East. All four authors in my study fall into this category.

Said, however, does a very biased and inadequate analysis of Richard Burton's *Pilgrimage*. He argues, on the one hand, that Burton was able to participate completely in a foreign culture and see "Oriental life from the viewpoint of a person immersed in it" (ibid., 196). However, Said goes on to reason, Burton was able to integrate himself completely with another culture only because he had "a European's self-awareness of society as a collection of rules and practices" (ibid., 197). Since, he continues, this kind of know-ledge is accessible only to a European, Burton's informed participation in Oriental life is also an aspect of European domination. This is a cyclical argument: damned if you do not understand the Orient, damned if you do.

However, an important contribution of Said to the study of literary texts is his recognition of the different techniques of character portrayal and narration that reduce the Orient and its people to a set of objects to be observed by the Western world. Typology in literature, for example, is one of the ways in which a character is reduced to a static object with a static set of qualities. Said's brilliant analysis of Gertrude Bell's reductive rhetorical style is worth quoting. In a letter to her stepmother about Damascus, in 1905, Bell claims that

> The defeat of Russia stands for a great deal, and my impression is that the vigorous policy of Lord Curzon in the Persian Gulf and on the Indian frontier stands for a great deal more. No one who does not know the East can realize how it all hangs together. It is scarcely an exaggeration to say that if the English mission had been turned back from the gates of Kabul, the English tourist would be frowned upon in the streets of Damascus.

This innocent looking description of events insinuates a very reductive picture of the Arabs. Said analyzes the Orientalist implications of this passage crisply: "In such statements as these, we note immediately that "the Arab" or "Arabs" have an aura of apartness, definiteness, and collective self-consistency such as to wipe out any traces of individual Arabs with narratable life histories" (ibid., 229). The Arabs, as Said correctly observes, have been reduced to single, homogenous types by Bell.

This book of travel accounts of the Orient both builds on and questions Said's work. His definition of Orientalism as a system of European domination and his analysis of the stylistic manifestations of this discourse in literature is the basis of this study. However, unlike Said's, my work aims to be more receptive toward the individualistic, non-Orientalist tendency in Western writing on the Orient.

Although Said initiated this type of close study of Western perspectives of the Orient he often unfortunately undermined his arguments, as seen here, by his "Occidentalism". Some other scholars who preceded and followed him, as will be seen, achieved a more balanced, middle-of-the-road, perspective on Orientalism. In his study, *Oriental Essays: Portraits of Seven Scholars*, 1960, A.J. Arberry, a Western scholar of the Orient himself, recognizes that there is much that is wrong with Oriental studies, and with the overall Western approach to the Orient; but he also realizes that there were some scholars who used their skills "to help build a bridge between the peoples and cultures of Asia and Europe" (7).

Arberry is as aware as Said of the static Western conception of the Arabs:

> For instance, from what sources has the average Englishman or American drawn his idea of the Arabs? First and foremost I suppose the *Arabian Nights*. . . . For him . . . the life, the manners, the ideals, the dreams of the Arabs down the ages are all contained within the pages of the *Arabian Nights* (Arberry 1960: 252–53).

He is also aware that even academicians have been responsible for perpetrating this attitude: "he [the reader of the Koran] will have been repelled by the most widely circulated travesties which masquerade as translations of that sacred and poetical work" (ibid., 253). The true scholar, he argues, must courageously take on the frustrating task of clearing a "vast accumulation of nonsense and misapprehension and deliberate lies" about the East.

Arberry's study is not an analysis of the causes of this "vast accumulation of nonsense," but he knows it exists and does not hesitate to give an honest portrayal of it. The bulk of his study is about the life and work of seven Oriental scholars who used their knowledge to bring the East and the West closer together. Two of the scholars he studies are Simon Ockley, and E.G. Browne, the great Persian scholar.

Arberry's study of Simon Ockley is of particular interest because of the way it differs from Said's image of Ockley. Arberry recognizes the courage and true scholarship that Ockley demonstrated in insisting that academicians should study Arabic and read the

Koran in the original. This was a remarkable demand, states Arberry, considering that the only existing English version of the Koran was translated from the French, and was written with the express intention of showing that it was a trivial book, "a gallimaufry of Errors" and "a misshapen issue of Mahomet's Brain" (ibid., 15). However, in spite of his insistence on an honest portrayal of the history and the achievements of the Arabs, Ockley maintained that the Prophet Mohammad was an imposter. Arberry tries to understand why Ockley adopted this attitude in spite of his "advocacy of things Arabic." He argues convincingly that Ockley's "small means and a large family make a combination little apt to encourage nonconformity" (ibid., 22). Moreover, as an aspirant for the Arabic chair at Cambridge, maintains Arberry, Ockley had to remain within orthodox limits. Ockley was so poor that he wound up in debtor's prison in 1717. And Cambridge was so orthodox that in 1710 it expelled Ockley's colleague, William, a physicist who occupied Issac Newton's chair, for a heretical claim that he made based on a translation of an Arabic manuscript.

Said, on the other hand, refuses to consider Ockley's situation and ignores his scholarly work and his sympathetic understanding of Arab history. The only observation Said makes is that Ockley "made it clear that Islam was an outrageous heresy," whereas the courageous William got expelled from Cambridge for his "Islamic enthusiasm" (Said 1979: 76). Without considering the situation he adopts an "us" Orientals versus "them" Occidentals attitude toward Ockley. We know that Said is aware of Ockley's financial condition because he quotes from Arberry's essay on Ockley; but Said has used the material as selectively, and as unjustly, as the Orientalists themselves.

Anouar Abdel-Malek is another scholar who takes a more balanced approach toward Orientalists. His short article "Orientalism in Crisis", 1963, influenced Said considerably. Said has quoted extensively in *Orientalism* from Abdel-Malek's article, and expanded on it considerably. There are, however, two major differences between Said and Abdel-Malek: (*i*) Abdel-Malek does not perceive knowledge of the Orient as intrinsically an act of domination; and (*ii*) he does not view academic Orientalists as deliberately evil individuals (as the harshness of Said's attitude toward them tends to suggest), but rather, like Arberry, he sees them as victims of a socio-political system.

Abdel-Malek differentiates between two kinds of Orientalism: the traditional or academic Orientalism, and the politically motivated Orientalism. He then proceeds to divide the traditional Orientalists into two categories, the humanists and the special interest groups. The humanists group, he argues, tried to build a bridge between two cultures rather than make binary divisions. However, while not denying the existence of genuine scholars of the Orient, nor the excellent work they did studying ancient civilizations and rescuing old manuscripts, Abdel-Malek does question their methodology and conclusions which, he argues, were compromised by the political climate of the day. Such scholars (he does not name them) were, in a sense victims of their society because they were *"objectively"* led to the "politico-philosophical positions of the other group of researchers" (Abdel-Malek 1963: 106). The other academic Orientalists, he continues, are comprised of special interest groups like merchants, politicians, and intelligence officers "whose only objective was to gather intelligence information in the area to be occupied, to penetrate the consciousness of the people in order to better assure its enslavement to the European powers" (ibid., 107). Abdel-Malek does not mention any specific people, but Gertrude Bell and her colleagues who worked at the Arab Bureau in Basra immediately come to mind.

As a result of the influence of one group of Orientalists on the other group, Abdel-Malek argues that the two different schools share a similar conception of the Orient, and use a common methodological approach to it. It is this approach to the Orient that Said, sixteen years later, termed "Orientalism." Abdel-Malek did not give it a critical term, but he defined it far more clearly and succinctly than Said. This article is therefore very helpful though the translation makes the following passages seem a bit choppy and abrupt.

1) *General conception*, that is the vision of the Orient and Orientalism . . . :

a) On the level of the *position of the problem*, and the *problematic*, the two groups consider the Orient and Orientals as an "object" of study, stamped with an otherness — as all that is different, whether it be "subject" or "object" — but of a constitutive otherness, of an essentialist character. . . . This "object" of study will be, as is customary, passive, non-participating, endowed with a "historical" subjectivity, above all non-active, non-autonomous, nonsovereign with regard to itself: the only Orient or Oriental subject which could be admitted . . . is the alienated being, philosophically, that is, other than itself in relationship to itself, posed, understood, defined — and acted — by others.

b) On the level of the *thematic*, both groups adopt an essentialist conception of the countries, nations and peoples of the Orient under study, a conception which expresses itself through a characterized ethnist typology; the second group will soon proceed with it to racism.

According to the traditional orientalists [both groups], an essence should exist . . . which constitutes the inalienable and common basis of all the beings considered; this essence is both "historical," since it goes back to the dawn of history, and fundamentally a-historical, since it transfixes the being . . . within its inalienable and non-evolutive specificity, instead of defining it as all other beings, states, nations, peoples and cultures — as a product . . . in the field of historical evolution.

Thus one ends with a typology — based on real specificity, but detached from history, and, consequently, conceived as being intangible, essential — which makes of the studied "object" another being, with regard to whom the studying subject is transcendent . . . the man — the "normal man" it is understood — being the European man . . . (107–8).

In section 'a' Abdel-Malek is defining what Said was later to call the "binary" conception of the world. The West regarded the Orient as a "constitutive otherness"; as something that is by its very nature different from the West. The "object", the Orient, is absolutely dehumanized, and exists only as it is defined by the West. In the historical survey I have already demonstrated how Western scholars, travelers, and colonialists — people like Cuvier, Lady Montagu, and Lord Curzon — dehumanized and "Orientalized" the Orient. The paradox of Orientalism is that it was based on "real specificity", as Abdel-Malek explains in section 'b'. Orientalists gathered data about different cultures, but they perceived this research material in a static sense; they reduced the Orient to a "type" which always possessed, and will always possess, certain attributes. Lady Montague's vision of the Orient as the sensuous world of *Arabian Nights* is a manifestation of this static approach to the Orient.

The Western conception of the Orient as a static world determined, according to Abdel-Malek, the very methods by which it was studied. The Orientalists studied only the past of the Oriental nations because the past alone was considered its most glorious period. "This past itself was studied in its cultural aspects — notably the language and religion — detached from social evolution," and this led to many erroneous conclusions because they studied a living culture as if it was a dead culture: "[h]istory, studied as 'structure' was projected, at its best, on the recent past. That which re-emerged, appeared as a prolongation of the past, grandiose but extinct. From historicizing, history became exotic" (Abdel Malek 1963: 110). Obviously, such an attitude was going to affect the selection and description of the Orient in literary works. As will be seen in subsequent chapters, the works of Morier, Kinglake, Burton, and Bell use various literary devices that reveal a reductive conceptual and methodological approach to the Orient.

Mary Louise Pratt's article "Conventions of Representation: Where Discourse and Ideology Meet," 1982, is not on Orientalism, but it is relevant to this subject because it is an analysis of the ideological dimensions of the aesthetics of novels and non-fictional travel literature. Of particular interest is her analysis of a landscape description by Burton (in *The Lake Regions of Central Africa*). Burton's descriptive style, his choice of adjectives, and selection of detail, are all shown to be images of domination. Her study demonstrates that Burton's portrayal of the scenery surrounding Lake Tanganyika is like the description of a painting. Burton finds that it lacks the "finish of Art", and suggests various changes that would make it more beautiful. Burton's description, according to Pratt, is a "depiction of the 'civilizing mission' as an esthetic project . . . an

old and familiar strategy in Western imperialism" (Pratt 1982: 147).
"Landscape descriptions" thus "in some cases embody, esthetically
and ideologically a kind of discourse of empire" (ibid., 144–45).
Although Pratt's study enables us to see that a variety of different
techniques can be used to dominate the "object", it is impossible
to identify and catalogue the different literary devices available to
the creative writer. Ethnist typology and ahistorical descriptions
are only a few of the modes that a writer utilizes.

Domination of the Orient can even take the form of psychological instrumentality. As noted earlier in the historical survey,
the Western world's hidden desires led to a portrayal of the Orient
as a place of sexual freedom. In his study, "Orientalism and the
Problem of Civil Society in Islam", Bryan S. Turner, a sociologist,
observes that even comments on the political systems of the Orient
had an underlying psychological necessity. Turner views the Orientalists' distorted attitude toward Islamic polity as an expression
of the West's anxieties about its own monarchy:

> The debate about Oriental Despotism took place in the context
> of uncertainty about Enlightened Despotism and Monarchy in
> Europe. . . . These problems and anxieties were consequently
> transformed onto the orient which became, not a representation
> of the East, but a caricature of the West (Turner 1984: 39-40).

In "Orientalism and the Arab Elite", 1982, M'hammad
Benaboud identifies some other factors that dominated the ideological orientation of the Orientalists from the mid-nineteenth to
the first half of the twentieth centuries. One of these is very relevant
to this study: colonialism. According to him, although many European Orientalists supported and promoted colonialism "even
through their pursuit of Arabic and Islamic studies," the actual
conditions of their work were very complex in that they too were
in some ways victims of their political system since they had to
depend on colonialism for "financial resources, [and] their recognition as scholars" (Benaboud 1982: 7, 9). So like Simon Ockley
in the early eighteenth century, even nineteenth century Orientalists had to cater to the system. Benaboud discusses only the political
environment of the Orientalists; he does not explore the various

different ways in which it would have affected them. But from his description of the political context of the Orientalists one can theorize that strong individuals must have felt the tension between their private opinions and their dependency on colonialism.

Other studies examine different aspects of Orientalism, but this selection surveys the major issues relevant to this work. In my analysis of the writings of four nineteenth century British travelers I wish to study not only the literary manifestations of Orientalism, but also the areas of tension and conflict between individual perspectives and the Orientalist tradition. While Said's definition of Orientalism is pertinent it would be a mistake to generalize about Western writers since the West did not always use the Orient but also made a genuine attempt to understand it.

Travel Writers

A considerable number of travel accounts of the Orient were written in Britain in the nineteenth century. Some of the very popular writers and their works were James J. Morier's *The Adventures of Hajji Baba of Ispahan*, 1824; Alexander W. Kinglake's *Eothen*, 1844; Sir Richard Francis Burton's *Personal Narrative of a Pilgrimage to Al-Madinah and Meccah*, 1855; and Gertrude Lowthian Bell's *Syria: The Desert and the Sown*, 1907.

Travel literature was immensely popular in the nineteenth century and therefore a good indicator of cultural attitudes. In a letter dated August 28, 1813, Lord Byron advises his friend, the poet Thomas Moore, to "stick to the East — the oracle . . . told me . . . it was the only poetical policy. The North, South and West have all been exhausted; but from the East we have nothing . . . the public are orientalizing and pave the path for you" (Marchand: 1974). Considering the huge number of people who published records of their travels we can conjecture that such literature must have been a flourishing industry. In his history of Persia, *Persia and the Persian Question*, Lord Curzon writes that "the entry to Persia having been reopened by European diplomacy [in the nineteenth century], a stream of travellers has followed in the wake of plenipotentiaries, ministers and envoys, both classes devoting themselves with equal assiduity to the literary record of their experiences" (Curzon 1892: vol. 1, 20).

These travelers not only reflected their culture, they also challenged its assumptions about the Orient — some with greater intensity than others. Unlike Thomas Cook's tourists, who would be served a typical British breakfast even in the middle of a desert, independent travelers received considerable exposure to the Orient because they had to make their own travel arrangements and often live and work with the locals. Under these circumstances, they were likely to distance themselves from the biases of their homeland or at least feel uneasy about expressing their cultural biases. Just as Britain's political culture see-sawed between alliance and arrogance, so did the British traveler to the Orient fluctuate between cultural biases and opinions formed through personal contact with the locals. As a result, such a traveler could, and did, challenge "manifest Orientalism", and even questioned the so-called "differences" between West and East, civilized and uncivilized, progressive and backward.

These travel writers not only reflected and resisted cultural stereotypes, they also influenced their culture. After Kinglake's *Eothen* was published, every visitor to the East felt he just had to read it. On board ship *en route* to the Orient, Thackeray could not even obtain a copy of *Eothen* because of the general scramble for it. Morier's *Hajji Baba of Ispahan* was read throughout the nineteenth century by politicians and generals as a way of understanding and manipulating the Persian people.

The unease that these travel writers felt with their culture's assumptions about and attitude towards the Orient and the popularity of their travel accounts suggest that the nineteenth century British view of the East was not as homogenous as it has often been considered. While there is no denying that the dominant view of the East was typically Orientalist and imperialist in nature, there was another perception of the East that ran counter to this view. This counter-current, which can be seen in the travel accounts of popular writers like Morier, Kinglake, Bell and Burton, is more visible in the writings of less known nineteenth century travelers like Harford Jones Brydges, Charles Frederic Moberly Bell, and

Frederick William von Herbert. These writers not only sought to perceive the East in a non-Orientalist manner, they also challenged the traditional Western perception of the Orient. In fact, Harford Jones, in his account of his travels (*Transactions*), consciously sought to distance himself from the image of the Orient conveyed by Morier's *Hajji Baba of Ispahan*.

One can only conjecture why some travel writers challenged their culture's view of the Orient more vigorously than others. As Raymond Williams put it in his study, *The Long Revolution*, "though the members [of a community] share an area of common meaning, the actual process of organization [Williams defines art as the organization of experience] in each individual is necessarily personal" (Williams 1961: 29). Each chapter therefore consists of a two-part analysis. The first part explores the unique influences on the author's life and thus provides a background to the present work; the second part concentrates on an analysis of the text and the way it reflects the author's personal and cultural influences.

Notes

1. I hesitate to use the word "forced" because to some extent it probably reflects a Western–Christian perception of the spread of Islam. Whether the followers of Islam forced conversions after the first impetus and enthusiasm of conquest is regarded as a debatable point by historians. Moreover, "forcing" slaves to convert was actually advantageous to the converts because, since Islam forbade Muslim slavery, it meant that they would soon be given their freedom. Perhaps the fear generated by the expansion of the Arab and Turkish empires led to such assumptions about their religious attitudes.

   From the sixth to the eighth centuries the Arabs conquered Mesopotamia, Persia, Palestine, Syria, and Egypt. They expanded through North Africa to the Atlantic, toward the East up to the Indus, and North into Central Asia. Twice they besieged Constantinople unsuccessfully, but they did obtain a foothold in Europe by their capture of Spain. The Ottoman empire rose to power in the fourteenth century, and from the fourteenth through the fifteenth centuries they expanded as far West as the Danube, and then later encroached even further into Europe up to the northern shores of the Black Sea.

2. Why did nineteenth century Europe persist in this sense of fear and rivalry toward a militarily weak (relatively) Islamic Orient? It is not possible to explore such hidden aspects of the human psyche and we can only guess at the reasons. Perhaps, as we can see from the situation in Kosovo, this rivalry continued simply because old religious and cultural fears and enmities die hard.

3. See Byron Porter Smith's, Marie E. de Meester's, and Martha Pike Conant's surveys of the numerous works of English literature and scholarship on the "Orient", or influenced by the "Orient". Meester's study on English literature of the nineteenth century reveals the influence of writer's on each other. Her analysis shows that even purely fictional works like William Beckford's *Vathek* contributed to the Western conception of the Orient.

Chapter 2

The Dual Orientations of James Morier

Different Perspectives of the Orient

James Justinian Morier (1782–1849), author of *The Adventures of Hajji Baba of Ispahan*, was no ordinary Englishman sent on a British mission to Persia. He was brought up in Turkey, educated in England, and worked as a merchant in Smyrna, and had had a complex set of influences on his perspective of the Orient. This complexity is evident in his most famous and enduring work, *Hajji Baba*.[1]

Morier's father, Issac, a naturalized British citizen, was born in Smyrna in 1750 where his family had been settled for many years. Naturally he had first-hand direct knowledge of Turkey, and as a result, after he lost his family fortune he was able to obtain a job in the British Levant Company in 1803. He was ultimately appointed Consul General at Constantinople in 1803. In 1806 the Company was dissolved and the post converted into that of His Britannic Majesty's Consul, a position Issac Morier held until he died of the plague in 1817.[2]

Like many of his countrymen Issac Morier sent his family to the home country so that his children could receive an education, but even though James Morier and his brothers spent a good portion of their childhood in London they were so used to living in Smyrna that, according to his great-niece Alice Wemyss, in "The Birth of Hajji Baba", "even when the family moved to London it maintained as far as it could the Smyrna way of life." This is of course a very vague statement, and Wemyss unfortunately does not elucidate it further, but it clearly suggests that they were used to non-English customs.

Ava Inez Weinberger, who provides us the most recent and well-researched biographical sketch in her dissertation, "The Middle Eastern Writings of James Morier: Traveler, Novelist and Creator of Hajji Baba", informs us that in 1800 James Morier returned to Turkey to join a mercantile firm in Smyrna, but in a few years, according to Alice Wemyss, in 1806, he gave up his job and joined his father in Constantinople. It is here that we see Morier develop an academic interest in the Orient, an interest evidenced by the fact that he "mingled with the many distinguished Orientalists then to be found in the European Quarter" (Wemyss 1978: 165). Wemyss does not provide us with any specifics of this interaction, but from Morier's works we can see that he had considerable interest in and exposure to traditional Orientalist literature. In his first literary endeavor, *A Journey Through Persia, Armenia and Asia Minor, to Constantinople, in the Years 1808 and 1809*, Morier refers extensively to the works of eighteenth century Orientalists, and even corroborates or develops their research.

It was also here in Constantinople, in 1808, that Morier met the envoy to Persia, Harford Jones, who was kind enough to fund his trip home to England and to "accede to his [James Morier's] wish of accompanying me to Persia as my private secretary" (in *An Account of the Transactions of His Majesty's Mission to the Court of Persia in the Years 1807–11*). Morier's first trip to Persia was short, from 1808 to 1809, covering only about six months. He was sent back home in May 1809 to accompany the Persian ambassador to England, but he soon departed for Persia again, in July 1810, this time as Secretary of the Legation headed by Ambassador Sir Gore Ouseley. On his second trip he remained in Persia for five years, until 1815, even taking over the reins of diplomatic power after Sir Ouseley's return to England in 1814.

Morier's background reveals two influences on his perspective of the Orient: experience of life in an Oriental community, and a traditional European academic perspective on it. Both these influences can be traced in his first two recorded accounts of his trip to Persia, *A Journey Through Persia, Armenia and Asia Minor, to Constantinople, in the Years 1808 and 1809* and *A Second Journey Through Persia, Armenia and Asia Minor, to Constantinople, in the Years 1810 and 1816*. In the first *Journey* we see an empathetic personal approach that treats Persians like individual human beings, mingled with a reductive tendency to stereotype them, and a conscious desire to present himself as a contributor to Western scholarly studies of the Orient. In the second *Journey* there is a marked shift toward a reductive Orientalist attitude which sought to study the Orient only to demonstrate or claim Western superiority.

Morier's attitude in the first *Journey* was probably more humane because he traveled under the auspices of Harford Jones, a person who had "adopted both the habits and the mores of the people with whom he transacted business" (Wemyss 1978: 165). Harford Jones was a man who treated Persians as equals and as friends. In his record of his mission to Persia, Jones writes, "I have said already, and I repeat it, that the greater part of the vices of which the Persians are accused, arises from the nature of their government. For instance, when force can, at any time deprive a man of his all, does it not follow, that he will easily reconcile himself to not being over nice in the means he takes afterwards to recruit his finances? He who attempts to make us believe that the inhabitants of Persia and the Persian peasantry are, in moral character, the same, knows little or nothing of what he is talking about, and he who imagines that the Persian peasants of Fars, Irak, Azarbaijan, or any other province, all possess the same moral qualities, is equally ignorant" (Jones 1834: 1, 92). For Jones, Persians were simply people, both good and bad, as anywhere else in the world.

Harford Jones' attitude naturally rubbed off on his private secretary, Morier. Morier too notes that there is no single Persian type, but simply people in all their variety. At an ox and lion fight in a fête he observes that "the bloody scene was pleasing to the

Persian spectators in general, although I thought that I perceived some who sympathized with us for the helplessness of the ox" (Morier 1812: 127). Undoubtedly there is an air of Western ethical superiority in this statement, but what one also observes is that, in spite of the Orientalist jargon of "us" and "them", Morier refuses to make a generalizing comment on what he perceives to be Persian character without modifying it with a personal statement that challenges the distinction of "us" and "them".

Underlying this personal response to Persia and the Persians was also perhaps the political situation. Jones had been sent to Persia to eliminate the French influence, and in such a situation arrogance was hardly the appropriate attitude. With the French and British both begging for alliance with Persia, the Persians had a diplomatic edge. Courtesy, respect, and equality were the pass-words, and, as Morier says, even when they were permitted to follow their own inclinations they preferred to follow Persian customs: "Sir Harford made the compliments required, when the prince desired us to sit at our ease. We, however, as in a former circumstance, chose to be respectful and uncomfortable, and to continue in the fashion of Persia" (ibid., 116). Harford Jones' own political problems led to something more than a diplomatic friend-ship. The then Governor-General of India, Lord Minto, had wanted his favourite, Sir John Malcolm, to be the envoy to Persia, and he tried to make Jones' Persian mission politically uncomfort-able and even dangerous. It is not clear which one of the Governor-General's disturbing activities Morier refers to in his journal be-cause he asserts that it would be "improper to disclose the contents [of the Governor-General's letter], further than to remark that they placed his majesty's envoy extraordinary in a situation of peculiar embarrassment, from which nothing but the most friendly disposition in the Persian court could have relieved him" (ibid., 220). And it was the support of the Persians at this time that made Morier feel that Persia was like home and Persians like country-men: "Throughout the whole management of a new and very delicate situation, their proceedings were so plain, so upright, and so cheering, . . . that we regarded them with the liveliest gratitude; and felt relieved in finding among strangers all the heart and principle of countrymen" (Morier 1812: 220). Personal experience was teaching Morier that "brothers" could be found even among easterners.

At the same time, Morier was also considerably influenced by the Orientalist tradition. He viewed Persia as a land to be "discovered" by the West, and made immense notes in his journal on the horticulture, climate, geology, art, and architecture of the place, as though it had not existed till a westerner had ratified its presence. Undoubtedly, Morier had to write in a detailed manner for his ignorant Western audience, but the fact that he does not refer to Persian writers and, instead, only to earlier Western explorers makes one feel almost as if he was exerting a cultural domination of the place. Morier was also very conscious of a sense of Western cultural superiority, and was very happy that the mission was scrupulous in matters of religion because he felt certain that this piety would make an impact on the natives: "We never omitted to perform divine service on Sunday; suffered no one to intrude upon us during our devotions; and used every means in our power to impress the natives with a proper idea of the sanctity of our Sabbath" (ibid., 57).

This tendency to make binary distinctions of "superior" and "inferior" is far more visible in his account of his second journey to Persia by which time he was promoted to Secretary of Legation. This time the group consisted of Ambassador Sir Gore Ouseley, Lady Ouseley and her maids, and his brother and private secretary Sir William Ouseley. The change in political climate, along with Morier's own loneliness due to his exclusion from Ouseley's close-knit family group, were perhaps the causes that led to his close-minded, conservative attitude.

In Morier's second travel account there is a strong consciousness of the East–West difference and a tendency to view the East as a homogenous, alien world. In the preface to his account he claims that "whatever differences of creed, of government, or of language may exist between them, there is still no line of separation between any two Eastern nations so strong as that which is between Europeans and Asiatics" (Morier 1818: viii). Not only is there a strong difference between the two cultures, there is also, for Morier, a

marked sense of Western superiority. Morier finds Eastern manners noteworthy only because they serve to elucidate Western
antiquity; apart from that he finds the morality underlying these
Oriental manners degenerate in its hypocrisy.

Morier does not merely relate everything Eastern to scripture,
the religious root of Western civilization as he knew it; he also
likes to observe that Oriental manners are degenerate because they
observe only the external forms of scripture. The following is a
somewhat lengthy quote because it elucidates his attitude very
clearly. At a party hosted by the Ameen-ud-Dowlah (the treasurer),
Morier notes that:

> When a Persian enters a *mejlis*, or assembly, after having left his
> shoes without, he makes the usual salutation of selam alekum,
> (peace be unto you) which is addressed to the whole assembly, as
> it were saluting the house (Matthew, X.12.); and then measuring
> with his eye the degree of rank to which he holds himself entitled,
> he straightway wedges himself into the line of guests, . . . It may
> be conceived that among a vain people, the disputes which arise
> on matters of precedence are numerous; and it was easy to observe,
> by the countenances of those present, when anyone had taken a
> higher seat than that to which he was entitled. Mollahs, the Persian
> scribes, are remarkable for their arrogance in this respect, and they
> will bring to mind the caution that our Saviour gave to the Jews
> against their scribes, whom among other things he characterizes
> as loving the uppermost places at feasts (Mark, IX.39). The master
> of the entertainment has, however, the privilege of placing any one
> as high in the ranks of the mejlis as he may choose, and we saw
> an instance of it on this occasion; for when the assembly was nearly
> full, the Governor of Kashan, a man of humble mien, although of
> considerable rank, came in, and had seated himself at the lowest
> place, when the Ameen-ud-Dowlah, after having testified his
> particular attention to him by numerous expressions of welcome,
> pointed with his hand to an upper seat in the assembly, to which
> he desired him to move and which he accordingly did.
>
> The strong analogy to be discovered here between the manners
> of the Jews, as described by our Saviour in the first of the parables
> contained in the fourteenth chapter of St. Luke, and those of the

Persians, must be my best apology for quoting the passage at full length, particularly as it will more clearly point out the origin, and more strongly inculcate the moral of that beautiful antithesis with which it closes. *When thou art bidden of any man to a wedding, sit not down in the highest place, lest a more honorable man than thou be bidden of him, and he that bade thee and him, come and say to thee, Give this man place, and thou begin with shame to take the lowest place; but when thou art bidden, go and sit down in the lowest place, that when he that bade thee cometh he may say unto thee, Friend, go up higher: then shalt thou have worship in the presence of them that sit at meat with thee. For whosoever exalteth himself shall be abased, and he that humbleth himself shall be exalted* (Morier 1818: 143–44).

In the parable Christ, as a Jew, is using the manners of the semitic culture illustratively whereas Morier is using the manners of the Persians to imply that they are an essentially vain people who observe only the external forms of Scripture. In fact, it seems that he is using the parable to suggest that the Western tradition, as opposed to the Persian, is moral and superior, for while he perceives the Western as being genuine he views the Eastern as a hollow tradition, a mockery. And in the process he also implies that the courtesy and humility of the Governor of Kashan too consists of external forms only. Morier has become so conservative, so much a part of the Orientalist tradition, that he has forgotten (or has chosen to ignore) his own personal experiences with the shabby intrigues of an English Governor-General and his protégé.

The Persians, however, he believes are "pliable", and if only "they had enjoyed all those advantages of situation and converse with Europeans which the Turks possess, they would have been far more their equals in all the arts of war and peace" (ibid., 23). In other words, they would have become more Western, that is, more civilized. Morier believes that

the Persians might be entirely civilized; and if it were ever the policy of any one of the European nations to give a further impulse to the eagerness with which they have already begun to acquire some of our arts [of manufacturing modern weapons], it is not to be doubted, but that the whole of Persia would soon exhibit a very different aspect from what it does at present; and ... their darkness in religion would perhaps be gradually dispelled (ibid., 227).

The Persians are thus objects representative of "the White Man's burden" because they have to be moulded by superior Western technology and morality and are regarded as inherently incapable of developing by their own effort.

Alice Wemyss believes that this attitude developed out of his sense of exile from the home country. She writes that "the blame [for Morier's narrow opinions] should not be laid entirely at the door of the Persians. Seven years with but one short break is a long time to live in an alien country. The loneliness inherent in this situation was aggravated by the strange behavior of Sir Gore Ouseley, who would not allow his First Secretary to share either in the diplomatic activities of the mission or the privacy of his home" (Wemyss 1978: 172). To put it in Morier's own words,

> He [Gore Ouseley] literally did everything for himself: he made music; he wrote despatches and he looked through the kitchen accounts; he paid out hundreds and thousands of pounds and he counted broken pots and pans; he gave the richest shawls as presents and distributed candles and cheese to the servants. He did everything, and the Chargé d' Affaires did nothing but yawn and count the days till the Ambassador's departure (ibid., 1911: 170).

Morier's sense of isolation from regular activities and all that was familiar probably made him retreat more and more into the sanctuary of the Western-centered approach to the East.

The changing political climate, which Morier was very aware of as a diplomat, also perhaps gave support to this Eurocentric view of the world. A Persian alliance was no longer critically important to the English while an English alliance had now become vitally important to the Persians. England had required Persian support as a buffer against France and Russia, but with Napoleon's invasion of Russia in 1812, Russia became an important ally for the British, not an enemy. Consequently, according to historian Malcolm Yapp in *Strategies of British India, Britain, Iran and Afghanistan 1798–1850*, rather than try to stop the Russian incursions into Persia, "British diplomats were instructed to contrive a peace which would free Russian troops for the war with France" (Yapp 1980: 83). In 1812 Ouseley withdrew all British officers from active service with the Persian troops whom they had trained; and in 1813 he negotiated the peace treaty of Gulestan between Russia and Persia which conceded Persian territories to Russia. The Persians had become so dependent on British support that when the British revised their treaty with the Persians and rewrote it to remove those clauses which ensured their help to Persian forces, the Persians had no choice but to sign it. According to Denis Wright in *The English Amongst the Persians During the Qajar Period 1787–1921*, "the Persians could scarcely afford to be choosers and almost any treaty with Britain, then the only European power capable of affording them protection against the Russians" (Wright 1977: 15). This awareness of Persian dependence on superior British power was very evident to the diplomat Morier, and he comments on it in his account of his journey: "Fear of Russians was their [the Persians] strongest feeling" (Morier 1818: 185).

In 1817, Morier retired from foreign service (except for a special service in Mexico in 1824) and spent his time recording his experiences in Persia in the form of a fictionalized narrative by a Persian, *The Adventures of Hajji Baba of Ispahan. Hajji Baba* is more than just a narrative of events in the life of an ordinary Persian; the very recording of events and people reflects stylistically Morier's attitude toward Persia and the Persians. In this novel we can observe the same dual approach that we witnessed earlier: one based on intimate personal knowledge of individuals, and the other based on the traditional Orientalist framework.

The fictional introductory epistle to *Hajji Baba* clearly establishes these two conflicting attitudes. While reminding Dr. Fundgruben of an earlier conversation they had on writing a novel on the Orient, Morier, masquerading as Peregrine, subtly caricatures European learning which makes an artifact of the East. He gives a very comic description of the learned Orientalist who is the author of *The Biography of Celebrated Mummies*, and who is currently "seeking another oasis in the wilds of the desert (that emblem of yourself [Dr. Fundgruben] in hieroglyphic lore), to which, so I was informed, you expected to have been guided by information gained in the inside wrappers of one of your most interesting mummies" (xixa). Dr. Fundgruben treats the Orient only as an interesting piece of antiquity, an attitude that Morier clearly caricatures in the above description.

And yet Morier feels that he is part of the world that he caricatures because he attributes the impulse to write a novel on the Orient to Dr. Fundgruben. It was in conversation with Dr. Fundgruben that he realized the need for a work that gives a true picture of the Orient: "true picture" in that it does not make "sweeping assertions" about the Orient. Even as he wishes to present a more realistic portrayal of Orientals, he claims that the "manners of the East are, as it were stereotype," and in a state of decay, like the "last impressions from a copperplate engraving where the whole of the subject to be represented is made out, although part of it from much use have been obliterated": a traditional Western perspective of a static but degenerate Orient. (Although this novel is on Persia, Morier uses "Persia" and "Orient" synonymously. Any observations in my study about Morier's attitude toward Persia should be taken to be synonymous with his attitude to the Orient, and vice versa).

The following pages will further examine these two opposed perspectives on the Orient. Unlike nineteenth century criticism which debated the morality and the realism of Persian character portrayal, or twentieth century studies which either examined the art of the novel or uncovered the historical figures underlying the characters in the novel, my work will explore the attitudes underlying the much praised art and "realism" of *Hajji Baba*. This study will examine the different perspectives of the Orient that the novel represents and reflects.

The "Realism" of *Hajji Baba*

Nineteenth century reviewers invariably compared Morier's book with Thomas Hope's *Anastatius: or the Memoirs of a Greek*, 1819, and in fact some thought that the book had been written by Hope since both novels portray an Oriental picaresque hero. Those who preferred Anastatius felt that Hajji Baba was too morally degraded, or that he was too unromantic to excite any interest. The *Oriental Herald* (based in London) felt that although Hajji has "conveyed to us a very lively notion of the state of manners in most classes of Persian life," he cannot be tolerated because "he is so very unattractive a mixture of knave, fool and coward, that we have conceived an unmingled contempt towards him; and have no desire whatever to hear anything he may have to say relevant to England in particular" (465). The reviewer for *Blackwood's Edinburgh Magazine* is convinced that Hope is the author of *Hajji Baba*, and is of the opinion that "Anastatius was not merely *one* of the most vigorous, but absolutely *the* most vigorous, of the 'dark-eyed and slender-waisted,' heroes that had appeared," and that Hajji Baba's tale should be given no further encouragement because "an Oriental gentleman, who can neither fight nor make love, will never do to buckle three more volumes upon the back of" (51, 57).

However, the taste for a romantic portrayal of the Orient was dying out, and the British audience now preferred to view the Orient as uncivilized and decadent, not romantic. In a vigorous critique of Thomas Moore's long romantic poem, "Lalla Rookh: an Oriental Romance," in the *British Review*, 1817, the reviewer declares that "these miserable Turks and Greeks and Persians and Albanians make a figure only in the sickly pages of our epicurean poets; there is scarcely an individual among them whom an English gentleman of cleanly habits could endure by his side; and yet because they lie in the free indulgence of animal pleasures, . . . the thoughts of our countrymen are turned by our poets of nature, . . . " (32). The perspective of the Orient had shifted from that of "sickly" lovers to a place of "sickly", inferior culture.

Hajji Baba was therefore a welcome relief to those who believed in the technological and moral superiority of the West. The *Quarterly Review* felt that although "as a novel Anastatius . . . must bear away the palm. . . . As the map of manners, as the effort of a foreigner to impregnate his style of thought and opinions . . . the Memoirs of the Greek must yield in the perfection of dramatic truth and propriety to the adventures of the pure Asiatic [Hajji] before us" (200). An article in the *New Monthly Magazine*, 1877, which expresses the belief that *Hajji Baba* is a "complete thorough-going exposition of the interior life and manners" of the Persian, defines very vividly what it means to be a "pure Asiatic": "in the European spirit . . . there exists an honesty of motive, a steadiness of purpose, a fixedness of principle, and a truthfulness and sincerity of conduct which is rarely discernible among Oriental people," and therefore *Hajji Baba* is an accurate depiction of Persian character, "its innate treachery, deceit, and falsehood, its absolute hollowness and insincerity . . ." (Keegan 1877: 681). One assumes that neither of these reviewers had visited the East for if they had, they probably would have mentioned it; instead, they simply voice a popular Western concept of the East and praise Morier's accuracy in corroborating it.

Up to a point these reviewers are correct in claiming that *Hajji Baba* is a realistic portrayal of Persia and of Oriental manners. Morier has described Persian traditions and customs with such accuracy that Hassan Kamshad, a Persian literary critic, observes that "the author displays such amazing knowledge and understanding of the private lives, customs and practices of some sections of Persian society that it is difficult to credit a foreigner with these meticulous observations" (Kamshad 1963–64: 70). However, Kamshad, like some other twentieth century critics, goes on to argue that *Hajji Baba* is not a "true" picture but an "exaggerated" depiction of Persia and the Persians. Hasan Javadi notes that "it must be admitted that Morier's obsession with the vices of the Orient produces a decidedly unbalanced portrayal of the Persian character" (Javadi 1970: 170).

Some of Morier's contemporaries also felt that the portrayal of all Persians as knaves was highly misleading. Harford Jones, in his preface to his account of his travels (*Transactions*), writes that "[o]ne may allow oneself to smile at some of the pages of Hajee [*sic*] Baba, but it would be just as wise to estimate the national character of the Persians, from the adventures of that fictitious person, as it would be to estimate the national character of the Spaniards, from those of Don Raphael, or his worthy coadjutor, Ambrose de Lamela" (Jones 1834: viii). The *London Magazine*

(1824) commented that "the total absence of virtue in any country is untrue in nature as well as unpleasing in fiction" (quoted in Weinberger, 1984: 26). Later in the century, the great Persian scholar, Edward Granville Browne, cautioned the reader, "Let not the reader, then, be so far carried away by the charm of Morier's pages as to lay down the book in the belief that every Persian is a Hajji Baba, a Mirza Ahmak, or a Mulla Nadan" (Browne 1895: xi).

Twentieth century criticism has shifted to a discussion of the relationship of *Hajji Baba* to *Gil Blas* and to the picaresque tradition, and also to a study of the artistic realism of the work. However, these scholars have either not explored these aspects fully in the context of Morier's attitude toward the Orient, or they have simply ignored the relationship between technique and attitude. The much praised artistic realism, use of Persianisms, and the humorous and "satiric" aspects of the novel demonstrate not just the narrative skill, but as will be seen, also portray the Western "realism" or perception, of the East as a place to be dominated and manipulated, as nothing more than an object, inferior, mute, and ridiculous. In *Hajji Baba* this domination can be seen most clearly in the way the Persian characters, their personalities and their outlook on life, are depicted. Both the narrative style and the picaresque form of the novel, as we shall see, work to subjugate the Orient by defining it in the way the West chose to perceive it.

The Mute Persian Character and the Dominating Western Voice

The narrative consists of the memoirs of a Persian, but only superficially so. The *Oriental Herald*, 1824, was quick to observe that Peregrine's story about meeting Hajji and obtaining his memoir, just when he was hoping that one day he should run across an "imaginary manuscript of some imaginary native of the East," is "very awkward and unprofitable — not to say impertinent; because the work [*Hajji Baba*] is evidently intended to come forward as an example of the plan suggested first" (453). This "first" plan refers to Peregrine's original intention to collect anecdotes of Mussalman life and weave them into a continuous narrative, as in Le Sage's *Gil Blas*. So what we have here is a nominal first-person narrative by Hajji, and the real first person, Morier, behind the scenes. The reading public had just recently received one novel, *Anastatius*, that had been written by an Englishman but narrated by an Oriental so they were not unused to this stylistic device. However, what they expected from such a novel, as can be seen from the reviews cited earlier, was a truly Oriental novel written from an Oriental perspective. Since Morier is not able to conceal his identity or his values, what Wallace Cable Brown called (in "Prose Fiction and English Interest in the Near East, 1775–1825") his "British conscience", such a piece of work conveys the impression that only a westerner can truly explore and express Persian life. Even Morier's contemporary, the *Edinburgh* reviewer, recognized and protested against the authorial intrusions which resemble "a rolling up, as it were, of knowledge into little hard pills, and giving us dozens of them to swallow, (without dilutent), one after the other. . . . It makes the book read like a judge's notes of a trial . . ." (53).

In the introductory epistle we are informed that Hajji maintained a record of his life because

> Ever since I have known your nation [the English], I have re
> marked their inquisitiveness and eagerness after knowledge.
> Whenever I have travelled with them, I observed they record their
> observations in books; and when they return home, thus make
> their fellow-countrymen acquainted with the most distant regions
> of the globe. Will you believe me, that I, Persian as I am, have
> followed their example; and that during the period of my residence
> at Constantinople, I have passed my time in writing a detailed
> history of my life, which although that of a very obscure and
> ordinary individual, is still so full of vicissitude and adventure, that
> I think it would not fail to create an interest if published in Europe
> (Morier 1897: xviia).

Underlying Hajji's explanation is the image of a mute Persia, unable to represent itself unless touched and improved by the West. Had Hajji not been inspired by the world that seeks knowledge, he, "Persian" that he is, would not have seen any need to express his thoughts about his life and adventures. And even then his portrayal of his country would be incomprehensible to the Western audience unless, according to Peregrine, a westerner edited it for "European readers, divesting it of the numerous repetitions, and the tone of exaggeration and hyperbole which pervade the compositions of Easterners" (ibid., xviia).

Even though the tale is narrated in the first person by Hajji, there are important sequences that allow the reader to realize that he is no more than a puppet on a string. For example, to backtrack a bit, Hajji's comment that Persian though he is, he still wrote about his life sounds most unnatural because he is referring to himself not as an individual but as a representative of a country. Hajji does this quite often in the novel claiming that he is heartless or vain because he is a Persian or because he is a Muslim. When he tries to overcome his sorrow at his separation from Zeenab, he talks as though he is a representative Muslim: "I endeavoured . . . to show myself a true Mussalman by my contempt for woman kind" (ibid., 314). He also describes his own vanity as a Persian failing: "The ninety five pieces of gold in my girdle . . . made it difficult for me to restrain that vanity of display so common to all my countrymen" (ibid., 479). Only a westerner could have put such words in Hajji's mouth. Behind the so-called first person we hear the real voice, the voice of the westerner interpreting Persia and Islam for us.

Morier has not managed to make his tale sound as truly Hajjian as Weinberger would have us believe, nor does he keep his "British conscience" in check as Wallace Cable Brown claims in *Prose Fiction and English Interest in the Near East, 1775–1825*. There are some major contradictions in character portrayal and action that reveal Morier's voice behind the Persian mask. Hajji is presented to us as a religious, although not a devout person, and yet he is sometimes presented as capable of taking advantage of the religious beliefs of other Muslims. When Hajji requires suitable provisions for his life as a nasakchi (officer attached to the chief executioner, or bailiff) he cheats other Muslims to gain his ends:

> As for instance, I wanted a bed, a quilt, and a pillow; a poor man happening to die under our charge, I assured his relations, whom I knew to be the most bigoted of Mussalmans that his death could

be no fault of ours, for no one could doubt the skill with which he had been treated, but that the bed upon which he lay must be unfortunate; for, in the first place, the quilt was of silk [silk is unclean], and in the next, the foot of the bed had not been turned towards the Kebleh, as it ought to have been; this was enough for the family to discard the bed, and it became mine (Morier 1897: 216).

We are expected to believe that Hajji, who is a Muslim, would have been capable of taking advantage of customs and norms which he should have respected and feared as much as the family members of the deceased. The same Hajji who had earlier felt very conscious that he had "broken the commandment by taking a cup," (a crime he never again committed) could not possibly do such a deed. Moreover, would it be probable for him, a Shiah, to call someone else bigoted for being concerned about one of the most common and sacred forms of the religion, the turning of the bed to the Kebleh?

A little while later Hajji Baba appropriates Mirza Ahmak's trunks by making them "unclean" and thus participating in a sacrilegious act himself. Hajji places a whole litter of pups in the trunks, forcing the doctor, who was "scrupulous . . . to a fault about things forbidden as unclean," to discard them. Hajji, the great critic of infidels, who calls the English ambassador a "dog of an unbeliever," and the Turks "the most accursed heretics," appropriates the "unclean" trunks. The narrative voice is uncertain: Hajji is speaking to us, and yet it is not the voice of Hajji. The reader is not always presented a narrative from Hajji's point of view, as Weinberger maintains, but is instead presented with the voice of the westerner, manipulating, dominating, and laughing at the customs of the Orient.

In fact, the Hajji who is capable of taking advantage of "bigoted" Muslims acts in a way that bears striking resemblance to the Western strategy for gaining political power in the East. As already mentioned in the first chapter, Napoleon, realizing that he could not take Egypt by force, used Comte de Volney's and other Orientalists' knowledge of Egypt to pit the local Egyptians against the ruling Mamelukes, and then presented himself to the Egyptians as their savior. The manipulation of Hajji, and the manipulated Hajji's actions, parallel this technique of domination of the East.

This behind the scenes narrative voice not only uses its knowledge to exploit the religious biases of the Persians, but it also very obviously gathers the knowledge of another culture for presentation to a Western audience and delivers it without any "dilutent". Hajji, as a born Persian, should know the norms of behavior too well to have to explain them or even be conscious of them. And moreover, as he had informed Peregrine, he wrote a travel account in imitation of the English who used this technique to acquaint their fellow-countrymen with the rest of the world. If Hajji maintained an account of his travels for his countrymen the last thing he should do is inform them about their own customs. Yet, in a most unnatural fashion, he describes customary forms of his culture when he greets the doctor, and also informs us that they are of common usage:

> As soon as I appeared, the doctor invited me into the room and requested me to be seated; which I did with all the humility which it is the etiquette for an inferior to show towards his superior for so great an honour. . . . I bowed repeatedly as he spoke, and kept my hands respectfully before me, covered with the border of my sleeve, whilst I took care that my feet were also completely hid (Morier 1897: 115–16).

According to Weinberger, this description adds to the realism of the novel because "here Morier weds fact to fiction, using his travel material to enhance Hajji's character as the canny picaro, and thus the description of manners is apt in terms of the novel's story" (Weinberger 1984: 188).

However, this interpretation is unconvincing since it does not address the tone of the narrative. Had Hajji been self-consciously behaving in this humble manner to deceive the doctor, surely he would have demonstrated some glee at his success instead of giving us a dead-pan recital of his manners and his "humility". It is not as though Hajji is incapable of expressing such delight at his abilities. Later on, when he deceives the duenna of a Turkish lady who is in love with him, by telling her that he is descended from a rich and noble family, he literally dances for joy: "Ahi Hajji, friend Hajji, . . . by the beard of your father, and by your own soul, for this once you have shown the difference between a fool and a sage. Well done . . . " (Morier 1897: 511). One does not see any trace of this tone in his description of his meeting with the doctor.

Morier's half-concealed voice also emerges in inconsistencies in the narrative voice to give us its picture of Persian character. In the description of the chaoush who was to escort their caravan from Tehran to Meshed, Hajji says that the chaoush was "a character well known on the road between Tehran and Meshed, and enjoyed a reputation for courage, which he had acquired for having cut off a Turcoman's head whom he had found dead on the road." How could Hajji have known that the chaoush had cut off a dead man's head? He had just arrived in Tehran from Ispahan, and was just a naïve boy, away from home for the first time. It is through asides like these, placed in Hajji's mouth, that Morier presents a so-called "realistic" Persian commentary on cowardly Persians.

Under the guise of first person narration, the guise of realism and authenticity, we are presented a Eurocentric "realism", that is, what the Western world chose to define as authentically Oriental. The two voices are so obvious that one wonders why they have not been noticed before. Perhaps such a state of affairs exists because westerners unconsciously endorsed Morier's perspective, and therefore did not question his subtle, and often unsubtle, intrusions. The best example of this close-mindedness, an extreme example I should say, is Wallace Cable Brown, writing in 1938, who is so bold as to assert that because other Western observers have noted Persians to be knaves and cowards, *Hajji Baba* is a correct portrayal of their national character. In his article, "Prose Fiction and English Interest in the Near East, 1775–1825", he says:

[by analysing himself and his companions Anastatius] . . . gives [the reader] a clear-cut picture of the Near East in all its shameless hypocrisy, its glitter, and its romance. . . .
    In point of character Morier's hero is a more typical native of

the Near East than Anastatius. This is the result partially of a
happy accident, for Morier set his novel in a country which, of all
countries, was notable for its solidarity of national character. The
Persian's craftiness and prevarication, his cowardice and credulity,
his vanity and mobility, his alacrity in making a compromise with
conscience — these traits were attested by everyone [nineteenth-
century Western travellers and diplomats] who came in contact
with the race. Thus in building Hajji Baba's character, Morier could
follow a fairly simple formula. . . . It must have not been so simple
for the author to still the voice of a very active British conscience
into acquiescence with his eastern design.

   In this situation one suspects that Hope was guilty of compromise: for him Anastatius's nominal Christianity was an avenue of
escape from this dilemma (Brown 1938: 835).

In the light of such an attitude, Brown cannot be expected to realize
that "realism" is a subjective term, or to understand that Morier is
imposing his Western centered realism on the Persian narrator of
the story.

   Morier's narrative technique also serves to portray characters in
a manner which reflects his Western orientation to the East. To the
Western world, the Orient was just one imaginary entity, different
and inferior, and it could not see the Orient as composed of people
of various traits and personalities. Consequently, although they
observed the Orientals in minute detail, they ultimately reduced
them to objects, to stereotypical beings who have no individual life
history or development, but are merely "specimens". It was as
though Western observers could not cope with this alien world
unless they fitted it into some preconceived category. Morier, in
spite of his personal experiences in the Orient, too tends to reduce
his characters to types which embody the Western notion of Orientals. The portrayal of Hajji is, however, more complex because
although at one level he is depicted as an unchanging character, and
hence appears to represent the "unchanging East," at another level
he is also presented as an individual human being, not just a Persian,
with an inner life of emotions and concerns. Morier's early friendship with some individual Persians (Meerza Bozurg, for example,
who was an old and good friend of Harford Jones to begin with)

may have inspired him to present such a personality, or perhaps his creation, Hajji, developed a life of his own as often happens with writers and their characters.

Hajji, as we have already noticed, often voices attitudes and acts in a way alien to him; and these variations reflect Morier's Euro-centric notions of the East. In addition, it seems as if Hajji himself is an embodiment of Western notions of the East, of that "singu-larly unchanging Oriental people," as Lord Curzon said in his introduction to the 1895 edition of the novel. Lord Curzon was referring to the lack of change over a time span of a few decades, but the *Quarterly Review*, 1824, felt that this Oriental stagnation covered centuries. The reviewer felt that *Hajji Baba* reminded him of the Arabian Nights, and adds that "Asia is the only part of the universe where the form of society continues changeless and im-perishable, amidst the revolutions of ages and the ruin of empires" (201). Hajji embodies this unchanging quality in the essentially unchanging nature of his character. We see him through various adventures, trials and tribulations, we see him as a young boy just starting out in life, and finally as secretary to the Persian ambas-sador, but we see no change in his personality. He starts life as a vain young man and as a rogue, and when we last see him he is still vain and roguish, but much older.

In spite of the fact that he himself has been cheated, Hajji never questions this way of life, instead he merely attributes his misfor-tunes to fate and proceeds in his life as a trickster. Hajji has also learnt that vanity can lead to disaster, he knows that strutting before the Persian merchants in Constantinople led to their jealousy and his exposure; but at the conclusion of the novel we see him pre-paring to return to Ispahan to make a display, "with all the parade of a man of consequence" (579). Hajji never changes, even though he sees examples of the "noble" Englishmen, and he thus fulfills the expectations of the Orientalist C.J. Wills that "Persia does not change" (preface to 1897 edition of *Hajji Baba*, viii).

Hajji's life is thus depicted in externals: a number of events take place, but they leave no mark on his personality. Since no attempt is made to understand why Hajji is what he is and what drives him to behave the way he does, it seems as if the portrayal of Hajji is subservient to the Western notion of the uniformity of the Oriental character. Perhaps Morier believed, like Dr. Fundgruben, that the Oriental mind was inaccessible, and therefore he did not even care to present the inner life of his central character.

It is of course not possible to determine for certain why Morier portrayed Hajji in this flat, unchanging manner. Perhaps this depiction does not indicate, consciously or unconsciously, any specific Western approach to the East and this choice of character portrayal might simply have been dictated by the nature of the picaresque genre itself, a genre in which the hero is often a non-developing person with no stability or growth in personality. On the other hand, perhaps Morier selected the picareque genre for his Oriental novel because it enabled him to depict what he thought was typical of a Persian's nature. (A discussion of the picaresque genre in the context of *Hajji Baba* shall follow in the subsequent pages.)

However, in spite of the restrictions of the Western attitude toward the Orient, or the constraints of the picareque genre, the inner life of Hajji does emerge, if only for brief moments. There are times when we get an opportunity to understand his doubts, apprehensions, desires, and we catch a glimpse of his reflections on his actions. Hajji's involvement with the Mollah Bashi, for example, allows us to see the man behind the "Persian rogue". Mollah Bashi's death in the bath and his servant's mistake in taking Hajji to be the Mollah, throws a wonderful opportunity into Hajji's hands, an opportunity that he exploits to the fullest. But Hajji is not just a rogue delighting in his good fortune; he is a nervous, excitable youth who exults in joy and "shiver[s] with apprehension" at the same time, and so alarmed is he at his own activities that

> to say the truth, when pausing to breathe, I was so alarmed at the extraordinary turn which my fortunes had taken, that like one dizzy on the brink of a precipice, invaded by a sort of impulse to precipitate himself, it was with some difficulty that I could persuade myself not to return, and deliver up my person to justice (Morier 1897: 452).

Instead of merely depicting a rogue we are able to enter into Hajji's anxieties, tensions, and reflections about his actions.

It is this "confessional" mode, as Weinberger calls it, that permits us to view Hajji as a person, and not just as a Western representation. We are given an opportunity to observe Hajji's personal feelings, and not just his actions. Hajji's life's experiences do not lead to any change in his behavior, but his rare responses to the events in his life enable us to see his inner trials and concerns, and hence instead of "the Oriental" we glimpse the "Hajji", the pilgrim.

The other characters in *Hajji Baba* do not develop a life of their own even though they either narrate their own life histories and/or are described by other Persians in the novel. These two techniques — first-person narration and observations made by people of their community — lend a realistic air to the novel because they make the reader feel as though the local characters are expressing their own views about themselves and each other, whereas Morier is actually speaking through them and imposing his own Western attitudes. Actually, "character portrayal" is hardly the appropriate term because Morier does not so much portray character as present specimens, depicting only their external life.

The portrayal of Sefer and Zeenab makes one wonder if Morier's one-dimensional characters reflect a Western approach toward Orientals, or merely imitate the picaresque technique of depicting characters, or whether there is a connection between his Orientalist attitude and his style. Ultimately only Morier can clear up our doubts, if he was at all conscious of what he was doing, but considering that the personalities of Zeenab and Sefer embody Western stereotypes of Eastern sexuality and decadent religious beliefs one feels that probably the style of their character portrayal was subconsciously, at least, related to his reductive perception of Orientals.

Morier's tendency to reduce individuals to generalizations can be seen in the first interpolated tale, the story of the dervish Sefer. The dervish begins his tale by inviting Hajji to become one of them, and then follows by giving an account of his life and adventures as a dervish. But instead of talking about himself, his feelings and his fears, he informs us only of the events of his life. We are being told a story in the first person, yet we hear nothing about the person, only about the incidents that pertain to the fraudulent nature of dervishes. Dervish Sefer's manner of referring to dervishes in the plural pronoun further reduces any trace of individuality: he sprinkles his entire dialogue with "us" dervishes, and "we", and "our". Undoubtedly he is seated with two other dervishes, but the plural pronouns refer not to them but to the entire dervish sect, as if they were all just like him. "Little do you know of dervishes," he informs Hajji, and adds, "I lead a life of great ease, and am feared and respected by those who do not know what dervishes are" (Morier 1897: 61).

It seems unnatural that a villain should describe his crimes to one who is not even of his own group of select friends, and that he should do so to persuade a naïve Hajji, a Hajji who believes that dervishes are very learned men, to become a dervish. It is interesting to observe that when Sefer himself was a naïve young man, the dervish Bideen encouraged him to become one of their group by telling him tales of the magical powers he would acquire if he learned their arts. Dervish Sefer, on the other hand, is using a very poor rhetorical strategy, surprising in a man adept at deception, because he is speaking for Morier who wants to convey to the reader what he believes to be the common nature of all dervishes.

Dervish Sefer not only lacks individuality in spite of the fact that he gets to narrate his own life story; he becomes thoroughly a pawn of Western conception of the Oriental character, and even their spokesman when he makes some derogatory comments about the Prophet. To the Western world the success of Islam was very threatening because its very basis challenged and superseded their religion, and one of their ways of coping with it was by attributing the Prophet's success to cunning and trickery. According to Sefer, or rather according to Morier, Sefer says, "If I chose to give myself the trouble, and incur the risks which Mahomed himself did, I might even now become as great a prophet as he" (ibid., 61). Sefer has no life of his own, he has merely become a specimen in a Western, sociological laboratory, studied by a scientist who first forms his conceptions of the object and then in a "realistic" manner applies it.

Characters in the novel are also depicted by other Persians, primarily Hajji, the supposed narrator of the work. These descriptions do not automatically qualify as "realistically" Persian, as we shall see, even though they are presented by Hajji in meticulous detail. Hajji's description of his beloved is a case in point because it conveys the Western image of the sexually-appealing Oriental woman:

> Her blue veil was negligently thrown over her head; and as she stooped, the two long tresses which flowed from her forehead hung down in so tantalising a manner as nearly to screen all her face. . . . Her hands were small . . . her feet were equally small; and her whole air and form bespoke loveliness and grace . . . [she] had the most enchanting features that the imagination can conceive . . . . At this moment she let her veil fall, as if by chance, and I had time to look upon her face, which was even more beautiful than I had imagined. Her eyes were large and peculiarly black, and fringed by long lashes, which . . . formed a sort of ambuscade from which she levelled her shafts. . . . Her sweet nose was aquiline, her mouth small, and full of sweet expression. . . . Nothing could equal the beauty of her hair; it was black as jet and fell in long tresses down her back (ibid., 137–39).

This picture of Zeenab conveys the Western image of the mysteriously veiled Eastern woman who conceals her charms, her sensuous and enchanting features, behind her drapery. She is not only a sexual object whose tresses "tantalizingly" screen her face, but she is also a sexually uninhibited person who "levels her shafts" and who drops her veil "as if by chance." This description is not unlike the one that Lady Montagu gives of the dazzlingly beautiful and sensuous women in a Turkish bath "negligently" displaying their charms, women who under the protection of the veil move out of their husband's harems to rendezvous with their lovers.

Weinberger claims that this description of Zeenab is realistic and "fitting" because we see Zeenab from Hajji's point of view. According to her it is appropriate that Hajji give great attention to Zeenab's beautiful eyes because of the value Persians attach to them, and that it is fitting that Hajji pay careful attention to her features because a Persian woman's face is customarily hidden from view. The description, she continues, is also realistic because we see Zeenab in the same order Hajji would have: "while Zeenab's face is concealed from Hajji, he first focusses on her long hair, small hands . . . and her 'air and form' . . . " (Weinberger 1984: 197).

As far as the technical appropriateness of the presentation is concerned, Weinberger's analysis is convincing. But one must not ignore the fact that underlying this technical realism lies a Western conception of the Orient as the exotic, erotic and mysterious land. It would be simplistic to state, like Weinberger, that "[a]lthough Morier viewed Persian society through the prism of his British and Christian prejudices, in this novel he convincingly portrayed Persian manners and customs through Persian eyes," (ibid., 336) because this portrayal cannot be separated from the implied British and Christian attitudes.

The Picaresque and the Picaro

Morier wrote *Hajji Baba* in the picaresque form, and he naturally made his central character, Hajji, a picaro. It has been argued that Morier chose this form because it expressed his conceptions of Persian life. It is the nature of these conceptions that have to be explored through an analysis of the narrative style: the dual narrative voices, and the portrayal of the numerous Persian picaros in the novel. Morier's deviation from the traditional portrayal of the picaro, in particular his deviations from his avowed model *The Adventures of Gil Blas of Santillane*, will also be explored because they reveal his attitude toward the Islamic Orient.

In the introductory epistle itself Morier explains his intention to write a novel in the picaresque tradition. Of course he does not use the word picaresque, but he does say that he wants to write in the style of *Gil Blas*, which was a well-known and popular picaresque novel. He also stated his plan "to collect so many facts and anecdotes of actual life as would illustrate the different ranks which compose a Mussalman community, and then work them into one connected narrative, upon the plan of that excellent picture of European life, *Gil Blas* of Le Sage" (Morier 1897: viia). Obviously, he plans to use an episodic, picaresque structure, and the "imaginary manuscript" he claims to have translated does follow this plan that he has outlined.

The concept of the picaresque novel has undoubtedly undergone changes over the years, but what concerns us here are some of the essential elements of this technique. Frederick Monteser, in *The Picaresque Element in Western Literature*, 1975, and Stuart Miller, in *The Picaresque Novel*, 1967, have identified some of the basic elements of this class of literature. According to Monteser, the picaro must be of the lower classes, a rogue and not a villain, and "must be conscious, either during his adventures or later as a mature author, of the reflections upon society which his tale points up. He need not criticize it, but he must be aware of what the reader is to criticize" (3). Miller explores the character of the rogue further, arguing that the picaro is a "relative innocent developing into a picaro because the world he meets is roguish" (Miller 1967: 56). He also examines the episodic plot which he describes as symbolic: "The picaresque plot expresses an intuition that the world is without order, is chaotic," and the "rapid action sequences have the effect of dazzling . . . with the accumulated chaos of life's action" (ibid., 10, 21).

Hajji Baba, which Monteser has classified as a picaresque novel, by and large fits the above description. Hajji, the son of a barber, is a rogue who can even rob his master of fifty ducats, and his life rapidly takes him from "milieu to milieu," (as Miller would say), from barber, trader, water carrier, tobacco seller, dervish, apprentice physician, lover, officer of the chief executioner, holy man, trader, and finally secretary to the Persian ambassador to England — his world is undoubtedly chaotic. However, there are important variations to Morier's use of the picaresque, and variations from the narrative style of *Gil Blas* which, upon analysis, reveal that Morier was making a Eurocentric comment on the people he was writing about.

According to Terry H. Grabar, in "Hajji Baba of Ispahan: A Critical Study", Morier used the picaresque form because it accurately depicted what he conceived to be the nature of Persian life and character. In his second *Journey*, Morier often referred to the Persians as false and deceitful, and, "in short, he thought that the ordinary Persian was a typical *picaro*" (Grabar 1962: 143). But, as Grabar goes on to observe, Morier felt that such behavior was the natural outcome of life under a despotic government where one's life was dependent on the whims and fancies of one's superiors, and also natural considering that they did not have any contact with Europe.

However, despite what Morier says in his two travel accounts about the corrupting influence of a despotic government, in *Hajji Baba* he presents a picaro who is leading a life of roguery because he wants to, and not because he is subject to any man. A summary of Hajji's adventures demonstrates his inherent roguishness very clearly. Hajji starts life as a naïve young man who has never seen the outside world, but longs to be something more that just a barber all his life, for "he had a soul above razors." He accepts a job with Osman Aga because it will give him an opportunity to see life outside Ispahan, but when their caravan is captured by the Turcomans his first act is to steal his master's money because it might be useful in case he succeeds in escaping from the bandits. Hajji is a "relative innocent," naïve about the other tricksters in the world who will appropriate his stolen goods in a short while, but he does not need anyone to teach him roguery. After he escapes from the Turcomans Hajji becomes a water carrier, but because of a sprained back he shifts to selling tobacco. Unfortunately, to make a quick profit, Hajji starts selling adulterated tobacco, for which he gets punished by the officers of the law. After this he becomes a dervish, a teller of traditional folk tales in this case, but when he accidentally runs into a messenger carrying the court poet's letter to his family, he steals the letter and the messenger's horse, and delivers the letter himself in the hope of a reward. When the poet returns home he begs him for some kind of employment, and the poet obliges, placing him in the royal physician's service. But Hajji soon gets weary of working for the physician because he sees no future in it, and he requests the doctor to recommend him to the chief executioner to replace an officer who had recently died. As an officer, Hajji is up to mischief again because his comrade, Shir Ali, "gave me such an insight into the advantages of the situation, that I could dream of nothing but bastinadoing and getting money"

(Morier 1897: 227). Hajji is evidently a rogue because he finds it monetarily advantageous. Hajji soon has to leave this job and run for his life for having seduced Zeenab, one among the Shah's harem, but ultimately after living for some time as a holy man in the protection of a religious sanctuary, he obtains the Shah's pardon. But soon after that he engages in illegal work, arranging temporary marriages, or in other words dealing in prostitution, until finally — when his ill-doings lead to the harrassment of the Christians — the Shah expels him from Tehran. Partly through luck, and partly by connivance, Hajji steals a horse and some money and crosses the frontier into Turkey. Here, with the help of Osman Aga, his first master, he sets up a business, but his greed, vanity, and deceit soon bring him down, and penniless, he turns to the Persian ambassador who offers him a job. Instead of being persecuted by an unjust government, it seems as though Hajji is the culprit making a nuisance of himself to the citizens of Persia.

When Morier wrote his two travel accounts he did feel that the vicissitudes of a Persian's life were due to the despotic government he lived under (probably because this was also Harford Jones' opinion), but his depiction of Hajji's life suggests that he now feels that these vices are inherent in a Persian's nature. Weinberger's assumption that in *Hajji Baba* Morier believed Persians were corrupt because they lived under a despotic government is based on her interpretation of Hajji's statement that as an officer he became a very vigorous "beater" to impress his superiors. This is a very shaky argument because the need to impress superiors to gain promotion is part of the human situation and exists even under democratic governments. Besides, Hajji's entire career reveals his inherent roguish nature, a character trait that was evident even before he became "one of the beaters."

As the outline of the narrative shows, the picaro in this particular case is not corrupt because of the nature of the society around him. Even when he is away from the corrupting influence of court life, working among honest merchants, he continues with his tricks. It is this deviation from the development of the picaro in a picaresque world that leads one to conclude that it was Morier's deliberate intention to demonstrate what he regarded as the inherently decadent nature of the Persians, not to treat them like human beings and attempt to understand what made them develop into rogues. The picaresque form was ideal for Morier because while it enabled him to depict a chaotic world and to survey its rogues, a slight, but important, change in the genre also permitted him to represent his conception of the inherent ethical inferiority of the Orientals.

Hajji's character is also different from that of the traditional picaro, and this deviation too reveals the Western assumption of cultural superiority. A picaresque novel, as defined earlier, is written by a mature narrator who, even if he does not criticize his society, at least knows what there is to criticize. Hajji, however, is far from mature, and he never looks back and comments on his society. Only once, when he observes that he is not cruel by nature but has become hardhearted by the example of the other nasakchis, does he implicitly comment on the brutality of the society. Generally speaking, Hajji is content to describe events in a dead-pan tone, neither implying criticism, nor directly commenting on the nature of the incident he is presenting to us. For example, he describes how the Shah subtly extorts money from his senior officials to pay his own servants:

> In the course of his [the Shah] eating he ordered one of the pilaus, of which he had partaken, to be carried to Mirza Ahmak, his host, by a servant-in-waiting. As this is considered a mark of peculiar honour, the mirza was obliged to give a present in money to the bearer. . . . And in this manner he contrived to reward two persons, the one who received the present, and the other who bore it (Morier 1897: 196).

Hajji does not comment on this injustice in so many words, or even in the tone of his voice. In fact, he is so uncritically accepting of his society that he even calls the Mollah Nadan the most devout man in Persia. And even when he remarks on the "Persians", as mentioned earlier, he does not intend any criticism. Hajji may comment on the envy and malevolence of the Persians, but it is not a moral issue for him because he revels in this kind of behavior and he deliberately tries to make other people jealous because it makes him feel important.

In Hajji's comments on the English we realize that he has never matured simply because Morier regarded any other kind of behavior to be totally foreign to Persians. Observe his shocked and contemptuous response to the Englishman's direct style of address: "The speech made on the occasion by the elchi [the English ambassador] was characteristic of the people whom he represented — that is, unadorned, unpolished, neither more nor less than the truth, such as a camel driver might use to a muleteer . . ." (ibid., 565). Even when faced with examples of the westerner's altruism, Hajji dismisses all such notions with "I had nothing to do with their tastes . . . " (ibid., 570).

Hajji is obviously a very different character from Gil Blas who observes and comments on the ills of his society, and ultimately retreats from it completely. Morier borrowed considerably from *Gil Blas* — both themes and incidents — and therefore any significant change in the narrative of *Hajji Baba* is worth noticing.[3] The alterations that Morier made in the presentation of the rogues is particularly important because it reveals his conscious intention of demonstrating that the vices he is presenting are specifically Oriental and Islamic, and definitely not English or Christian.

When Le Sage exposes the vices of his society, he often does so by presenting an ideal in the form of an individual, or a critic, from within that same community. In *Gil Blas* we witness corrupt doctors and ministers, but we also see doctors who critique the corrupt among them, and noble lords who use their influence to protect their friends from corrupt ministers. Dr. Sangrado, the incompetent, unethical, and comical doctor, is mocked by Dr. Cuchillo who even gets into a fight with the doctor's apprentice, Gil Blas. And for all the corrupt officers we meet at court, particularly the Duke of Lerma, prime minister to the Spanish Crown, we are presented with a counterbalance in the Lords of Leyva who consistently assist Gil Blas. For all the Sirenas we also have the virtuous wives, Seraphina, Antonia, Beatrice, and Dorothea.

Morier's narrative, however, consists of a series of oppositions between English and Christians on the one hand, and Persians and Muslims on the other hand, which serves to make it very clear that these vices are connected with origin and religion, not despotism.

According to Weinberger, "Morier's . . . themes of greed and hypo-crisy . . . [account] for the novel's universal appeal, for if his subject matter is geographically foreign, the moral behaviour of his char-acters is not" (Weinberger 1984: 203); and, says Grabar "[t]he faults, errors and follies that he finds in Persian dress are universal, and there is almost never any hint that Morier's satiric intention was limited to the Persians who are its immediate objects" (Grabar 1962: 179). However, although these faults and vices of greed, hypocrisy, and deceit are universal in nature, Morier presents them not only as essentially Persian in nature, but also as absent in the English and the Christians.

The pairs of contrasts that the narrative carefully sets up dem-onstrate that the vices are indeed "foreign" to a superior Western, Christianized culture. Hasan Javadi, in "James Morier and His Hajji Baba of Ispahan", analyzes one such contrast: the "parallel stories" of Zeenab and Hajji, and Yusuf and his Mariam. Zeenab gladly leaves her lover when a better opportunity presents itself, whereas Mariam, risking her life, escapes to her lover; and as for the two men, Yusuf risks his life to save Mariam, even keeps his oath to Hajji, a Muslim, whereas Hajji, although deeply troubled, does nothing to save Zeenab, and even involuntarily participates in the death of Zeenab and his own child. The Christians alone possess the values of loyalty, love, truthfulness, and of course, ultimately gain the reward of a safe and secure life.

There are other pairs too: Mollah Nadan and the Frank dervish, and Mirza Ahmak and the Frank physician. Mollah Nadan is a fanatic and a rogue, trying to make himself more important than the Mollah Bashi, and of course attempting to make as much money as possible by arranging temporary marriages. The corrupt Mollah may be a stock figure "within the oriental scene, in puppet pantomime," as Grabar argues, and the image of the corrupt man of religion is, as Weinberger states, a universal one, but in *Hajji Baba* the Mollah is not merely a traditional or universal figure but instead a contrast to the courageous and intelligent Frank dervish. The Mollah himself informs us that the Frank was "of a wit so sharp, that the Shaitan in person was not fit to be his father. His eyes were like live charcoal, and his voice like a high wind. He never lost an opportunity of entering into an argument with our most learned men . . . with the heart of a lion . . . " (Grabar 1962: 462). This apostolic Frank dervish's actions too reveal him to be a very capable and rational man who can stand his ground and reason with a mob of Muslims intent on harrassing him. Mollah Nadan clearly does not embody the "universal" image of the corrupt priest: he embodies the corruption of the Muslim clergy.

Mirza Ahmak, the royal physician, is presented as a contrast to the two Frank doctors in Persia. It is not just that the Mirza's knowledge is limited compared to the "modern" science of the Franks, but his attitude toward his patients is also highly unethical. He is annoyed that the Franks have invented a vaccine for small pox because "[t]he small pox had always been a comfortable source of revenue to me; I cannot afford to lose it because an infidel chooses to come here and treat us like cattle" (Morier 1897: 116). The Frank doctors, on the other hand, not only treat their patients gratis (Morier of course does not choose to inform us that they were salaried people), they also believe that "the blessing [the vaccine] must be spread throughout the world" (ibid., 571). Persian and Islamic ethics are thus immediately labelled as inferior to the supposedly altruistic Western culture, which was at that time making Persia a pawn of European power politics. The Eurocentric view of the world never sees anything as universal because it never judges itself by the same standard it applies to the Orient, and since Morier's narrative of cultural contrasts eliminates any hint of universality it endorses this attitude. (Harford Jones, who is aware of this tendency to divide the world into simplistic Western/Oriental divisions, remarks sarcastically, "[i]n every part of the East which I have visited, if Europeans have not increased the propensity of the natives to vice, it has not been their fault for (generally speaking) they have exhibited to them very perfect examples of selfishness, rapacity, chicanery, and the very *crapule* of debauchery; . . . " [Jones 1834: 1, 349].)

The Muslim response to the British political system also represents an inherently static quality of Oriental life. When the narrative takes us beyond Persia to other parts of the Islamic world we encounter the Turkish Reis Effendi (foreign minister) who finds the concept of any form of control on a king a species of madness: "he [the English 'Shah'] does not dare even to give the bastinado to one of his own viziers, be his fault what it may; whereas the aga, if expedient, would crop the ears of half the city and still receive nothing but reward and encouragement. . . . Let us bless Him and our prophet, that we are not born to eat the miseries of the poor English infidels . . . " (Morier 1897: 549). The Reis Effendi's inability to comprehend the English infidels' political system is a device by which Morier suggests that such enlightened concepts are beyond the pale of Muslims.

Morier has been very selective about his picaros: "good" is Western or Christian, and "bad" is Persian and Muslim. However, in spite of this selectivity one notices a tension in his attitude toward the nature of Eastern character. He does present good, loyal, generous Persians and Turks, but at the same time glosses over them so fast that they are not noticed, or sometimes he deliberately, as an afterthought, distorts their personalities. Among the good characters who get glossed over are the kind muleteer, the cadi (police officer-cum-magistrate), and the Mollah who rescues the Frank dervish. The characters who suffer distortion are the Turk Osman Aga, Hajji's mother, and teacher.

The good muleteer actually helps Hajji twice, on two caravan trips. The first time he looks after his needs free of charge, and the second time, when Hajji and his new acquaintance, the dervish, ask him for help he maintains both of them for the duration of the caravan trip. Not only that, when Hajji was utterly destitute, he advised him, and helped set him up as a saka, or water-carrier. Little attention is paid to him, however, and he is never referred to when not part of the narrative. The usually prolix Hajji is silent about this person. The kind Mollah figures only once, in Mollah Nadan's narrative, and he too is disregarded and diminished. The Mollah has rescued the Frank dervish from a mob incited to fanaticism by Mollah Nadan, but strangely enough, the aggressive Mollah Nadan does not even express disgust or anger at being thwarted by the humane and generous Mollah's actions, thus reducing him to merely a line in the narrative, not a character with different opinions and attitudes.

Such presence and absence of decent Persian characters suggests a tension in Morier's perception of the Orient. He acknowledges their presence, and yet resists it by quickly passing over it, thus falling back into the traditional Orientalist mode. Like Lord Curzon he stereotypes Orientals as a degenerate lot, but unlike Lord Curzon, in the introduction to an 1895 edition of *Hajji Baba*, he is not comfortable with the claim that anyone who thinks there are any noble Persians must be soft-headed. This uneasiness with a single, rigid attitude is even more striking in his distortion of the personalities of some of the individuals in *Hajji Baba*.

Hajji Baba's mother changes drastically and suddenly from a loving, fussy, and concerned mother, who was in tears at his departure from Ispahan and, deeply worried for his welfare and safety, into a greedy and selfish woman. When Hajji returns home to claim his inheritance, he discovers that his mother has intrigued with his schoolmaster to deprive him of his inheritance. The character has been drastically altered with no explanation but the implied one that either Orientals have no predictable core of character, or are by nature greedy and treacherous and will show their true colors sooner or later. The change in the schoolmaster is equally surprising because when we last saw him he was educating Hajji free of charge, only demanding Hajji's father's services as a barber in exchange.

Osman Aga, the Turkish merchant, does not suffer such a sudden change in his character, but in fact experiences something as bad: he is reduced to a comic figure. Osman Aga took Hajji to his heart and always trusted in him and helped him. He set up Hajji as a trader in Constantinople, welcomed him in his home, looked after him in his illness, and like a father advised him against greed and vanity. At the same time, this wise and kindly old man is also portrayed as a comic, avaracious figure, easily recognized by his one famous line: "What is the price of lambskins in Constantinople?" His character of the comical profit-seeking merchant is at odds with, and overrides, the image of the generous father figure.

Morier's uneasiness with the portrayal of these characters suggests that he did resist, although feebly, the rigid Orientalist tradition which would refuse to recognize anything alien to its conception of the Orient, anything that could not be fitted into preconceived categories or explained away. Unlike his armchair readers in England, he could not glibly comment on the degenerate nature of Orientals, of their "innate treachery, deceit, and falsehood" (P.Q. Keegan in "Gleanings From Anglo-Oriental Literature, Vathek-Anastasius-Hajji Baba" 1877).

Satiric or Orientalist Novel?

Is *Hajji Baba* a satire on the Persians? After all, one-dimensional, generalized characters are often found in satire, and are the means by which a satirist lashes out at his society's vices. To determine whether *Hajji Baba* is satiric in intent one has to, as we shall see, examine evidence within and without the novel. To the nineteenth century reviewers *Hajji Baba* was a true depiction of the Persians, and even in 1905, Major D.C. Phillot, editor of the Persian translation of the work (and in fact the man who rescued the manuscript of the Persian translation when he was the British consul in Kerman), claimed that "*Hajji Baba* must, in fact, be regarded as serious history and not as burlesque" (in Phillot's introduction to the 1905 Persian translation, ix). Only E.G. Browne and Sir Harford Jones cautioned the reader not to draw their conceptions of that nation from Morier's novel. Browne observed that Morier lived chiefly at the court, in the midst of political intrigue, and "[n]ot among these [court politicians], as a rule, would one seek for the noblest types of national character" (introduction to the 1895 edition of *Hajji Baba*, xiii).

Twentieth century critics, with the exception of Wallace Cable Brown (in "Prose Fiction and English Interest in the Near East, 1717–1825", 1938), have realized that although Morier depicted the customs and manners accurately, the characters are considerably distorted and the vices exaggerated. To put it in Marzieh Gail's words, in *Persia and the Victorians*, Morier "reported with photographic accuracy, but obviously selected and slanted his material." The novel has thus, according to Hassan Kamshad, a "dual character". As a result of this awareness *Hajji Baba* has been termed not "history" but "satire". The word "satire" has been used by Weinberger, Javadi, Kamshad, Gail, Grabar, and Fatma Moussa-Mahmoud (in

"Orientals in Picaresque: A Chapter in the History of the Oriental Tale in England") with reference to *Hajji Baba* — it has remained stable throughout the twentieth century.

According to Grabar and Weinberger's studies, Morier attacks only universal vices, such as greed, hypocrisy, deceit, and religious corruption. Grabar goes so far as to claim that not only are the vices universal, they are also not specifically directed at Persians. Marzieh Gail implies the same when she asserts that Morier could even have found a Hajji Baba in Manhattan. However, as we have already observed, there is a marked Persian–English and Islam–Christian contrast that clearly implies that even though the vices may be universal in nature, the criticism is directed selectively at the Persians.

The one important point that these critics have neglected is that in intent, and in fact, the novel was clearly aimed at a Western audience. In the introductory epistle we are informed that Morier wishes to write an Oriental novel to educate a Western audience. Peregrine and Dr. Fundgruben both feel that although the *Arabian Nights* "gives the truest picture of Orientals," it unfortunately cannot be thoroughly understood by westerners who have "not lived some time in the East, and who have not had frequent opportunities of associating with its inhabitants" (*Hajji Baba* via). *Hajji Baba* is born out of this need for a true "delineation of Asiatic manners." Moreover, the contents of the novel very obviously presuppose a Western audience. The Persian–British, and Islam–Christian contrasts in *Hajji Baba* illustrate that the norm of sound human behavior is considered typically Western, and that only the westerner can be expected to identify the deficiencies of the Orientals. A good portion of the humor, especially the linguistic humor, presupposes a Western audience. By translating Persian phrases and words literally into English, Morier has not just given it a "Persian flavour", he has also made Persian speech sound ridiculous. Phrases and metaphors like "[love has made] roast meat of my heart", "his face was to be whitened", "their faces shall be truly whitewashed", "seated on the carpet of hope", "quench the flame of covetousness by the waters of prudence", or "wrap myself in the folds of my own counsel", serve to create an amusing, or

archaic and picturesque impression because they are directly translated, and not transliterated. This kind of humor — and the novel
is replete with it — would be lost on the Persian audience because
to them it would be normal, everyday speech; a Western audience
is required to respond to it.

If a novel is written by an Englishman, for the entertainment
and education of a Western audience, but levels its criticism at the
Persians, can it be called satiric? The concept of satire, observes
Alvin B. Kernan (*The Plot of Satire*), has changed and developed
over the years from mere invective to an art form, but the purpose
of satire, to criticize vices in the hope of reforming the readers, has
remained constant. Morier's work can hardly be called satiric because it is not directed toward reforming Persians, nor toward the
people whose vices it exposes and exaggerates, but toward a Western audience in the hope of eliciting a smug laugh at the vicious-
ness, folly, and ignorance of the Persians, just as in the novel the
British laugh at the Persians' ignorance of their customs concerning
court dress. Morier consistently exposes the vices of the Persians,
but not once does he show a Persian critiquing these vices. On the
other hand, as we have already seen, he demonstrates the scientific
and moral superiority of the English, and so we can assume that
he expected the Western audience, and not the Persian, to recognize the extent of the degradation of Persian character. Major-
General Sir Frederic Goldsmid (who was engaged in diplomatic
activity with Persia from 1871 to 1872) comments on the nature
of the humor in *Hajji Baba* and articulates this awareness of
Morier's "satiric" intent. In the introduction to the 1897 edition of
Hajji Baba he writes:

> The humour of 'Hajji Baba', though quite as thorough and pervad-
> ing, is possibly less direct and more inferential than that which has
> contributed so much to the reader's enjoyment of Dickens, though
> the appreciation of it is due to the same sense of the ludicrous
> within us. To the ordinary English apprehension, the fun of the
> latter writer, displayed to its full extent in 'Pickwick', . . . emanates
> from the idiosyncrasies of the author's fellow-countrymen; whilst
> Morier's is produced by the doings and utterances of a foreigner
> who acts and talks in a way which would be impossible to an

Englishman, yet which is irresistibly ludicrous to the English reader in its sober assumption of truth. To the ordinarily-educated Persian the relish of such fictitious biography — supposing it to be translated or otherwise placed intelligibly before him — would consist in its incident and adventure, but the salt of the satire would be wanting. He would see himself reflected in an English mirror, and the likeness would be more striking and complete than that obtained from his own *áina* or looking glass, to which he has been in the habit of resorting; but there is nothing in it with which he would be dissatisfied, in which he could detect a moral lesson (Morier 1897: xx).

The Persians are simply the objects of humor in *Hajji Baba*, not its true audience.

The notion that *Hajji Baba* is a satire, that it was intended to reform the Persians, derives from Morier's introduction to its sequel, *The Adventures of Hajji Baba of Ispahan in England*, 1828. Morier's comment is, however, tongue-in-cheek, just as his introduction is nothing more than an advertisement for his novel. A close reading reveals that Morier's intent was to ridicule the Persians from his status as an Englishman and a westerner.

In his introduction to *Hajji Baba in England* Morier claims that not having received any encouragement to complete his translation of Hajji's journal, he had decided to "bid adieu to ambition," and not follow it up with a sequel. However, one day he received a letter from a Persian "high in office," in fact from the Persian ambassador whom he had accompanied to England, complaining that:

> I am offended with you, and not without reason. What for you write Hajji Baba, sir? King very angry, sir. . . . All people very angry with you, sir. That very bad book, sir. All lies sir. Who tell you all these lies, sir? Persian people very bad people, perhaps, but very good to you sir. . . . English gentlemen say, Hajji Baba very clever book, but I think not clever at all — very foolish book. . . .But why you write 'bout me? God know I your old friend. . . . As you write so many bad things 'bout Mirza Firouz [the name of the Persian Ambassador in the novel], I think you send me some seed and roots [for his garden] not bad; and because I defend you to

the king and swear so much, little china and glass for me very good (Morier 1828: xii–xiii).

It was this letter that, Morier claims, prompted him to carry on with the sequel because it showed that he "produced" some "sensation among the Persians, by which they may be led to reflect upon themseves as a nation. . . . Let them see that they can be laughed at, you will make them angry. Reflection will succeed anger; and with reflection, who knows what changes may not be effected? But having produced this effect, let me ask what further good may not be expected by placing them in contrast with the nations of Christianity, and more particularly with our own blessed country?" (ibid., xiv).

This fictional anecdote probably engendered the notion that *Hajji Baba* was written with a satiric intent. However, Javadi makes a pertinent remark when he asks why Morier took so long, about four years, to state that he sought to reform the Persians through his first novel? To that we might add that if Morier intended to reform the Persians why did he not publish the so-called "Hajjian manuscript" in Persian? And if, as he says, he did not receive encouragement for the sequel in England, would it not be folly to pursue it further in that country? Morier's explanation is unrealistic not only because it comes too late, but also because it is lame. It is more of an eye-catching device than a serious statement of intent.

Morier's own fictional respose to the ambassador's letter reveals that his intent is merely to be derogatory rather than satiric. Instead of writing an explanatory letter to a deeply offended friend, he ridicules his linguistic abilities by writing to him in broken English:

> I have received your letter, and I pray that your shadow may never be less. As for Hajji Baba, what for you not read that book before you write me such letter, Sir? Sheik Abdul Russool great fool; but you, Mashallah! you very clever man, sir, now vizier, how you not read before you write? . . . You say Persian people very good to me. Perhaps not kill me, not make me Mussalman; that very good; thank you, sir, for that; but that's all. . . . But why you write such bad letter to me! God know I your old friend (ibid., xiv–xv).

This letter does not apologize or explain his purpose to his "old friend", instead, all it does is ridicule a foreigner's inability to master another language, completely forgetting that in his early days in Persia he spoke a "barbarous foreign accent," and could scarcely make himself understood (Jones 1834: 1, 412). His dismissal of the Persians' kindness toward him as "that's all" makes it evident that he is now unable to judge by personal experience, and instead only voices the traditional Western notions of superiority.

If the novel is a sample of Western conceptions of the Orient, why did the Persians enjoy it immensely, and why did they perceive it to be satiric? According to D.C. Phillot's introduction to the 1905 Persian translation of *Hajji Baba*, the Persian version circulated widely in manuscript form in Persia and "was copied with eagerness; it was read with excitement . . . [and] was equally well received in Shiraz and Ispahan" (Phillot 1905: ix). Marzieh Gail makes the interesting comment that her father enjoyed the book immensely but was "furious" when he realized that it was written by an Englishman. Gail's remark suggests that the answer to our question lies in the nature of the translation and perhaps in the liberties that the translator took. I am unable to read Persian, but Hassan Kamshad's summary of the omissions and transformations of the translation provides sufficient clues to answer the question.

Hassan Kamshad notes some major characteristics of the translation which make a significant difference to the novel. First, he observes that the translator added a considerable number of proverbial poems, and popular everyday sayings to *Hajji Baba*. Second, the extended Mariam–Yusuf tale, which runs parallel to the Hajji–Zeenab relationship, was shortened to a mere five pages in the translation. And third, instead of referring to Persian officials by their ranks, as Morier did, the translator refers to them by their actual names or titles. Hassan makes it clear that he has provided us with only a few examples of what he defines "as a very loose and free rendering of the original," but these are sufficient for our analysis.

Morier's direct translation of Persian phrases and metaphors lent a picturesque and comical air to the novel for a Western audience. By so doing he not only added to the humor and "realism" of the novel, he also implied that Persians were to be taken no more seriously than charming little children. After all, to regard a people as picturesque is to suggest that they are inferior to solid, noble Western norms. This picturesqueness would disappear in the translation to the original Persian because then they would sound like natural, everyday, grammatically normal, speech. Marzieh Gail observes that "[t]he Western reader is reminded that the Persianisms translated back into Persian would lose their foreign quality . . . " (Gail 1951: 73). The fact that the translator retained these Persianisms, and in fact added to them, also suggests that this elaborate and strange speech would sound natural in Persian. The Western assumptions underlying Morier's use of these turns of speech would therefore, it appears, automatically disappear by the act of translation.

The abridgement of the Mariam–Yusuf story also makes a vast difference to the intent of the translation. The Mariam–Yusuf story in the original follows Zeenab's joyful departure to the Shah's harem, and develops with Mariam's escape from the Governor's palace, concludes with Yusuf's courageous rescue of Mariam and his family, which is soon followed by Hajji's cowardly self-preservation and Zeenab's death. The tale is clearly intended as a contrast between good Christian behavior, and that of typical self-serving, Mussalman lovers. To compress this tale is to mitigate the implied comments, and to probably also disturb the sequence of events, a sequence which highlights the contrast between Christianity and Islam.

The third change is the most important of all because it is this which makes the novel a political satire, not a document attesting Western superiority. By changing the references to officials in *Hajji Baba of Ispahan* to recognizable, well-known, corrupt politicians, the translator was commenting not on the nature of Persians, but on the characters of specific, notorious, individuals. Thus we now have a novel, written by a Persian, and which is truly directed toward a Persian audience, because only a Persian audience would recognize the figures being satirized. The British–Persian contrasts in the novel would cease to be comments on Persian culture, and instead become a criticism of specific individuals.

I have no further evidence of what other changes were made in this "loose and free rendering of the original," but it is credible to assume, from our knowledge of the translator's life, that he turned *Hajji Baba* into a political document. Mirza Habib, who was identified as the translator in a letter by his friend Shaykh Ahmad to E.G. Browne, 1892, was, according to Hassan Kamshad, a resolute advocate of democracy and liberalism, opposed to the Persian government, and as a result, had to fly to Turkey and live there until the end of his life. Mirza Habib died "soon after" this letter was written, but he left his manuscript, which the Censor of the Press in Constantinople had refused to print (probably because of its political implications), with Shaykh Ahmad. Shaykh Ahmad himself was actively involved in anti-government activities, and he belonged to a group which was suspected of assasinating Nasir-ud-din Shah in 1896. Shaykh Ahmad and a friend of his had at this time been extradited from Turkey by the Sultan, and were to be tried in Persia for their subversive activities, when, on the road to Tehran, the news of the Shah's assasination was announced. D.C. Phillot, the British consul in Kerman at that time, writes that "the two suspects were secretly butchered in a kitchen in the presence of the governor" in Tabriz, on the road to Tehran.

The Persians themselves viewed the book as a political satire, for according to Phillot, the Persians appreciated "the skill with which their countryman had depicted certain notable characters and well marked types" (Phillot 1905: ix). It was only when "the English original reached me [Phillot] from India, . . . [that] *Haji* [*sic*] *Baba* ceased to be popular," because the Persians now realized the true intent of the book. Phillot's reference to a Persian's reaction to the English version shows this new awareness: "This author has overstepped his bounds; he has made fun of everyone from the Shah downwards" (ibid., ix).

Hajji Baba is undoubtedly a fast-paced, exciting narrative, full of characters whose foolish behavior evokes laughter and whose unethical conduct is comical in their innocent acceptance of it. However, we must not be insensitive to the attitudes underlying the novel, nor to the attitudes that we reflect when we find it comical or satiric. To do so would be to ignore the individuality and humanity of the people it describes, and, from a literary stand-point, a failure to see the relationship between form and content.

In the Persian "translation", or version, *Hajji Baba* became a political satire, but in Morier's original work it took the shape of a dangerous document on what Johannes Kolmodin called the "inegality of human races." No wonder that the racist French philosopher, Comté Joseph Arthur de Gobineau (1816–1882), praised it in his *Nouvelles Asiatiques* for having depicted "the im-morality of the Asiatics, and the spirit of falsehood which rules them." Although *Hajji Baba* expressed some understanding and empathy for the Persians, by and large it reflected the notion of Western superiority, and even the techniques of Western domina-tion and manipulation of the Orient. James Morier, born in the Orient, ultimately became a representative of his Western roots.

Notes

1. All page references to *Hajji Baba* in this study will be from C.J. Wills' 1897 edition.
2. See Rosslyn Wemyss' *Memoirs and Letters of the Right Hon. Sir Robert Morier, G.C.B. From 1826–1876*. Unless otherwise stated, the rest of the factual information is available in *The Dictionary of National Biography*.
3. See Terry H. Grabar's "Hajji Baba of Ispahan: A Critical Study", 1962, Ava Inez Winberger's "The Middle Eastern Writings of James Morier: Traveller, Novelist and Creator of Hajji Baba", 1984, and Hassan Javadi's "James Morier and his Hajji Baba of Ispahan", 1970, for extensive details on the similarities between *Gil Blas* and *Hajji Baba*.

Chapter 3

Alexander Kinglake: "The eternal Ego that I am!"

Palmerstonian Days

In 1834, a young gentleman, Alexander William Kinglake, set out on a tour of the East. He returned after a year, in 1835, but he took ten years working on his travel account, and finally published it in 1844, at his own expense, after being turned down by several publishers. Despite the attitude of the publishers, Kinglake's book *Eothen, or Traces of Travel Brought Home From the East* was an immediate and resounding success.

Eothen was a high-spirited, witty, and arrogant account of approximately a year's adventures in the Ottoman empire. Kinglake and his friend Lord Pollington (known as Methley in *Eothen*) crossed over into Ottoman dominions at Semlin on the river Save, and accompanied by an interpreter, a bodyguard, and an English manservant, they journeyed on horseback to Constantinople via Servia and Adrianapole. Together Methley and Kinglake explored the Troad (or road to Troy) and then moved on to Smyrna where they encountered an old friend, Henry Stuart Burton (Carrigaholt). While at Smyrna, Methley received letters that obliged him to return to England and so Kinglake continued onward on his own. He sailed to Cyprus and Beirut on a Greek brigantine, enjoying himself enormously listening to sailors' yarns on board ship. Like Lord Byron before him, Kinglake rode over from Beirut to an old convent in the Lebanon range to meet the legendary Lady Hester Stanhope who had established herself there as a prophetess and the Queen of the Desert. After passing a day in her company he proceeded on his route, engaging an Arabic speaking interpreter, Dthemetri, and a new guide (referred to as "the Nazarene"). Kinglake now traveled on through the Holy Land to Gaza, across the deserts on camel-back into Egypt, up to Cairo. He recrossed the desert on his return journey, proceeded to Damascus, and finally concluded his Eastern adventures in a struggle for power with the Pasha of Satalieh who wanted to quarantine him for a few days since he had traveled through the plague-ridden cities of the Ottoman empire.

European power, and particularly English power, was on the rise in the Ottoman empire when Kinglake traveled in the East, and continued to increase and establish itself firmly during the years that he worked on his narrative. In 1827, during the Greek Revolution, British, French, and Russian forces crushed the military might of Sultan Mahmud II and his Pasha (of Egypt) Mehmet Ali, and appropriated part of the Ottoman empire to form Greece. And in 1840–41 the arrogant and popular British foreign minister, Henry Temple Palmerston (1830–1851), at the risk of war with France, persuaded four European powers, Britain, Russia, Austria, and Prussia, to mediate a peace between the warring Turks and Egyptians. The net result of his maneuverings was the elimination of Russian power in Turkey, and Franco–Egyptian power from the Arabian peninsula. In war and in diplomacy, the British reigned in the Ottoman empire.

Kinglake was very conscious of Western, and specifically English, power in the Levant, and in fact, his arrogance has often been explained as typical of a British citizen in the days of Palmerston. In *English Travellers in the Near East*, Robin Fedden observes that Kinglake's "careless assumption of the Englishman's natural superiority, [was] characteristic of his time and nation. Palmerston was in power and all Englishmen were in some degree Palmerstonians" (Fedden 1958: 17). Kinglake was well-aware that Palmerston's aggressive foreign policies had considerably raised British prestige in the Orient and that "so strong and strenuous was England (Lord Palmerston reigned in those days) that it was a pride and delight for a Syrian Christian to look up, and say that the Englishman's faith was his too" (Kinglake 1845: 216–17). While recognizing that Europe in general was very influential in "Western Asia", Kinglake felt sufficiently confident to claim that "[t]he credit of the English especially was so great that a good Mussulman flying from the conscription, or any other persecution, would come to seek from the formerly despised hat, that protection which the turban could no longer afford, and a man high in authority (as for instance the Governor in command of Gaza) would think he had won a prize, or at all events a valuable lottery ticket, if he obtained a written approval of his conduct from a simple traveller" (ibid., 204–5). Kinglake knew that Europeans had considerable power in the Orient, but he also felt that the English "reign" and have excellent "credit".

Given such a position and awareness of power, it is not surprising that Kinglake manifested strong Orientalist attitudes. What is remarkable, however, is that even though he endorsed his culture's assumptions of the Oriental "other", he simultaneously challenged them in his travel account. In *Eothen* we see him mocking other travelers who try to possess and dominate the Orient, while he himself is actually behaving in a similar manner. One can only speculate why "Eothen", as he was often called, expressed such contradictory views. His complex personality is our only clue to his response to the Orient and toward his own culture. His biographer Gerald de Gaury, in *Travelling Gent*, describes him among other things as a practical cynical personality, a self-confessed atheist, and at the same time a romantic who loved heroic wars and manly duelling (which was illegal at that time). Perhaps it is this combination of youthful rebellion and pride in his nation's "manliness" that made him share in, and resist, his cultural codes.

From a well-to-do family, and educated at Eton and Cambridge, Kinglake mingled with the upper classes of society, but he was a shy man, not given to speaking much on social occasions. So shy was he that, according to his friend William Tuckwell, in

A.W. Kinglake, even when he was in his mid-forties he would purposely arrive early at parties because there would be fewer people to hear his name being proclaimed! (His shyness affected future literary studies since he requested his brother to burn all his papers on his death.) Kinglake was very reserved even with his friends, perhaps because he was cynical about their romantic aspirations. Although a contemporary and good friend of Tennyson (at Cambridge) he declined joining the Apostles because, as Tuckwell informs us, "he shrank from camaradrie, shared Byron's distaste for 'enthusmusy'; naturally cynical and self contained, was repelled by the spiritual fervour, incessant tilting at abuses of those young Apostles" (Tuckwell 1898: 11). Kinglake's "realism" is evident in the way he put down a friend: "to one rhapsodizing about the 'plain living and high thinking' of Wordsworth's sonnet, he answered: 'You know that you prefer dining with people who have good glass and china and plenty of servants' " (ibid.).

A balanced, no-nonsense young man who would not hesitate to question his society, Kinglake was known for his well-bred, softly spoken, subtle but incisive comments. Tuckwell describes his wit with a stanza from Don Juan on the pirate Lambro: "He was the mildest mannered man / That ever scuttled ship or cut a throat, / With such true breeding of a gentleman, / You never could divine his real thought" (ibid., 15). The major problem in a study of Kinglake's *Eothen* is precisely this inability to "divine his real thought." For in addition to being a calm, cynical personality he was also in his own way, strangely enough, the romantic individual that he mocked. Given this contradiction in his personality the reader is hard put to decipher the intentions underlying his witty observations in *Eothen*.

Staid English gentleman though he was, Kinglake was romantic enough to feel stifled under the "social conventionalisms and shams" of his society, writes Tuckwell. Even as late as 1872, records Tuckwell, Kinglake "chaffed at restraint: 'when pressed to stay in country houses,' he [Kinglake] writes in 1872, 'I have had the frankness to say that I have not discipline enough.' Repeatedly, he speaks with loathing of the 'stale civilization', the 'utter respectability' of European life . . . " (ibid., 13–14). Kinglake longed for excitement and glamor, particularly the thrill of soldiery. Because of his weak eyesight he could not join the army, but he still always sought to somehow or the other get close to war zones. Even though he was an established solicitor in 1845 (he was called to the bar in 1837) he took a month's holiday in Algeria to observe the French army's occupation of that country — an exciting but extremely uncomfortable vacation. And in 1854 he followed, on horseback, the armies in the brutal Crimean War of 1853–54 even though he was neither a combatant nor a reporter.

Since *Eothen* reflected the author's personality in that it was witty, lively, and cheerfully cynical of social prejudices it was, not surprisingly, both a popular and a controversial book. In *At John Murray's* George Paston informs us that nineteen publishers, apart from Murray, had turned down the book. Recognizing his error of judgment, Murray ultimately procured the copyright of *Eothen* and by way of explanation and apology — after *Eothen* was a success — wrote to Kinglake that he would have printed the book "were it not for that wicked spirit of jesting at everything which forms the essence of the book [and] might I feared have raised a clutter and proved for my Colonial library a place on the list of prohibited books."[1] In 1845, Macvey Napier, editor of the *Edinburgh Review*, wrote to the famous lawyer and writer Abraham Hayward asking:

> Who is 'Eothen'? I know he is a lawyer and highly respectable; but I should like to know a little more of his personal history. . . . He is very clever, but very peculiar. I know he is one of Lockhart's men [John Gibson Lockhart, then editor of the *Quarterly*]. I do not (honestly) think the *Quarterly* is improving (Hayward 1886: 106).

Although Napier was still showing some hesitation in spite of the success of *Eothen*, Murray, like an alert publisher, had already invited Kinglake to write articles for the *Quarterly*.

While publishers and editors initially felt uneasy about *Eothen*, the public loved it. Tuckwell recalls the first appearance of the book: "It arrested old and young men of the club and library, undergraduates, schoolboys, even domestic servants: the messenger at New College, an eccentric college scout . . . knew the book by heart, and used to linger talking of it in our rooms." [2] In *Cornhill to Grand Cairo* Thackeray, *en route* to the Orient (1848), recounts that he could not obtain a copy of *Eothen* because of the general scramble for it on board ship. *Eothen*'s popularity continued to increase throughout the century and, according to an issue of *The Dial*, "*Eothen* reappeared in edition after edition, usually with a diminishing interval between each later edition and its successor. In England alone, nineteen editions have been issued between 1844 and 1910, and the twentieth [published in America] . . . is now on the market" (*Dial* 55 (1913): 482).

Unfortunately for Kinglake the controversial aspect of the book and the "peculiar" image it conveyed of him damaged his career as a lawyer. When his friend Richard Monckton Milnes (1809–1885) was trying to collect literary works for a dying friend's magazine as a way of raising money for him Kinglake stated that he preferred to submit cash than a piece of writing because he felt that his art had already damaged his legal reputation: "My frailty in publishing a book has already, I fear, hurt me in my profession, and a small sin of this kind would bring me into still deeper disgrace with the solicitors." [3] As Richard B. Ince said in *Calverly and Some Cambridge Wits of the Nineteenth Century*, "[l]awyers who write 'peculiar' books on any subject of less weight than Torts or Charter-parties do so at their peril. In traveling through Asia Minor and permitting the East to inspire him with a perverse distrust of Western Progress, Kinglake could scarcely have 'fortified himself for the business of life' to worse effect. Not thus are Lord Chancellors made" (Ince 1929: 247–48). No wonder the next book Kinglake wrote was an account of the invasion of the Crimea — a serious, ponderous work.

Early reviews of *Eothen* reveal both the praise and the uneasiness that it elicited among Kinglake's contemporaries. Eliot Warburton (the friend to whom Kinglake addressed the narrative), in his review in the *Quarterly* (1844) dwelt on the stylistic brilliance of *Eothen* and its "accurate" portrayal of the Orient. However, he also expressed some misgivings toward the author's irreverent attitude toward the Holy Land. On the other hand, the *Athenaeum* reviewer of 1844 sensed that the irreverence and ambiguity of intent were inherent in the light-heartedness of Kinglake's style itself.

Twentieth century critical debate has centered around Kinglake's use of the persona and his distancing of the narrator from the Orient. In *Orientalism* Edward Said argues that Kinglake does no more than use the Orient to discover himself, and that the East existed to him as only an object for his self-fulfillment: "he is more interested in remaking himself and the Orient than he is in seeing what there is to be seen" (Said 1979: 194). What Kinglake sees, Said continues, is not the Orient, but what he is expected to perceive. Charisse Gendron and Benjamin Dunlap both, on the other hand, feel that this romantic attitude is deflated in *Eothen*. While Gendron (in *"Eothen* Again") views this deflation as a form of Kinglake's self-mockery, Dunlap regards it as a comic put down of the romantic persona of the narrative. In "Kinglake's *Eothen*" Dunlap argues that *Eothen* is an autobiographical narrative that reflects Kinglake's growth from the twenty-five-year-old traveler to the thirty-five-year-old author, from the romantic youth who regarded the East as an escape from civilization, to the grown man who realizes that "there was better company in England than in the harem." He perceives the relationship between the elevated, romantic style and its comic deflation as the voice of the older author humorously dismissing the young man's romanticism.

The truth, to use an old adage, lies somewhere in between. A close study of the narrative style, persona, character portrayal, and imagery of *Eothen* reveals that the complexity of this travel account lies in the tension between Kinglake's Orientalist assumptions of the East and his simultaneous deflation of not only his youthful persona but also the ethnocentricity of the Englishmen in the Orient. On the one hand, Kinglake is the dominating Western traveler who views the East as a mysterious, dangerous place that he must conquer and subdue; on the other hand, he is a remarkably self-aware traveler who ridicules the arrogance that underlies this Western approach to the East. He is both the traditional Orientalist who dominates the Orient and its people, and also the objective observer who feels uneasy about such attitudes and depicts his unease through ridicule of himself and other Englishmen. Perhaps the one reason why *Eothen* will remain popular, even with Orientals, is the amazing self-awareness he displays of Western cultural assumptions of the East even while he endorses them. Unlike Morier, he is often sufficiently objective to realize what the East means to the West, and the different ways in which the West represents and uses the Orient.

The Conquering Hero

Kinglake was a very careful and precise writer who took ten years (and two failed attempts) to write *Eothen* exactly the way he wanted. Lady Augusta Gregory, the future patron of the poet W.B. Yeats, wrote in "*Eothen* and the Athenaeum Club" that Kinglake recalled his manuscript eleven times from the publisher to revise it! Given that Kinglake was such a self-conscious writer we may conjecture that he was well-aware of the duality of his attitude toward the Orient that he expressed in *Eothen*. It is in his careful structuring, character portrayal, and tonal effects that one should study his complex approach to the Orient.

An understanding of the persona's voice and its development is essential to any interpretation of *Eothen*. *Eothen* is an unusual travelogue in that it tells us nothing about the places that the author visited except in the way they affected him; from Belgrade through the Ottoman empire and its Egyptian province, and across the deserts we are aware of only Kinglake's feelings. The entire narrative hinges around the persona and there is no pretense at objectivity. Kinglake had consciously written such an account as can be seen in his prefatory address to his friend Warburton in which he took on the role of a cheerful, light-hearted young man who does not care two straws about society or propriety:

> Whilst I feigned to myself that you only were listening, I could not by possibility speak very solemnly. Heaven forbid that I should talk to my own genial friend, as though he were a great and enlightened Community, or any other respectable Aggregate! . . . It is right to forewarn people (and I have tried to do this as well as I can, by my studiously unpromising title-page) that the book is very superficial in character. I have endeavoured to discard from it all valuable matter derived from the works of others, and it

appears to me that my efforts in this direction have been attended
with great success; I believe I may truly acknowledge that from all
details of geographical discovery, or antiquarian research — from
all display of 'sound learning, and religious knowledge' — from all
historical and scientific illustrations — from all useful statistics —
from all political disquisitions — and from all good moral reflections the volume is thoroughly free (vii).

Thus wrote the thirty-five-year-old solicitor, merrily refusing to
cater to society's expectations and writing only on the "traces of
travel" as he experienced them and not as he ought to have. However, although his tone has a mocking quality it is not offensive
because of its light-heartedness and its youthfulness. This trait in
fact made the contents of his book acceptable as the *Athenaeum*
reviewer had observed.

As already mentioned, some modern critics see two, not one,
voices in *Eothen*: the voice of the romantic youth being constantly
deflated by a more rational and mature voice that prefers the
"civilized" West with all its drawbacks to the East. Some key passages in *Eothen* clearly indicate these two voices, and Kinglake's
trick of romantic deflation does suggest a rejection of the romantic,
exotic view of the Orient. While one acknowledges the presence of
this deflation, one should also notice that the mature voice too
romanticizes the East as a mysterious, threatening entity that has
to be not just rejected but also conquered. Even the laughter, the
comic deflation, perhaps indicates (as we shall see) not so much a
mockery of a romantic view of the Orient but a triumph over the
Orient. The structure, images and events of the narrative portray
not merely a dismissal of one voice by the other but, as will be
demonstrated, a domination of a feminine East by a masculine
West.

The two key sections of the book which indicate the two voices
in *Eothen* have already been observed by Dunlap. One passage
occurs toward the centre of the narrative:

If a man, and an Englishman, be not born of his mother with
a natural Chiffney-bit in his mouth, there comes to him a time for
loathing the wearisome ways of society — a time for not liking

tamed people — a time for not dancing quadrilles — not sitting in pews — a time for not pretending that Milton and Shelley, and all sorts of mere dead people, were greater in death than the first living Lord of the Treasury — a time in short for scoffing and railing — for speaking lightly of the very opera, and all our most cherished institutions. It is from nineteen, to two or three and twenty perhaps that this war of man against men is like to be waged most sullenly. You are yet in this smiling England, but you find yourself wending away to the dark sides of her mountains — climbing the dizzy crags — exulting in the fellowship of mists and clouds, and watching the storms how they gather, or proving the mettle of your mare upon the broad and dreary downs, because that you feel congenially with the yet unparcelled earth. A little while you are free and unlabelled, like the ground that you compass, but Civilization is coming, and coming; you, and your much loved waste lands will be surely inclosed, and sooner or later, you will be brought down in a state of utter usefulness — the ground will be curiously sliced into acres, and roods, and perches, and you, for all you sit so smartly in your saddle, you will be caught — you will be taken up from travel, as a colt from grass, to be trained, and tired, and matched, and run. All this in time, but first come continental tours, and the moody longing for Eastern travel; the downs and the moors of England can hold you no longer; with larger strides you burst away from these slips and patches of free land — you thread your path through the crowds of Europe, and at last on the Jordan, you joyfully know that you are on the frontier of all accustomed re-spectabilities. There on the other side of the river (you can swim it with one arm), there reigns the people that will like to put you to death for *not* being a vagrant, for *not* being a robber, for *not* being armed, and houseless. There is comfort in that — health, comfort, and strength to one who is dying from very weariness of that poor, dear, middle-aged, deserving, accomplished, pedantic, and pain-staking governess Europe (Kinglake 1845: 97–98).

This passage both expresses and undermines the romantic mood, for while Kinglake writes as if he truly felt the "moody longing" for the wild, free, uncivilized life he recognizes at the same time that this is just a phase that one passes through before reaching adult-hood: it is "a time for pretending" and for not praising "all sorts of mere dead people." Like Wordsworth he sorrows over the loss of childhood freedom, and echoing the Intimations Ode he writes, "[h]eroic days were these, but the dark ages of schoolboy life came closing over them" (ibid., 33); but he ultimately makes his choice and willingly consents to enter into a "state of utter usefulness" as he stands at the Pass of Lebanon in the last but one chapter of *Eothen*:

> My place upon this dividing barrier was as a man's puzzling station in eternity, between the birthless Past and the Future that has no end. Behind me I left an old decrepid [*sic*] World — Religions dead and dying — calm tyrannies expiring in silence — women hushed and swathed, and turned into waxen dolls — Love flown, and in its stead mere Royal and 'Paradise' pleasures — Before me there waited glad bustle and strife — Love itself, an emulous game, — Religion a Cause and a Controversy, well smitten and well defended — men governed by reasons and suasion of speech — wheels going, — steam buzzing — a mortal race and a slashing pace, and the devil take the hindmost — taking me, by Jove (for that was my inner care), if I lingered too long upon the difficult Pass that leads from Thought to Action.
>
> I descended, and went towards the West (ibid., 222–23).

Like Wordsworth at the Simplon pass, Kinglake finds his position in life as he stands on this dividing barrier. The exotic and primitive he now rejects as dead and dying and he greets the restrictive business of civilization joyfully as a competitive, fast-paced game. The excitement that he sought for earlier in the East he now discovers in the West.

Not only does Kinglake reject the romantic view of the East toward the end of his account, he also deflates such a perspective in his narrative, as Dunlap had observed. The romantic voice and its deflation is most prominent in the first chapter when Kinglake crosses over into Ottoman territory. He starts off by portraying a dark, gloomy, frightening East, the East imagined by a terrified Europe when the Ottoman empire was at its zenith:

> whenever I chose to look southward, I saw the Ottoman's fortress — austere, and darkly impending over the vale of the Danube —

historic Belgrade. . . . Of the men that bustled around me in the streets of Semlin, there was not, perhaps, one who had ever gone down to look upon the stranger race that dwells under the walls of the opposite castle. It is the Plague, and the dread of the Plague, which divide the one people from the other. All coming and going stands forbidden by the terrors of the yellow flag (ibid., 1).

This awed mood is quickly disrupted by a comic description of the "terrors" of the plague:

If you dare to break the laws of the quarantine, you will be tried with military haste; the court will scream out your sentence to you from a tribunal some fifty yards off; the priest, instead of gently whispering to you the sweet hopes of religion, will console you at duelling distance, and after that you will find yourself carefully shot, and carelessly buried in the ground of the Lazaretto. . . . [Before crossing the river] they asked if we had wound up all our affairs in Christendom, and whether we had no parting requests to make. We repeated the caution to our servants, and took anxious thought lest by any possibility we might be cut off from some cherished object of affection — were they quite sure that there was no faithful portmanteau — no patient and long-suffering carpet bag — no fragrant dressing case with its gold-compelling letters of credit from which we might be parting forever? No — all these our loved ones lay safely stowed in the boat, and we were ready to follow them to the ends of the earth (ibid., 1–2).

And so with his "patent portmanteaus," as he later calls them, Kinglake enters Dante-like into the nether regions. The tone and the images again become dark and gloomy: "We soon reached the southern bank of the river, but no sound came down from the blank wall above, and there was no living thing that we could yet see, except one great hovering bird of the vulture race, flying low and intent, and wheeling round and round over the Pest-accused city" (ibid., 3). Again the serious, ominous tone is comically displaced: "But presently there issued from the postern, a group of human beings — beings with immortal souls, and possibly some reasoning faculties, but to me the grand point was this, that they had real, substantial, and incontrovertible turbans ... " (ibid.). And so the tale commences, with romantic elevation followed by comic displacement.

But this laughter does not necessarily indicate merely a rejection of the romantic conception of the East as an alien, mysterious, frightening entity as Dunlap maintains it does. Terrors and nightmares continue to stalk the East without comic deflation and whole chapters are devoted to the death-dealing plague that roams Stamboul, Izmir and Cairo. And even if we find him laughing at people's fears about the plague, or his own nightmares about pyramids, he describes these fears so vividly that one finds it hard to believe that he is dismissing them. Instead of simply rejecting the romantic approach it seems as if he is acknowledging what he perceives as the terrors of the East, and then conquering them. Even his very cheerfulness, as we will see in his treatment of the plague, seems to be not so much a dismissal but an act of resistance against the deadly disease.

Eothen, the romantic journey of self-discovery, as Dunlap regards it, appears to be also a journey of conquest. While Dunlap is correct in emphasizing the importance of the Pass of Lebanon one should not forget that it is but the second to last chapter of the book. The last chapter is called the "Surprise of Satalieh" and describes in military terms the bullying of the Pasha to enable them (Kinglake and his companion of the moment, a Russian general) to break quarantine orders. *Eothen* thus concludes with the conquest of an Oriental and the Oriental terror, the plague.

This conquest of the Orient manifests itself in the images and events of the narrative that depict the Orient as a feminine entity — as threatening, mysterious, irrational, timid and passive — that can be and requires to be controlled and bowed down by the manly, rational, brusque, efficient West. While these qualities are traditionally associated with femininity and masculinity, to fully appreciate Kinglake's association of femaleness with the Orient one should first survey his portrayal of women in general, and specifically, his portrayal of Oriental women. This may seem a digression, but it is essential to briefly glance at this aspect of Kinglake before proceeding to his depiction of a feminine, vanquished Orient.

Overcoming the Female "Other"

There are numerous women in *Eothen*, both natural and immortal, for example, the skipper's wife (the "skipperina"), the stranger in the streets of Cairo, and the Sphinx, to name a few. These women are either threatening and dangerous in their eroticism, or are childlike creatures, lacking in mental faculties, sometimes even like soft, innocent animals. In addition to being considered inferior, women are ultimately viewed as beings who can be stripped of their power and defeated or overcome by laughter and caricature.

Kinglake regarded women as inferior beings who must serve the male of the species, their masters. Early on in *Eothen*, when he runs into his friend Carrigaholt (alias Henry Stuart Burton) we see his concept of women as unreasoning beings that are a nuisance to men. When Carrigaholt jumped on board the first attractive looking ship at the docks (in England) to escape a law suit, he naturally received a lecture from the skipper's wife for his irresponsibility :

> [i]f the dons at Oxford could have seen poor Carrigaholt thus absolutely 'attending lectures' in the bay of Biscay, they would surely have thought him sufficiently punished for all the wrong he did them, whilst he was preparing himself under their care for the other, and more boisterous University. The voyage did not last for more than six or eight weeks, and the philosophy inflicted on Carrigaholt was not entirely fatal to him; certainly he was some-what emaciated, and for aught I know, he may have subscribed somewhat too largely to the 'Feminine-right-of-reason Society;' but it did not appear that his health had been seriously affected (Kinglake 1845: 38).

From one single aspect of one individual woman he generalizes on the reasoning capacity, or rather incapacity, of all women. That Kinglake did view women as possessing a limited intellect, and that he did view them as uniform types is borne out in an article of a definitely serious nature written within a year of the publication of *Eothen*. In "The Rights of Women" Kinglake stated:

> we think that the faculty of the woman's mind consists rather in refracting than in reflecting the truth — and that one of her most

fascinating powers is that of subduing mere facts by feeling, and putting the hard realities and formal rules of life in a charmingly wrong point of view (Kinglake 1844–1845: 114).

While this charmingly silly aspect of women relegates them to a position of inferiority vis-à-vis men, a limited intellect is also considered desirable in women. After all, the essential role of women, as he comments in the same essay, is to "entertain their lord." This duty, he goes on to argue, is more gratifying when freely performed by the Western woman than by the slave-like women of the harem.

Kinglake's non-English women are not only desirable creatures but also dangerously attractive, for their beauty is associated with power and with deathliness. However, they do not seem to constitute an uncontrollable force since he is able to overcome their attractiveness. The stranger Kinglake encounters in the streets of Stamboul is draped in a "coffin-shaped bundle", and her beauty, which she briefly reveals,

> is the beauty that dwells secure in the perfectness of hard, down-right outlines. . . . There is fire, though, too — high courage, and fire enough in the untamed spirit, or whatever it is, which drives the breath of pride through the scarcely parted lip.
>
> You smile at pretty women — you turn pale before the beauty that is great enough to have dominion over you. She sees, and exults in your giddiness; she sees and smiles . . . (ibid., 27).

But as the sentence continues the beauty that is great enough to have dominion suddenly becomes transformed into the image of a very pleasant, playful young lady:

> she sees and smiles; then presently, with a sudden movement she lays her blushing fingers upon your arm, and cries out, 'Yumourd-jak!' (Plague! meaning 'there is a present of the Plague for you!') This is her notion of a witticism: it is a very old piece of fun, no doubt — quite an oriental Joe Miller; but the Turks are fondly attached, not only to their institutions, but also to the jokes of their ancestors; so the lady's silvery laughter rings joyously in your ears, and the mirth of her women is boisterous and fresh, as though the bright idea of giving a Plague to a Christian had newly lit upon the earth (ibid.).

The mysterious, sensuous, threatening woman suddenly loses all power and becomes simply a charming, almost childlike person. And instead of possessing a "high courage" she in fact blushes at her own act of boldness.

Kinglake resists this stranger merely by deflating her dangerous qualities, but in his description of the Sphinx we see him asserting his power over her. In Kinglake's description of the Sphinx all the qualities of monstrosity, mystery, beauty, and sensuousness come together: she not only represents his stereotypical woman but is also, literally, the immortal woman. The Sphinx is both a "deformity and a monster," and also sensuous as the Coptic girls who have the same "big, pouting lips of the very Sphynx" (ibid., 179). She bears the "awful semblance of Deity," eternally watching generations wither away, but is also a "creature", a "beast", which will be the future possession of the "Englishman . . . [who] will plant a firm foot on the banks of the Nile." In the form of the Sphinx the woman truly becomes a type, cast permanently in stone.

Stereotypically silly, soft and childlike, and at times mysterious and dangerous in addition, the female is always portrayed as inferior to the male. Kinglake transfers these ideas he associates with women onto the Orient, and is in fact very clear about his sense of conquest over it. He not only resists the temptations and dangers of the Orient but he also vanquishes it. Kinglake does not necessarily always use feminine pronouns for the East but he does use feminine metaphors for it. He describes the East as gracious and soft, to the point of lifelessness, and in this form the East emerges as both desirable and pleasing and at the same time dangerous in its very antithesis to the masculine West. Kinglake also takes it upon himself to act like a crusading westerner annihilating what he regards as the East's mental and physical threats to his sanity and his health.[4]

The softness and mysteriousness of the Orient is evident as soon as Kinglake crosses over the river into the Muslim quarter of the city and meets the Pasha. He encounters a stillness that is overpoweringly deathly:

> the still air that you breathe is loaded with the scent of citron . . .
> with the dry, dead perfume of strange spices. You long for some

life, and tread the ground more heavily, as though you would wake
the sleepers with the heel of your boot; but the foot falls noiseless
upon the crumbling soil of an Eastern city, and Silence follows
you still (Kinglake 1845: 4).

He proceeds to the Pasha's castle where soldiers lie around "like
corpses upon cool stones" into a world which is ghostlike in its
mysteriousness. The Pasha has to merely "drop" a syllable "from
his lips . . . and [conjure] away the attendants like ghosts." The
"Asiatic contentment" that Kinglake enjoys as he smokes the tchi-
bouque with the Pasha is described sensuously: "when I pressed
the amber lip to mine, there was no coyness to conquer; the willing
fume came up, and answered my slightest sigh and followed softly
every breath inspired . . . " (ibid., 5). His mistress, unlike Andrew
Marvell's in "To His Coy Mistress", requires no persuasion before
conquest, perhaps because she has already felt the touch of death
that surrounds the city and the castle.

The Orient's gracefulness and graciousness indicate a mental
torpor to Kinglake, a passivity that is subject to and inferior to
Western physical and mental activity. The life of the Orient moves
slowly even in its commercial districts in Kinglake's description of
the bazaar in Constantinople:

> The vendor, perceiving that the unfolded merchandize has caught
> the eye of a possible purchaser, commences his opening speech. He
> covers his bristling broadcloths, and his meagre silks, with the
> golden broidery of Oriental praises, and as he talks, along with the
> slow and graceful waving of his arms, he lifts his undulating periods,
> upholds, and poises well, till they have gathered their weight,
> and their strength, and then hurls them bodily forward, with grave,
> momentous swing. The possible purchaser listens to the whole
> speech with deep and serious attention; but when it is over, his turn
> arrives; he elaborately endeavors to show why he ought not to buy
> the things at a price twenty times more than their value; bystanders,
> attracted to the debate, take a part in it as independent members
> — the vendor is heard in reply, and coming down with his price,
> furnishes the materials for a new debate (ibid., 29).

This passivity, slowness and grace take some hard knocks from a

British sailor at Smyrna which is literally and physically "the main point of commercial contact betwixt Europe and Asia." Here we find the "genuine Osmanlee smoking away with all the majesty of a Sultan, but before you have time to admire sufficiently his tranquil dignity, and his soft Asiatic repose, the poor old man is ruthlessly 'run down' by an English midshipman who has set sail on a Smyrna hack" (ibid., 37). Although this scene is comically portrayed, Kinglake does believe that Orientals need to be managed by the westerner. He agrees wholeheartedly with Lady Hester Stanhope, whom he soon meets in Beirut, "that a downright manner, amounting even to brusqueness, is more effective than any other with the Oriental" (ibid., 78).

Kinglake is thankful that other Englishmen before him have brought the Orientals to their knees, thus making his task easier. He speaks with appreciation of the Captain of a brig at Suez who threatened to bombard the place if his request for fresh water was not complied with, and thus forced the local governor to obey the English ever after out of fear. Kinglake writes that he felt "infinitely indebted to the gallant Captain" for having made his passage through the Suez so convenient and cordial. The strong-willed Mr. Farren, Consul-General of Damascus, did not have to use such crude methods against the citizenry; he triumphed over them merely by "firmness and temper" (ibid., 215). It is no wonder that in the last chapter Kinglake marches into Satalieh with all the pomp and dignity of an army captain, reposing "unbounded faith in the feebleness of Asiatic potentates" (ibid., 227).

This last scheme of conquest was suggested not by the Russian general accompanying him but by Kinglake himself as he admits to the reader. The general had merely worked himself up to a state of agitation and in consequence "adopted my suggestion" to "set the Pasha at defiance." And it was Kinglake who masterminded the landing too:

> My instructions to the Captain were attended to with the most perfect accuracy, for scarcely had my foot indented the sand, when the four six pounders of the Brigantine sublimely rolled out their brute thunder. . . . And we were allowed to disembark without the least molestation (ibid., 228–29).

Although the general leads the march to the Pasha's audience hall it was Kinglake who taught him how to "deal" with Orientals and how to appear before them in order to terrorize them. The Pasha in turn tries to intimidate them, but they outdo him in their aggressiveness, and claim and gain freedom from the quarantine. Victorious, they are even feasted by the Pasha and provided with horses; like the traditional hero Kinglake rides away into the horizon in the last paragraph.

The mental feebleness of the Orientals takes on not only this "soft", "bowing" quality but also a threatening aspect as an irrational force. Kinglake assumes the Orientals lack the rationality of human beings, and he regards the Orient itself as a place that seeks to deceive the West with mirages or cheats. After he becomes aware of this danger and the causes of its influence on westerners, Kinglake systematically proceeds to destroy its power. Kinglake first encounters what he considers the intellectual dark ages of the Oriental mind as he attempts an innovative technique to care for the ailing Methley (Lord Pollington) on the road to Constantinople. Methley had to be carried somehow and so Kinglake devised the plan of hitching horses instead of oxen to a Turkish araba (a lady's carriage) to accommodate him. As he tries to put his plan into action he complains that "[n]o one had ever heard of horses being used for drawing a carriage in this part of the world, but necessity is the mother of Innovation, as well as of Invention. . . . Thus poor, dear patient Reason would have fought her slow battle against Asiatic prejudice . . . " (ibid., 20). Although he writes in a comic tone here he soon takes the threat to reason seriously when he sees how drastically it affected Lady Hester Stanhope.

Lady Hester Stanhope and other Europeans, according to Kinglake, lost their reasoning faculties when they became infected by this subtle mental disease of the Orient. Lady Hester surrendered to the "intellectual regime" around her because "she seldom spoke to any body, except crazy old dervishes, who received her alms, and fostered her extravagances" (ibid., 82). So completely did she relinquish the battle that her behavior often came "perilously akin to madness" and in fact she felt unhappy when in a state of rationality: "I plainly saw that she was not an unhesitating follower of her own system, and I even fancied that I could distinguish the brief moments during which she contrived to believe in Herself [her divine self], from those long and less happy intervals in which her own reason was too strong for her" (ibid., 81). Kinglake opines that many others who come from Europe are, like her, prey to this environment:

> A man coming freshly from Europe is at first proof against the nonsense with which he is *assailed*, but often it happens that after a little while the social atmosphere in which he lives will begin to *infect* him, and if he is unaccustomed to the *cunning of fence* by which Reason prepares the means of *guarding* herself against fallacy, he will *yield* himself at last to the faith of those around him, and this he will do by sympathy, it would seem, rather than from conviction (ibid., 82) [emphasis mine].

There is no comic deflation anymore and Kinglake is evidently taking this insidious warfare seriously. He finds nothing laughable about this dark and gloomy picture of the secret plague of the Orient.

As if forewarned and forearmed by Lady Hester's fall, Kinglake resists deception by the forces of unreason for the rest of his journey and finally he "kills" the source of the threat. After visiting Lady Hester he continues toward Egypt via the Holy Land where at Nazareth he almost succumbs to the "insane" worship of the Virgin but recalls himself in time. Worship of Mary, as far as Kinglake is concerned, is "an insane devotion" from which his "watchful reason, if ever so slightly provoked, would drag [him] back to life" (ibid., 86). To lose his reason is to partake in the deathliness and torpor of the Orient, a state that Kinglake is nearly reduced to at Mary's shrine where he plunges into a fever:

> With a half consciousness — with the semblance of a thrilling hope that I was plunging deep, deep into my first knowledge of some most holy mystery, or of some new, rapturous and daring sin, I knelt, and bowed down my face till I met the smooth rock with my lips. . . . My bosom was lifted, and swung — as though I had touched Her warm robe. One moment — one more, and

then — the fever had left me. I rose from my knees. I felt hopelessly
sane. The mere world reappeared. My good old Monk was there,
dangling his keys with listless patience, and as he guided me from
the Church, and talked of the Refectory, and the coming repast,
I listened to his words with some attention and pleasure (ibid.).

The sensuous, unreasoning passion that almost makes Kinglake
lose his self-control here is not just dismissed or deflated but, as
can be seen from the description, consciously resisted by him.

As he continues on through the desert into Cairo he forces his
reason to challenge his doubts by logically exploring the situation.
The first example of desert magic encountered by him is an optical
illusion, a mirage:

About this part of my journey, I saw the likeness of a freshwater
lake; I saw, as it seemed, a broad sheet of calm water that stretched
far and fair towards the south — stretching deep into winding
creeks, and hemmed in by jutting, promontories, and shelving
smooth off towards the shallow side; on its bosom the reflected
fire of the sun lay playing and seeming to float upon waters deep
and still (ibid., 150).

The scene seems very convincing to him and it appears almost as
if the deity, the sun, is lying in wait for him. But this time Kinglake
does not fall into a fever. He guides his camel into the waters to
undeceive himself once and for all even though he "knew of the
cheat." In a detached, scientific manner he proceeds to analyze the
cause of the "phantasm":

A sheet of water heavily impregnated with salts, had filled this
hollow; and when dried up by evaporation had left a white saline
deposit that exactly marked the space which the waters had covered, and thus sketched a true shore-line. The minute crystals of
the salt sparkled in the sun, and so looked like the face of a lake
that is calm and smooth (ibid.).

Kinglake's reason has clearly become very active by this stage! In
fact his reason itself has acquired heroic proportions in that it has
given him the courage to literally walk straight into danger in order
to overcome the illusion.

Kinglake's second experience of desert magic is an even greater challenge because it is auditory and hence more difficult to deal with. It also carries additional conviction because it recalls his homeland to him:

> The sun, growing fiercer and fiercer, shone down more mightily now than ever on me he shone before, and as I drooped my head under his fire and closed my eyes against the glare that surrounded me, I slowly fell asleep, for how many minutes or moments, I cannot tell, but after a while I was gently awakened by a peal of church bells — my native bells — the innocent bells of Marlen, that never before sent forth their music beyond the Blaygon hills! (ibid.)

To further compound matters he realizes that at this very same time it would actually be Sunday morning in Marlen. But once more his reason reasserts itself and dismisses this as an illusion and attributes its cause to "the great heat of the sun, the perfect dryness of the clear air . . . and the deep stillness of all around" (ibid., 151).

Finally the great trickster, the sun itself, which had (according to Kinglake) bowed down the ancient Persians, stands before brandishing his sceptre:

> From pole to pole, and from the East to the West, he brandished his fiery sceptre as though he had usurped all Heaven and Earth. As he bid the soft Persian in ancient times, so now in his pride he seemed to command me and say, 'Thou shalt have none other gods but me.' I was all alone before him. There were these two pitted together, and face to face — the mighty sun for one, and for the other — this poor, pale, solitary self of mine, that I always carry about with me (ibid., 152).

Unlike the Oriental, his self, by sheer will, defied the sun and reached "the living world." The deathly mental stupor of the Orient did not engulf him; instead he emerged from it with his self intact, and in token of success he received from the West "an ear of rice, full, fresh and green" (ibid.). Like Noah, Kinglake maintained his faith and braved the terrors that surrounded him in his voyage.

Kinglake may have laughed at the romantic perception of the East initially, but he soon came to feel that this alien culture constituted a threat (even if not of a colorful 'romantic' nature) that must be overcome. Ultimately, in the death of the Wizard of Cairo he destroys this danger to his reason. He strikes a deal with a Wizard (as he calls him) to descend into the pyramids with him and there evoke the Devil. However, the Wizard makes no money on the agreement because on the appointed day he dies. Symbolically, not only has the mysterious East lost its power over Kinglake, he has also killed it.

The passive Orient also possesses a physical, literal danger that Kinglake has to face: the death-dealing plague. From Belgrade, Stamboul, to Cairo it pursues Kinglake, and unlike the relatively tame threat of the "coffin-shaped" temptress, the plague is the raging "Angel of Death". As Kathleen Zane has observed in her dissertation, "Paradigms of Place in Travel Literature: The Oriental Voyages of Nerval, Burton, Kinglake, and Chateaubriand", Kinglake specifically associated the plague with the Orient. On entering plague-ridden Stamboul (Constantinople) Kinglake remarks that

> [w]ith all that is most truly oriental in its character, the Plague is
> associated; it dwells with the faithful in the holiest quarters of the
> city: the coats and hats of Pera are held to be nearly as innocent
> of infection, as they are ugly . . . but the rich furs, and the costly
> shawls, the broidered slippers, and the gold-laden saddle cloth . . .
> these are the signs which mark the familiar home of the Plague
> (Kinglake 1845: 24).

The plague is not just specifically Oriental, and associated with the symbols of its splendor, its holiness and its rich furs, it is also the only source of majesty in the East, for:

> You go out from your living London — the centre of the greatest
> and strongest among all earthly dominions — you go out thence,
> and travel on to the capital of an Eastern Prince — you find but
> a waning power, and a faded splendor . . . but let the infernal Angel
> of Plague be at hand, and he, more mighty than armies — more
> terrible than Suleyman in his glory can restore such pomp and
> majesty to the weakness of the Imperial walls . . . (ibid.).

The plague is both the dividing line between the living West and the dying East, and the Eastern threat to the West, just as Eastern irrationality constituted a challenge to the westerner.

In its feminine form the plague takes the shape of a subtle enemy that ambushes the westerner. Although Kinglake uses the male pronoun for the awesome angel, he describes it in feminine, almost seductive terms: he views it as "mysterious" and "exciting", as a force that spreads its power gently, softly, through contact with clothes and silently creeps through the veins. According to Kinglake, it is the Oriental woman's pet trick, "a very old piece of fun," to pretend to spread the disease by touching Europeans. Although Kinglake maintains a bold front he is aware of the danger he faces, particularly in Cairo where the death toll has been exceedingly high. The plague was the "master of the city", and Kinglake knows himself well enough to admit that he truly lived in a state of fear:

> There is some semblance of bravado in my manner of talking about the Plague. I have been more careful to describe the terrors of other people than my own. The truth is, that during the whole period of my stay at Cairo, I remained throughly impressed with a sense of my danger. I may almost say that I lived in perpetual apprehension, for even in sleep, as I fancy there remained with me some faint notion of the peril with which I was encompassed (ibid., 154).

So terrible is the plague that on the seventh day after his arrival in Cairo the city is *"silenced"* and death begins to race down the streets as he hears the funeral howls:

> when his end appears to be approaching, and the moment that life is gone, they lift up their voices, and send forth a loud wail from the chamber of Death. Thus I know when my near neighbours died; sometimes the howls were near; sometimes more distant. Once I was awakened in the night by the wail of death in the next house, and another time by a like howl from the house opposite; and there were two or three minutes, I recollect, during which the howl seemed to be actually *running* along the street (ibid., 170).

No amount of cheerfulness deflates this threat and Kinglake never denies his underlying sense of anxiety: "For nearly three weeks I had lived under peril of death."

But as sheer will power enabled him to resist the illusions of the sun earlier he now concludes that he can deal with the plague in the same way. He decides that fear of the plague alone brings it on and that if he would refuse to believe in it, it would not be able to touch him:

> I took it into my pleasant head that all the European notions about contagion were throughly unfounded — that the plague might be providential, or 'epidemic' (as they phrase it), but was not contagious, and that I could not be killed by the touch of a woman's sleeve, nor yet by her blessed breath. I therefore determined that the Plague should not alter my habits and amusements in any one respect. Though I came to this resolve from impulse, I think that I took the course which was most prudent, for the cheerfulness of spirits which I was thus enabled to retain, discouraged the yellow-winged Angel, and prevented it from taking a shot at me (ibid., 163).

It is in the light-hearted style with which Kinglake deals with this threat that we see that laughter is more than a technique for deflating the romantic view of the Orient; it is also his way of guarding himself from the actual terrors of this alien world.

Kinglake's light-heartedness, it seems, is a "manly" tool for challenging the plague. It permitted him to play a game with death and to win as he rode down the crowded streets of Cairo on his donkey: "If I got through a street without being touched, I won; if I was touched, I lost — lost a deuce of a stake, according to the theory of the Europeans, but that I deemed to be all nonsense — I only lost that game, and would certainly win the next" (ibid., 164). And finally when the plague does literally breathe down his throat in the form of the dying medico of Cairo examining him for a throat ailment, he refuses to reveal his illness to any one of his servants till the "fever was extinguished." His will power combined with the help of the cheerful, courageous English doctor (the only one who has not left the city) who shakes his hand with "manly violence" give the death blow to the disease.

The persona of *Eothen* is not simply the mature man who laughs at the young man's romantic perception of the East, but an individual who through the course of his journey comes to feel that the "otherness" of the Orient by its very nature constitutes a threat to his way of life and his very being. The journey takes on the form of a conquest of the Orient and laughter develops into a serious technique of coping with this unseen enemy.

Perhaps Kinglake felt this strong need to dominate the Orient literarily not just because of a cultural will to power but also because the Orient represented to him the nameless, invisible terror of life he had experienced since early childhood. In a short chapter devoted to the Egyptian pyramids Kinglake describes the nightmarish feeling they give rise to and the old fears they revive:

> Yet it was not till I came to the base of the great Pyramid, that reality began to weigh upon my mind. Strange to say, the bigness of the distinct blocks of stone was the first sign by which I attained to feel the immensity of the whole pile. When I came, and trod, and touched with my hands, and climbed, in order, then, and almost suddenly, a cold sense and understanding of the Pyramid's enormity came down overcasting my brain.
>
> ... when I was very young (between the ages, I believe, of three and five years old), being then of delicate health, I was often in time of night the victim of a strange kind of mental oppression; I lay in my bed perfectly conscious, and with open eyes, but without power to speak, or to move, and all the while my brain was oppressed to distraction by the presence of a single and abstract idea — the idea of solid Immensity. It seemed to me in my agonies, that the horror of this visitation arose from its coming upon me without form or shape — that the close presence of the direst monster ever bred in Hell would have been a thousand times more tolerable, than that simple idea of solid size; my aching mind was fixed, and riveted down upon the mere quality of vastness, vastness, vastness; and was not permitted to invest it with any particular object. ... I could not of course find words to describe the nature of my sensations, and even now I cannot explain why it is that the forced contemplation of a mere quality, distinct from matter, should be so terrible. Well, now my eyes saw and knew, and my

hands and my feet informed my understanding, that there was
nothing at all abstract about the great Pyramid — it was a big
triangle, sufficiently concrete, easy to see, and rough to touch; it
could not, of course, affect me with the peculiar sensation which
I have been talking of, but yet there was something akin to that
old night-mare agony in the terrible completeness with which a
mere mass of masonry could fill and load my mind.

And time too; the remoteness of its origin, no less than the
enormity of its proportions, screens an Egyptian Pyramid from
the easy and familiar contact of our modern minds; at its base the
common Earth ends, and all above is a world — one not created
of God — not seeming to be made by men's hands, but rather, the
shear [*sic*] giant-work of some old dismal age weighing down this
younger planet (ibid., 176–77).

The pyramid weighs down his mind for it represents to him his
private nightmares of oppression, destruction, and indescribable,
mysterious terror; but it also threatens him as a westerner because
it represents a scale of time that is beyond his conception of history.
The Orient is thus an externalization of personal anxieties that he
must overcome and also an ancient world that he must destroy
because in its very age it weighs down his younger Western mind.

Ridicule of the Western Conqueror

Kinglake has been more successful than two other sojourners in the
East, Lady Hester Stanhope and Carrigaholt (Kinglake's friend,
Henry Stuart Burton) in that he both deflates the romantic approach to the East and vanquishes the terrors that inspired that
attitude. On the other hand, Lady Hester, who had established
herself in Lebanon with a small guard of soldiers as the Queen of
the Desert, succumbed to the influence of the East and reached a
stage of "fierce and inordinate pride perilously akin to madness."
Only partially did she manage to keep the Orient at bay, as Kinglake
proudly informs us, by deterring Ibrahim Pasha from attacking her
sanctuary for as "long as the Chatham's grand-daughter breathed a
breath of life there was always this one hillock, . . . which stood and
kept its freedom" (ibid., 76). And the dreamer Carrigaholt, an old
friend whom Kinglake encountered in Smyrna, that "practical

Plato" who attempted to "purchase (not only the scenery) but the many dramatis personae belonging to his dreams, with all their goodness, and graces complete," escaped this degenerate influence only by being suddenly married off in England.

And yet, even in his personal successful conquest of the East and its temptations and terrors, Kinglake finds the arrogant overbearing personality of himself and other Englishmen ludicrous. He does not hesitate to laugh or to express uneasiness at the very behavior that he himself endorses by his actions. This mocking and humorous aspect of his comic style, which is evident in chapter one where he first confronts the East, appears intermittently throughout the account, and manifests itself even in the "Surprise of Satalieh." Although Kinglake did not create a novel opinion (i.e. non-Orientalist) of the Orient as Said has argued, he did however express doubts about the dignity and humanity of his behavior and that of the "civilized" westerner toward it. Kinglake is so aware of the comic appearance that the proud Englishman in the East portrays that he can even provide us with an imaginary description of a fellow countryman's encounter with a Pasha. Since this scene follows his own meeting with the Pasha one wonders if this is his own way of perhaps laughing at himself. He refuses to provide us with the "substance" of his own conversation and instead presents us with a hypothetical drama:

> *Pasha* — The Englishman is welcome; most blessed among hours is this, the hour of his coming.
> *Dragoman* (to the Traveller) — The Pasha pays you his compliments.
> *Traveller* — Give him my best compliments in return, and say I'm delighted to have the honour of seeing him.
> *Dragoman* (to the Pasha) — His Lordship, this Englishman, Lord of London, Scorner of Ireland, Suppressor of France, has quitted his governments, and left his enemies to breathe for a moment, and has crossed the broad waters in strict disguise, with a small but eternally faithful retinue of followers, in order that he might look upon the bright countenance of the Pasha of Pashas — the Pasha of the everlasting Pashalik of Karaghlookoldour (ibid., 7).

The excessive number of honorifics mocks not only the Oriental style, but also, indirectly, the Englishman's pride in his nation and his love of ornate titles. The traveler's response, as the drama continues, reveals that he wishes the Pasha to be informed of his elevated status:

> *Traveller* (to his Dragoman) — What on earth have you been saying about London? The Pasha will be taking me for a mere cockney. Have not I told you *always* to say that I from a branch of the family of Mudcombe Park, and that I am to be a magistrate for the county of Bedfordshire, only I've not qualified, and that I should have been a Deputy-Lieutenant, if it had not been for the extraordinary conduct of Lord Mountpromise, and that I was candidate for Goldborough at the last election, and that I should have won easy, if my committee had not been bought. I wish to heaven that if you *do* say anything about me, you'd tell the plain truth (ibid., 7).

One wonders if Kinglake was mocking himself for, after all, he was a member of Parliament himself. The "plain truth", the traveler's belief in his own magnificence, gets further punctured by the Dragoman's interpretation:

> *Dragoman* (growing sulky and literal) — This friendly Englishman — this branch of Mudcombe — this head-purveyor of Goldborough — this possible policeman of Bedfordshire is recounting his achievements, and the number of his titles (ibid.).

In light of these "titles" the traveler's comments on the power and responsibility of the English toward the Orient sound absurd:

> I want to get his views, in relation to the present state of the Ottoman Empire; tell him the Houses of Parliament have met, and that there has been a Speech from the throne, pledging England to preserve the integrity of the Sultan's dominions (ibid.).

This is a very specific satire. In the form of this strutting Englishman it undermines precisely the same kind of behavior that we will soon see Kinglake indulging in. It is almost as though before he proceeds to arrogantly express his pride in his race he is setting the context for us to view it in.

Kinglake intermittently critiques Englishmen and their sense of superiority and their expression of their power, and finally concludes with the "Surprise of Satalieh" which constitutes a chapter full of satiric comments on the westerner in general. As the first chapter sets the undertones for his conquest of the Orient the last chapter looks back on it and draws our attention to all the subtle and unsubtle comments he made on the Englishman's assumed arrogance before the Oriental and the Oriental landscape throughout the journey.

Even the famous English impassiveness which distinguished them from the so-called childishly gregarious behavior of the Orientals comes in for its share of comic treatment. Kinglake describes with joy his sight of an Englishman in the desert and then paints a ludicrous picture of the awkwardness of their "civilized" behavior. First he builds up the emotional impact of the event:

> You, — you love sailing, — in returning from a cruise to the English coast, you see often enough a fisherman's humble boat far away from all shores, with an ugly black sky above, and an angry sea beneath, — you watch the grisly old man at the helm, carrying his craft with strange skill through the turmoil of waters, and the boy, supple-limbed, yet weather-worn already, and with steady eyes that look through the blast, — you see him understanding commandments from the jerk of his father's white eyebrow, — now belaying, and now letting go, — now scrunching himself down into mere ballast, or baling out Death with a pipkin. Stale enough is the sight, and yet when I see it I always stare anew, and with a kind of Titanic exultation, because that a poor boat with the brain of a man, and the hands of a boy on board, can match herself so bravely against black Heaven and Ocean; well, so when you have travelled for days and days, over an Eastern Desert, without meeting the likeness of a human being, and at last you see an English shooting-jacket and his servant come listlessly slouching along from out the forward horizon, you stare at the wide unproportion between this slender company, and the boundless plains of sand through which they are crossing their way (ibid., 147).

After this scene of exultation and human loneliness the "civilized", as opposed to "Oriental", behavior of the two Englishmen as they meet in the desert takes on a ludicrous aspect:

As we approached each other it became with me a question whether we should speak; I thought it likely that the stranger would accost me, and in the event of his doing so was quite ready to be as sociable and chatty as I could be, according to my nature. . . . The traveller, perhaps, felt as I did for except that we lifted our hands to our caps and waved our arms in courtesy, we passed each other as if we had passed in Bond Street. Our attendants, however were not to be cheated of the delight they felt in speaking to new listeners, and hearing fresh voices once more. The masters, therefore, had no sooner passed each other than their respective servants quietly stopped and entered into conversation. As soon as my camel found her companions were not following her, she caught the social feeling and refused to go on. I felt the absurdity of the situation and determined to accost the stranger. . . . He was the first to speak; he was much too courteous to address me as if he admitted of the possibility of my wishing to accost him from any mere sociability, or civilian-like love of vain talk; on the contrary, he at once attributed my advances to a laudable wish of acquiring statistical information, and accordingly, when he got within speaking distance, he said, 'I dare say you wish to know how the Plague is going on at Cairo?' . . . I thought him manly and intelligent; a worthy one of the few thousand strong English-men to whom the Empire of India is committed (ibid.).

Unable to communicate freely the two Englishmen can only discuss the death toll — "laudable" behavior indeed. Kinglake's last comments on the English stranger as "manly" become very suspect in light of this scene, for, since he has treated the terms "English" and "manly" so comically, one wonders how seriously to take them. In a very sly manner Kinglake has called into question the very qualities of himself and his countrymen — their innate Englishness and manliness — which supposedly make them superior to the Orientals.

The image of the conquering Englishman who is not only superior to the natives but who also puts them in their place too becomes a figure of fun. At one stage, when the Western attitude toward the Orient takes on lurid colors, Kinglake's satiric tone increases in sharpness. When Kinglake's faithful and zealous dragoman, Dthemetri, recommends the execution of the Nazarene for having taken them through the wrong route and endangering their lives he informs us that he found this suggestion

> fascinating . . . for the slaying of the guide was of course easy enough, and would look like an act of what politicians call 'vigor'. If it were only to become known to my friends in England that I had calmly killed a fellow creature for taking me out of my way, I might remain perfectly quiet and tranquil for the rest of my days, quite free from the danger of being considered 'slow'; I might ever after live upon my reputation like 'single-speech Hamilton' in the last century, or 'single-sin — ' in this, without being obliged to take the trouble of doing any more harm in the world (ibid., 108).

Kinglake clearly rebels here against the Western tendency to treat the Orientals as just so many decadent beings who have to be disciplined by them, and more interestingly, he also implies that if the Orient is considered barbaric, the West, in its arrogation of superiority, is no less cruel. Kinglake proceeds to seriously consider the issue, thus making fun of his "magnanimity" in letting the Nazarene live:

> I had no crotchet at that time against the punishment of the death, but I was unused to blood, and the proposed victim looked so thoroughly capable of enjoying life (if only he could get to the other side of the river), that I thought it would be hard for him to die, merely in order to give me a character for energy. Acting on the result of these considerations, and reserving to myself a free and unfettered discretion to have the poor villain shot at any future moment, I magnanimously decided that for the present he should live and not die (ibid.).

Kinglake has mocked not only the arrogant violence but also the equally presumptuous conviction of the Englishman in his so-called magnanimity toward the Orient. But by including himself in the description and making himself a figure of fun he successfully evades offending his readers while criticizing them.

Kinglake often undermines his own chauvinism — particularly his victory over the plague, the desert sun, and the Pasha of Satalieh

— by using a comic tone. As he wends his way through Cairo's bazaar which is full of the fragrance of "burial spice" he portrays his invasion of this plague ridden area in comic terms: "it seems to you that it is not the donkey but the donkey-boy who wafts you on with his shouts through pleasant groups and air that feels thick with the fragrance of burial spice. Eh! Sheik, — Eh! Bint, — reggalek — shumalek, &c., &c., — O old man, O virgin, get out of the way on the right — O virgin, O old man, get out of the way on the left, — this Englishman comes, he comes, he comes!" (ibid., 164). Such is the stuff of English heroes arriving on donkeys with donkey-boys ominously crying "he comes!"

Even his conquest of the awesome desert comes in for ridicule. On the one hand, he pits his will against it, on the other hand he laughs at his presumptuous domination of it:

> At the beginning of my journey, the night breeze blew coldly; when that happened, the dry sand was heaped up outside round the skirts of the tent, and so the Wind that everywhere else could sweep as he listed along those dreary plains was forced to turn aside in his course, and make way, as he ought, for the Englishman. . . .
>
> By and by there was brought to me the fragrant tea. . . . I feasted like a king — like four Kings — like a boy in the fourth form. . . .
>
> [as they depart] A speck in the broad tracts of Asia remained still impressed with the mark of patent portmanteaus, and the heels of London boots; the embers of the fire lay black and cold upon the sand, and these were the signs we left (ibid., 143–44).

The self-importance of the Englishman is humorously portrayed as nothing more than that of a boy in the "fourth form" and the mark of the Englishman dwindles into "patent portmanteaus" and "London boots". No wonder Kinglake exclaims as he completes the desert crossing, "the eternal ego that I am!"

The storming of Satalieh, the dramatic example of Kinglake's domination of the Orient, with which the book concludes is also the point at which Kinglake not only laughs at himself but also expresses his doubts about his imperial "right". Disinclined to observe quarantine restrictions that bar him from disembarking at Satalieh for a few days, Kinglake proposes a plan of attack. At the same time, however, he admits that the "impropriety of a traveller's setting at naught the regulations of another state is clear enough, and the bad taste of compassing such a purpose by mere gasconading is still more glaringly plain" (ibid., 227). He is only too relieved that he can shuffle off the responsibility on his Russian companion by the act of perpetrating the deed under the Russian flag.

Kinglake continues by deflating the heroism of the enterprise through a comic portrayal of it:

> We immediately formed a little column, or rather, as I should have called it, a procession, for we had no fighting aptitude in us, and were only trying as it were, how far we could go in frightening children. First marched the sailor with the Russian flag of war bravely fluttering in the breeze; then came the general and I; then our servants, and lastly, if I rightly recollect, two more of the Brigantine's crew. Our flag-bearer entered into the spirit of the enterprise, and bore the standard aloft with so much pomp and dignity, that I found it exceedingly hard to keep a grave countenance.... [and when they make a strategic mistake] I showed my comrade the danger he was running, and in the next instant we were both advancing more pompously than ever (ibid., 229).

Kinglake evidently has not changed in his approach toward Orientals since he still plays the game of frightening what he considers full-grown children, but he does find the act of domination absurdly comic and perhaps demeaning to the perpetrator himself. The description of the final confrontation — the debate with the Pasha — reminds one of the comic bullying style of the actor Eddie Murphy than the triumph of a superior power over an inferior:

> Therefore, without deigning to defend our conduct, he [the Russian] at once commenced a spirited attack upon the Pasha. The poor Italian Doctor translated one or two sentences to the Pasha, but he evidently mitigated their import; the Russian, growing warm, insisted upon his attack with redoubled energy and spirit; but the medico, instead of translating, began to shake violently with terror, and at last came out with his 'non ardisco,' and fairly confessed that he dared not interpret fierce words to his master.
>
> Now then, at a time when everything seemed to depend upon the effect of speech, we were left without an interpreter.

... [as the General continues to rage] the Pasha saw at his side a man, who not only seemed to be entirely without fear, but to be raging with just indignation, and thence-forward he plainly began to think that in some way or other (he could not tell how), he must certainly have been in the wrong. In a little time he was so much shaken, that the Italian ventured to resume his interpretation, and my comrade had again the opportunity of pressing his attack upon the Pasha; his argument, if I rightly recollect its import, was to this effect — 'If the vilest Jews were to come into the harbor, you would but forbid them to land, and force them to perform the quarantine, yet this is the very course, O Pasha, which your rash officers dared to think of adopting with *us!* — those mad and reckless men would have actually dealt towards a Russian General Officer and an English Gentleman as if they had been wretched Israelites! Never, never, will we submit to such an indignity. His Imperial Majesty knows how to protect his nobles from insult, and would never endure that a General of his army should be treated in matter of quarantine, as though he were a mere Eastern Jew!' (ibid., 231–32).

The bold and spirited attack is not more heroic than a clever use of words and in the process the Russian himself becomes a caricature akin to a comic, raging figure. Ultimately, it turned out that they were victorious not because of their skill with words but because the Pasha had a healthy fear of Russians having once been their prisoner of war.

Kinglake's comic style is what makes his criticism subtle and cutting. On the one hand, he satirizes the English ego vis-à-vis the Orient, but since he involves himself in this portrait and uses a light-hearted tone it is easy to note the comedy and miss the rest of the intent. The comic tone so effectively disguises the satire on the inflated English sense of self that it is hard to believe that this is the same man who, within a few months of the publication of *Eothen*, spoke out vehemently in "The 'French Lake'" (*The Quarterly*) against British occupation of Egypt. Referring to Warburton's comments in his travel narrative *The Crescent and the Cross* urging England to assert her dominion over Egypt, Kinglake writes:

> We will not seriously inveigh against a suggestion put forward as
> a mere piece of chat in the course of a traveller's narrative, but
> thinking that the indulgence of national covetousness at the ex-
> pense of friendly states is of itself an evil though never actually
> fulfilled, we would willingly chill this ardour for the spoliation of
> a Mahometan [*sic*] prince . . . (*Quarterly Review* 75 (1844–45):
> 534).

Although Kinglake did not question the British conception of the
Orient and Orientals as timid, stereotypical types that could easily
be controlled by the English, he was critical of the way Englishmen
imposed their ego on it and sought to possess it.

The Geographical East-West Dividing Line

Although Kinglake was uneasy with the Western attitude of domination toward the East, he had no doubts about Eastern inferiority
vis-à-vis the West. The East was a weak, dying place, unable to
shake off the torpor it had sunk into: "[the] Oriental, who, for
creative purposes, is a thing dead and dry — a mental mummy that
may have been a live King just after the flood, but has since lain
balmed in spice" (Kinglake 1845: 53). This cultural self-assurance,
however, did fail him in his confrontation with the European–
Oriental culture of the Greeks. One sees him struggling visibly
between a reductive approach toward the Greeks and a desire to
treat them as individuals affected by social and institutional forces.

Kinglake evidently associated the Greeks with European culture — as possessing imaginative and creative powers — rather
than with what he considers to be "Oriental" culture. He writes
how in his excitement he had turned his face "to the 'shining
Orient,' forgetful of old Greece, and all the pure wealth she has
left to this matter-of-fact ridden world" (ibid., 30). Greece, as these
lines indicate, is regarded as distinct from the Orient. In fact,
Kinglake feels so certain that the Greeks share the same characteristics as the "stirring" European world that he argues that since
the *Arabian Nights* have "so much of freshness of life, so much of
the stirring and volatile European character", they must have been
written by Greeks (ibid., 53).

As a traveler, however, his imaginative geography of what constitutes the "Orient" and the "European" has to face the physical,
historical reality. As next door neighbors of Turkey, Greece had for
centuries been a part of the Ottoman empire, and even in 1834
the bulk of the Greeks were still members of this Oriental empire
of the Turks. On the one hand, Kinglake wants to regard them as
Europeans, on the other hand he often treats them as Orientals,
and as a result his European/Oriental distinctions begin to blur.
His vacillations and doubts about the European-ness of the Greeks
expresses an uneasiness with the application of Orientalist conceptions to the cultural and geographical situation he encounters on
his journey.

Kinglake toured Greece with his friend Methley (Lord Pollington) very soon after they crossed the border into the Orient. With
a romantic yearning he leaves the Oriental city for Grecian skies:

> I sated my eyes with the pomps of the city, and its crowded waters,
> and then I looked over where Scutari lay half veiled in her mournful
> cypresses; I looked yet farther, and then higher, and saw in the
> heavens a silver cloud that stood fast, and still against the breeze;
> it was pure and dazzling white as might be the veil of Cytherea,
> yet touched with fire, as though from beneath, the loving eyes of
> an immortal were shining through and through. I knew the bear-
> ing, but had enormously misjudged the distance, and underrated
> its height, and so it was a sign and a testimony — almost as a call
> from the neglected gods, that now I saw and acknowledged the
> snowy crown of the Mysian Olympus (ibid., 30).

Greece is beautiful, pure and immortal, just as he had felt it to be
when his mother taught him "to find a home in his saddle, and to
love old Homer, and all that Homer sung" (ibid., 31). He recalls
his elation as a child with Alexander Pope's translation of *The Iliad*:
"it was history — poetry — revelation — . . . the works of men's
hands were folly and vanity, and would pass away like the dreams
of a child, but that the kingdom of Homer would endure for ever
and ever" (ibid., 32). This is Greece to him and this is how he seeks
to preserve it. While he is successful in this in the barren plains of
Troy, he does not find it an easy task in the cities.

As he wanders down what he calls the Troad (the road to Troy) with Methley he behaves very 'un-European' (unlike what he considers to be European, that is), very irrational, in his attempt to view Greece as the eternally pure and beautiful land:

> It was coldly, and thanklessly, and with vacant unsatisfied eyes that I watched the slow coming, and the gliding away of the waters [of the Scamander]. . . . Your feelings wound up and kept ready for some sort of half-expected rapture are chilled, and borne down for the time under all this load of earth and water; but let these once pass out of sight, and then again the old fanciful notions are restored, and the mere realities which you have just been looking at are thrown back so far into distance, that the very event of your intrusion upon such scenes begins to look dim and uncertain as though it belonged to mythology (ibid., 34).

This response is very different from his attitude of power and superiority toward the Orient. Here he consciously feels the need to elevate Greece just as he is certain of the West's superiority toward the East. Even his supposedly rational Western mind prefers to be deliberately illogical where Greece is concerned: "Nobody, whose mind has not been reduced to the most deplorably logical condition, could look upon this beautiful congruity between the *Iliad* and the material world, and yet bear to suppose that the poet may have learned the features of the coast from mere hearsay . . . " (ibid., 36).

While it is easy for Kinglake to preserve his image of Greece as the fount of civilization and poetic imagination on the Troad, it is not so easy for him to do so when he confronts individual Greeks in Smyrna, Greek sailors on a brigantine. It is here that we see him caricaturing them as flat, stereotypical characters just as he does the Oriental. However, he does at the same time attempt to rationalize and contextualize their behavior in terms of socioeconomic circumstances, something he does not do where Orientals are concerned. In Smyrna, he encounters the vices of the Greeks and realizes how badly they are treated in consequence. The Greeks, he writes, lack the virtues of veracity and fidelity (as did our Persian friend Hajji Baba), as a result of which they are highly unpopular among European merchants. They have such a poor reputation, he warns us, that "you must make up your mind to hear an almost universal and unbroken testimony against the character of the people whose ancestors invented Virtue" (ibid., 42). Kinglake thus views the Greeks as different from the Europeans and he observes how the other Europeans look down on them as scheming rascals; as we can see from his description of Orientals, he classes the modern Greeks with them instead. For example, he explains how on the desert march to Cairo his Arab companions pretended that they have no bread although they had initially agreed to bring their own food. Advised by his dragoman, Kinglake refuses to share his food and soon observes the deceitful trick played on him:

> In about ten minutes from this time, I found that the Arabs were briskly cooking their bread! Their pretence of having brought no food was false, and was only invented for the purpose of saving it. They had a good bag of meal which they had contrived to stow away under the baggage, upon one of the camels, in such a way as to escape notice. In Europe the detection of a scheme of this nature would have occasioned a disagreeable feeling between the master and the delinquent, but you would no more recoil from an Oriental, on account of a matter of this sort, than in England you would reject a horse that had tried to, and failed to throw you (ibid., 141).

Kinglake has reduced Arabs to stereotypes by generalizing about all Orientals from his companions. The difference between his treatment of Orientals and Greeks lies in the way he tries to analyze the causes of the Greeks' decline (spends two pages on that) whereas he treats deceitful behavior on the part of Orientals as something natural.

On the other hand, the Greeks, he argues, have changed from a past state and are not inherently corrupt. He also proceeds to place their change within their environment, claiming that it is the doctrines and practices of their religion that have ruined them, for the "Greek Church . . . seems to hang like lead upon the ethereal spirit of the Greek" and has reduced him to a figure with a "shaven skull, and savage tail pending from his crown, kissing a thing of wood and glass, and cringing with these base prostrations, and apparent terror, before a miserable picture . . . " (ibid., 43). So whereas he regards the Greeks as being as dishonest as Orientals, at the same time he tries to view them as essentially upright people, like Europeans, who have been corrupted only by their circumstances and have declined from an ideal and glorious past.

Kinglake was also given to caricaturing Greeks and Orientals, but whereas he tries to be sympathetic on the one hand, he is entirely reductive as far as the Orientals are concerned. On board the Greek brigantine he describes the anarchy on board with reference to the delegation of responsibility:

> the cook whom we had on board was particularly careful about the ship's reckoning, and when, under the influence of the keen sea breeze, we grew fondly expectant of an instant dinner, the great author of pilafs would be standing on deck with an ancient quadrant in his hands, calmly affecting to take an observation. But then to make up for this, the Captain would be exercising a controlling influence over the soup, so that all, in the end, went well. Our mate was a Hydriot, a native of that island rock which grows nothing but mariners and mariner's wives. His character seemed to be exactly that which is generally attributed to the Hydriot race; he was fierce, and gloomy, and lonely in his ways. One of his principal duties seemed to be that of acting as counter-captain, or leader of the opposition, denouncing the first symptoms of tyranny, and protecting even the cabin-boy from oppression. Besides this, when things went smoothly, he would begin to prognosticate evil, in order that his more light-hearted comrades might not be puffed up with the seeming good fortune of the moment (ibid., 49).

The generalization he arrives at from this comic picture is a noble one: "It seemed to me that the personal freedom of these sailors who own no superiors except that of their own choice, is as like as may be to that of their sea-faring ancestors" (ibid.). Their democratic freedom becomes even more heroic as he describes what in actuality seems like a mutiny. The anxious crewmen who refuse to cooperate with the completion of the journey as the storm gathers curiously take the form of Greek heroes:

But where was the crew? It was a crew no longer, but rather a gathering of Greek citizens; — the shout of the seaman was changed for the murmuring of the people — the spirit of the old Demos was alive. The men came aft in a body, and loudly asked that the vessel should be put about, and that the storm should no longer be tempted. Now, then, for speeches: — the Captain, his eyes flashing fire, his frame all quivering with emotion — wielding his every limb, like another, and a louder voice, pours forth the eloquent torrent of his threats, and his reasons, his commands, and his prayers; he promises — he vows — he swears that there is safety in holding on — safety, *if Greeks will be brave!* . . . and the angry growl of the people goes floating down the wind, but they listen—they waver once more, and once more resolve, then waver again, thus doubtfully hanging between the terrors of the storm, and the persuasion of glorious speech, as though it were the Athenian that talked, and Philip of Macedon that thundered on the weather bow.

Brave thoughts winged on Grecian words gained their natural mastery over Terror . . . (ibid., 54).

While this mock-epic scene obviously makes fun of the romanti-cization of Greeks, it does not undermine the heroic deed itself; the exciting nature of the description suggests gleeful participation than detached criticism of the sailors. This particular aspect be-comes evident when, in contrast, we hear Kinglake's derogatory description of the assistance rendered to him by the Orientals in the crossing of the Jordan.

While Kinglake both caricatures and appreciates the Greeks as he does the arrogant Lady Hester, he is extremely reductive about Orientals even when they are at their most efficient and helpful. Their heroism and leadership is portrayed in a cartoon like absurd manner even though without their help he would not have been able to cross the Jordan river. The Arabs build rafts, load them with all his provisions and swim over the swift waters to the other bank whilst their elders on the shore encourage them on:

The old men with their long grey grisly beards stood shouting and cheering, praying and commanding. At length the raft entered upon the difficult part of its course; the whirling stream seized and twisted it about, and then bore it rapidly downwards; the swimming men flagged, and seemed to be beat in the struggle. But now the old men on the bank, with their rigid arms uplifted straight, sent forth a cry and a shout that tore the wide air into tatters, and then to make their urging yet more strong, they shrieked out the dreadful syllables, 'brahim Pasha!' [Ibrahim Pasha of Egypt who had recently terrorized them] The swimmers, one moment before so blown, and so weary found lungs to answer the cry, and shouting back the name of their great destroyer, they dashed on through the torrent and bore the raft in safety to the western bank (ibid., 116).

Their commands certainly demonstrate no Homeric qualities to Kinglake! In fact, Kinglake has interpreted the scene to fit into his theory, which he often gives expression to in *Eothen*, that Orientals are such cowards that they respect only the individual who terrorizes them. In this case he assumes that it is fear of Ibrahim Pasha that motivates the Arabs to help him. Considering that Kinglake knows no Arabic, and that his dragoman does not understand the dialect of this particular tribe very well, for all we know they might even have been crying out 'Inshallah' (an invocation to God) to encourage the swimmers in God's name. Perhaps because Kinglake regards himself so unequivocally superior and powerful where Orientals are concerned that he cannot see them in any other light than the absurd and uncivilized. Ignorant though he was of their language he was certain that were he not accidentally playing with his pistols while the Arabs were debating the situation they would have robbed rather than helped him.

Kinglake unhesitatingly applies his Orientalist notions of inferior power and morality to the Oriental, but he indirectly questions such an approach through the trouble he has in applying them to the European/Oriental Greeks. The imaginative idea that there exist some type of beings who are essentially, by their very nature or genetic type, alien and inferior crumbles when he comes across a people he is used to regard as European but who seem to him to share what he considers the characteristics of "Orientals". Kinglake vacillates in his attitude toward them, now regarding them the way he views Orientals, and now as individuals who are acted on by their environment.

Dthemetri, the dragoman who joins him halfway through his travels and is mentioned fairly regularly until the end of the journey, is the only Greek who is pure caricature. Perhaps because Kinglake met him outside the independent Greek kingdom and away from the Greek populace he tended to perceive him as an Oriental and to caricature him outrageously. He regards Dthemetri as no more than an absurd but loyal animal and in fact even juxtaposes descriptions of him with that of animals:

> The man was a zealous member of the Greek church. He had been a tailor. He was as ugly as the devil, having a thoroughly Tartar countenance, which expressed the agony of his body or mind, as the case might be, in the most ludicrous manner imaginable; he embellished the natural caricature of his person by suspending about his neck, and shoulders, and waist, quantities of little bundles and parcels, which he thought too valuable to be entrusted to the jerking of pack saddles. The mule which fell to his lot on this journey, every now and then, forgetting his rider was a saint, and remembering he was a tailor, took a quite roll upon the ground. . . . Dthemetri never got seriously hurt, but the subversion and dislocation of his bundles made him for the moment a sad spectacle of ruin, and when he regained his legs, his wrath with the mule became very amusing. He always addressed the beast in a language which implied, that he, as a Christian and a saint, had been personally insulted and oppressed by a Mahometan mule. Dthemetri, however, on the whole, proved to be a most able and capital servant; I suspected him of now and then leading me out of my way, in order that he might have an opportunity of visiting the shrine of a saint, and on one occasion . . . a gross breach of duty; but putting these pious faults out of the question (and they were faults of the right side), he was always faithful to me (ibid., 65).

The patronizing tone of the last sentence is evident even as he observes Dthemetri struggling in an unfamiliar dialect to obtain the help of the Arabs in crossing the Jordan. Starved and exhausted as the rest of them, Dthemetri remains sufficiently alert to negotiate with the Arabs, but in spite of that noble behavior he is referred to as the "faithful terrier" who "was bristling with zeal and watchfulness" (ibid., 115). Faithful servant though Dthemetri is, his servitude is taken for granted as if it is the order of nature that a being like him should be a servant.

Dthemetri is viewed within the traditional Western perception of the Oriental: amusing, childlike, possessing a limited intellect. As Iran Banu Hassani Jewett has argued in his dissertation, "Kinglake and the English Travelogue of the Nineteenth Century", Dthemetri's character is the perfect foil to Kinglake's:

> Dthemetri's Greek–Oriental character provides a perfect contrast to the English temperament of Kinglake. His reactions to any situation are meant to be typical of the Eastern mind unhampered by any European inhibitions. He is the Eastern Mr. Jekyll to Kinglake's English Dr. Hyde [Jewett got the names backwards], and gets things done by threats, lies and intrigues. . . . Dthemetri is indeed, such a useful representative of the Eastern mind as popularly conceived by the English, that had he not existed, Kinglake might have had to invent him; perhaps he did (Jewett 1964: 103).

Perhaps Kinglake was able to view Dthemetri as the typical Oriental because he did not see him in the context of other Greeks. Or perhaps his Orientalist attitude toward Dthemetri was an indication of his growing unease with the traditional imaginary line between East and West when applied literally to geography.

Even as he made his choice between the Orient and the Occident at the Pass of Lebanon, maybe he felt unsure about applying an imaginative concept to actual physical geography. It is interesting to note that when he turned toward the West at the Pass of Lebanon he encountered not a westerner but an Oriental speaking Italian and using the "phrases of Oriental courtesy in an European tongue" (Kinglake 1845: 224).

Kinglake's journey seems to follow two trajectories, each one of which is self-contradictory, and both of which are, to some extent, mutually at odds. With a sense of assurance in his powers he cheerfully dominates the Orient and determinedly turns to the West; but even as he does so he expresses doubts about the West's arrogation of power, its use of it, and this power mania's self-reductive quality. He also expresses doubts about the application of an imaginative East–West division on the actual route of his journey when he is faced with the Greek culture that he cannot categorize easily or comfortably. It's almost as though he is not quite sure what this Orient is that he is dominating or that he regards as inferior. Kinglake knew very little about the history, traditions, or language of the Orient, but the very fact of travel forced him to indirectly raise some questions about convenient, simplified notions regarding the Orient.

Although Kinglake was not an Oriental scholar, he was a well-educated man who moved comfortably in literary and political circles. He was aware of the prevailing Orientalist assumptions, both political and cultural; yet he chose to write a book that questioned these assumptions and seriously harmed his legal career. Murray feared that the book might create such a "clutter" that it would wind up on the list of prohibited books. The fact that it became so popular suggests that either few readers (except solicitors) were able to notice that the book expressed a "distrust of Western Progress" or — and what seems more likely — that the nineteenth century British view of its elevated status with reference to the East was not as inflexible as it has often been perceived to be. Later in the century, scholars like Richard Burton and Gertrude Bell were more vocal not only in criticism of their culture, but also of the validity of its Orientalist assumptions.

Notes

1. Quoted in Gerald de Gaury's *Travelling Gent*, page 48. Original source Cambridge University Library, Add. 7633.4.
2. The source for this is William Tuckwell's introduction to the 1898 reprint of the first edition of *Eothen*, not his memoir of Kinglake.
3. In T. Wemyss Reid, ed., *The Life, Letters, and Friendships of Richard Monckton Milnes, First Lord Houghton*, vol. 1 (1891): 347–48.

4. In her dissertation, "Paradigms of Place in Travel Literature", Kathleen Zane argues that Kinglake has such a strong sense of his English identity that he regards both Orientals and Europeans as "other": "He [Kinglake] does not enter these other places as Said would have him do because he understands who he is and that he cannot be at home everywhere. . . . He is secure in his role as traveller-outsider-foreigner and describes from this displaced distance" (Zane 1984: 177). Although Kinglake does make "[subtle] distinctions between French and English" — only in chapter eighteen of *Eothen* — one should bear in mind that this is subsumed under the larger and pervasive East–West, Europe–Orient divisions. In addition one should also note that though Kinglake distinguishes himself from Frenchmen and Orientals, he regards the two very differently. He critiques only the French who are settled in the Orient and does not generalize from them to all Frenchmen, and in fact he even gives them a different label: Levantines. And even though he ridicules their fear of the plague, he does not reduce them to objects to bully or dominate. In short Kinglake does not regard the Levantines as stereotypical objects subject to his will to power as he does the Orientals. To argue that Kinglake distinguishes himself from Frenchmen is not necessarily antithetical to Said's statement that "Kinglake's views express a public and national will over the Orient."

Chapter 4

Captain Sir Richard Francis Burton: "The Haji from the Far-North"

The Myth and the Man

As an adventurer and scholar Richard Burton (1821–1890) was a giant compared to Kinglake and Morier. He explored Sind, the Arabian peninsula, Egypt, Abyssinia, Iceland, and South America, discovering new places, and often daring to go where no white man had dared to go before him. His gift for languages enabled him to master them within a few months, and his keen eye for cultural norms helped him imitate the social mores and customs of different people and travel in disguise. He was also a prolific writer and left behind immense scientific data on the peoples and geographies of the lands he traveled to, and numerous translations of Arabic, Persian, and Indian works. To recount his achievements is beyond the scope of this chapter, but to some extent we can at least survey the attitudes that he brought to bear on his explorations.

The Legend Develops

Given Burton's abilities and adventures, he was the ideal candidate for the myth of the great white explorer. Numerous other factors, however, contributed considerably, not just to his fame, but also to his notoriety. He was tall, dark, with flashing, mesmerizing, "gypsy" eyes, pursuing young women to the horror (much to his delight!) of their respectable mamas. He never concealed his sexual desires, or his interest in the erotica of different countries, and his "intentions", as he made clear to an aggressive mother, were "strictly dishonourable." Daring and dashing as he was, he also portrayed himself as one who was neglected by his narrow-minded countrymen, which, to some extent, was the case. To complete the romantic picture of this social and moral outcast, add to it an ancestry that traces itself back to the bastard son of Louis XIV, and, somewhere along the way, that of the gypsies, and it is easy to understand why he became a legend in his lifetime. Soldier, scholar, renowned fencer, romantic outcast, a Casanova with mesmerizing eyes, and royal and foreign blood in him, he was the true Renaissance-cum-Byronic hero.

Legends and tales gathered rapidly around him in his own lifetime. In a 1906 article, "Richard Burton", Ouida (Maria Louisa Ramee, 1839–1908), the fashionable authoress, described him as "a man who looked like Othello and lived like the Three Mousquetaires [*sic*] blended in one," and that "[m]en in Foreign Office in his time used to hint dark horrors about Burton, and certainly, justly or unjustly, he was disliked and feared, and suspected in English political and social life . . ." (Ouida 1906: 1040–42). Another contemporary and acquaintance of Burton, Frank Harris, wrote in *Contemporary Portraits*:

> I was exceedingly curious, and very glad indeed to meet this legendary hero. Burton was in conventional evening dress, and yet, as he swung round to the introduction, there was an untamed air about him. He was tall, about six feet in height, with broad, square shoulders; he carried himself like a young man, in spite of his sixty years, and was abrupt in movement. His face was bronzed and scarred, and when he wore a heavy moustache and no beard he looked like a prize-fighter; the naked dark eyes — imperious, aggressive eyes, by no means friendly; the heavy jaws and prominent hard chin gave him a desperate air; but the long beard which he wore in later life, concealing the chin and pursed-out lips, lent his

face a fine patriarchal expression, subduing the fierce provocation of it to a sort of regal pride and courage. 'Untamed' — that is the word which always recurs when I think of Burton (Harris 1915: 180).

Harris continues to inform us, in an extravagant style, of Burton's "encyclopaedic reading," his "ethnological appetite," his "intellectual curiosity," and the romantic melancholy, "that deep down in him lay the despair and gloom of utter disbelief. . . . Burton's laughter, even deep-chested as it was, had in it something of sadness" (ibid., 183).

The legend continued well into the twentieth century, and biographers fictionalized and romanticized his already exciting life. A few examples should sufficiently demonstrate his impact on the biographers' imaginations. Fairfax Downey, in *Burton: Arabian Nights Adventurer*, describes Burton's birth in a manner that resembles that of Sleeping Beauty:

> Shadowy ancestors extremely un-English hovered over the cradle that night and bestowed singular hereditary gifts. Sifting down through generations, their offerings formed a human pot pourri who became one of the most extraordinary mortals ever to redeem Mother Nature's pattern from its monotony.
>
> The name of Burton, one of the half-dozen distinctively Gypsy patronymics, signed the presence among the donors of the Romany folk. They bequeathed the child the curse of Ishmael. They gave him their gift of tongues and their Gypsy eyes which 'look at you, look through you, and then glazing over, seem to see something beyond you'. . . .
>
> The effulgent wrath of Louis XIV in all likelihood deigned to grace the mixed company of that night. . . .
>
> Jostling majesty, Rob Roy responded to the roll call of progenitors. The bold Scottish outlaw has in his bestowal an unruly spirit, a mighty sword arm. . . .
>
> And far in the background, most shadowy of the shadows yet most dominant, surely strode some mighty Arab, a warrior sage of the resplendent days of the Caliphates (Downey 1931: 1–3).

Burton's devil-may-care attitude, his powerful personality, and his un-Englishness, has appealed strongly to the romantic inclinations of some of his biographers. As late as 1962, Alfred Bercovici, in *That Blackguard Burton!*, writes:

> As Burton spoke he fixed his extraordinary black eyes on Sir James, who stared back, fascinated. He had never seen the like of Burton's eyes before; they were the eyes of a questing panther, eyes that glittered with repressed ferocity; eyes that were afraid of no man and no god (Bercovici 1962: 11).

The problem with this approach to Burton is that it does not help the reader understand Burton or the circumstances of his life. It merely presents a one-sided, romantic view of the complex personality underlying those glittering eyes and repressed ferocity.

Burton's Life

The best and most recent biography, *The Devil Drives*, 1967, by Fawn M. Brodie, is a highly researched and well-documented portrayal of Burton's life and personality. For an account of his early years, however, Brodie had to depend considerably on the *Life of Capt. Sir Richard F. Burton*, 1893, written by Isabel Burton (Richard Burton's wife). Although Isabel Burton's work reflects her own romantic and Catholic biases, it is the only source available on Burton's early years because she burned all his diaries and journals, to which only she had access, after his death. However, she claims her account of his early years was dictated by Burton himself and preserved by her as such.

For the purpose of this chapter it is important to review only the early period of his life, up to his journey to Meccah and Madinah. Rather than consider all the varied adventures he had as a child (he came from a traveling family), I shall recount only certain incidents and events of his life that demonstrate his complex attitude toward his country and its imperialism. This will enable us to see how different he is from Morier and Kinglake, and also to anticipate and grasp his peculiar attitude toward the East.

Although born in Britain, Burton was not raised there, for when he was only a few months old his family moved to the continent and traveled constantly from place to place. Burton was in England for only two short periods: for about a year, when he was nine years old, and for approximately two years, 1840–1842, while at Oxford. The major portion of his upbringing was conducted by numerous maids, nannies, and tutors in a very haphazard manner in small British colonies (or settlements) all over Europe. These colonies were intensely patriotic, according to Burton in *Life*, but being far removed from England did not cater to the "Miss Grundy" type of respectability. The Burtons lived in "an oasis of Anglo–Saxon-dom in a desert of continentalism," but with "the weight of English respectability . . . taken off them" (*Life* 1: 17). At the same time they were very nationalistic, and any

> Englishman who refused to fight a duel with a Frenchman was sent to Coventry, and bullied out of the place. English girls who flirted with foreigners, were looked upon very much as white women who permit the addresses of a nigger, are looked upon by those English who have lived in black countries. White women who do these things lose caste (ibid., 18).

So while Burton retained his English roots and his English pride to the extent that he could never feel like a Frenchman or Italian while living in these colonies, he could not at the same time fit into the English society back home. With mingled bitterness and nostalgia Burton writes that "[i]n consequence of being brought up abroad, we never thoroughly understood English society, nor did society understand us," and he regarded himself as a "waif" and a "stray" (ibid., 32).

Burton's brief experience of life in England was an unhappy one, and he found the English people and their social codes disgusting. He felt that

> The national temper [of England] was fierce and surly. . . . The little children punched one another's heads on the sands, the boys punched one another's heads in the streets, and in those days a stand-up fight between men was not uncommon. Even the women punched their children, and the whole lower class society seemed to be governed by the fist (*Life* 1: 27).

He regarded his native land as a crude, primitive, and inhospitable place, and when he and his brother finally left for the continent, they scandalized every one on board. We shrieked, we whooped, we danced for joy. We shook our fists at the white cliffs, and loudly hoped we should never see them again. We hurrah'd for France, and hooted for England, "The land on which the Sun ne'er sets — nor rises" . . . (ibid., 1: 32).

When he returned to England in 1840 as an undergraduate at Oxford he found the upper class society there no more attractive than the one he had experienced earlier. He regarded Oxford as a "hotbed of toadyism and flunkeyism," and academically beneath his linguistic abilities. In 1842, after barely spending two years there, he deliberately had himself expelled, and left jauntily, shocking the dons even as he walked out. Burton not only broke some rules concerning the social life of undergraduates, he also had the face, when summoned before the authorities, to criticize such restrictive rules and to moralize that only "trust begets trust." When expelled, he rode out of the college on a tandem (forbidden to undergraduates), while performing on a tin trumpet, stepping on the best flowers, waving to his friends and kissing his hand to the shop girls! His description of his feelings conveys the extent of his disgust: "In my anger I thoroughly felt the truth of the sentiment — 'I leave thee, Oxford, and I loathe thee well, / Thy saint, thy sinner, scholar, prig, and swell'" (ibid., 91). Burton was clearly an Englishman who did not belong in his country.

Burton's isolation from England was also perhaps heightened by his dislike of his parents. His mother, as he informs us on the first page of his account, cheated him out of a fortune for love of her brother. Whether she really cared for Burton we will never really know, nor does it matter; what is important is Burton's perception of his mother's attitude towards him. That he did feel neglected and rejected is evident from the way he starts his account of himself, and from the fact that he did not care sufficiently to return home from Aden at the time of her death. As Brodie observes, he was in good health to make the trip, but instead he preferred to stay back and work on his book. He disliked his father intensely and considered him a hypocrite, and called him, sarcastically, a "highly moral man." As the children grew up indisciplined and wild, his father took to beating them, and by 1840 "it was evident that the Burton family was ripe for a break up. Our father, like an Irishman, was perfectly happy as long as he was the only man in the house, but the presence of younger males irritated him" (ibid., 65). Burton's only memories of home and country were of distaste, humiliation, and neglect, and for the rest of his life he avoided England, residing there as little as possible.

Burton was, in a sense, always searching for a home, comparing his family to other families. In *Life* he mentions how tamely their mother parted from them, whereas in "Italian families, nothing is more common than for all the brothers and sisters to swear that they will not marry if they are to be separated from one another" (ibid., 66). We see these observations of domestic love in his *Personal Narrative of a Pilgrimage to Al-Madinah and Meccah* (1855–1856) too, where he describes the meeting of a mother and son "weeping aloud for joy as he ran around his mother's camel . . . standing on double in vain attempts to exchange a kiss . . . " (Burton 1893: vol. 1, 287). With sadness, and a sense of isolation, he describes the meeting of his servant Mohammed al-Basyúni, with his mother at Meccah: "The boy Mohammed left me in the street, and having at last persuaded the sleepy and tired Indian porter, by violent kicks and testy answers to twenty cautious queries, to swing open the huge gate of his fortress, he rushed up stairs to embrace his mother. After a minute I heard the *Zaghritah Lululú*, or shrill cry which in these lands welcomes the wanderer home; the sound so gladdening to the returner sent a chill to the stranger's heart" (ibid., vol. 2, 159). But soon enough Burton makes himself thoroughly at home, and wins the heart of Mohammed's mother, and even participates in family squabbles.

Given Burton's background, it is not surprising that he delighted in shocking British society and pointing out the faults of its government. What is difficult to determine is whether he always meant what he said, or if he intended only to horrify his audience. To further compound matters, he developed a pride in his countrymen's achievements, although he disliked them, and consequently he desired to be recognized and admired by them. In *Life* he writes that a man without a country is nothing but a "blaze of light without a focus," and that "no one ever gets on in the world . . . unless he is a representative of his nation" (*Life* 1: 32). Much though he despised English society, he did sentimentally wish England could be his country, for "it is a great thing, when you have won a battle, or explored Central Africa, to be welcomed home by some little corner of the Great World, which takes a pride in your exploits" (ibid.).

Burton's personal pride blended into national arrogance (to some extent) perhaps during his stay in India. In 1842, he begged his father to buy him a commission in the Indian army, and since officers were in demand due to the recent Afghan War, and since his father had by now given up his private hope of making him a bishop, he succeeded in getting what he wished. The Indian possessions, as we know, generated a sense of arrogance toward the easterners in the minds of the British. Burton was no exception, and he soon became a staunch supporter of British imperialism.

Burton writes that the possession of India was a heady experience to most Englishmen residing there, and confesses that he too behaved like the others. The transition to an Anglo-Indian lifestyle was exciting for the average Englishman: "Essentially a middle-class society, like that of a small county town in England, . . . was suddenly raised to the top of a tree, and lost its head accordingly. Men whose parents in England were small tradesmen, or bailiffs in Scotland, found themselves ruling districts and commanding regiments, riding in carriages, and owning more pounds a month than their parents had pounds a year" (ibid., 104). Like the others, Burton too was affected by the change in circumstances and proceeded to live in an extravagant style, hiring more than the usual number of servants assigned to officers. Like the other officers, he too developed a sense of superiority over the natives he ruled, and was in fact annoyed with the Company for not extending its power further in India, and like them he mocked the reformers who believed that Asia must be ruled by the Asians:

> His [Mr. Richard Cobden's] opinion as a professional reformer was, that Hindostan must be ruled by those who live on that side of the globe, and that its people will prefer to be ruled by its own colour, kith, and kin, than subject itself to the humiliation of being governed by a succession of transient intruders from the antipodes. . . .

All this was the regular Free-trade bosh, and the Great Bags-
man would doubtless have been thunderstruck, had he heard the
Homeric shouts of laughter with which his mean-spirited utter-
ances were received by every white skin in British India. There was
not a subaltern in the 18th Bombay N.I. who did not consider himself perfectly capable of governing a million Hindus (*Life* 1: 115).

Here, Burton is clearly expressing the traditional Orientalist notions
of the superiority of the West over the East, and of the white man's
natural right and ability to rule another people. Although Burton
may not have been a true Englishman, his style of thinking, as far
as the Orient is concerned, was in the mainstream of British political
thought.

Burton identified himself with the concept of empire, but he
was never happy with British society, and it was the social codes
of this society that brought his Indian career to an abrupt end.
While posted in Sind in 1845, Burton had submitted an explicit
and detailed report on homosexual brothels at the request of his
superior, Sir Charles Napier, a report that he had obtained only by
disguising himself as a Pathan and visiting a brothel. Although
this was a confidential report, one of Burton's enemies made it
public and successfully put an end to Burton's career. Burton,
suspected of homosexuality, was given four years of leave and sent
out of India in 1849.

Emotionally and physically ill at the way he was treated for his
work, he went to Europe and lived in an English colony at Bou-
logne. Unfortunately, his reputation had preceded him, and he was
"cut" by the British as a man of whom "something wrong" was
known. Burton, being what he was, felt frustrated that his talents
were not recognized, but at the same time delighted in shocking
British society, and consequently never attempted to clear himself
of the charge of homosexuality. Although we will never know the
truth, chances are that he did not indulge in any such activities
because, as Jonathan Bishop observes in his article on "The Identities of Sir Richard Burton: The Explorer as Actor," 1957, Burton
had not been circumcised till he undertook the Hajj, and to have
participated in brothel activities as a fake Muslim would have
culminated in certain death.

After recuperating for four years, Burton obtained an extra year of leave, and with the support of the Royal Geographical Society went on a trip to Meccah and Madinah in 1853. He went on this pilgrimage with mixed feelings toward his countrymen, desirous of their praise, and yet not interested in it. As we shall see, although Burton undertook the journey for national fame, the narrative criticizes his country's social norms and foreign policy viciously, a tactic that would gain him anything but popularity. And, although he complained all his life for not having been appreciated by England, he characteristically refused to return to England after his great exploit to receive the public's adulation: he turned a deliberate cold shoulder to the very public whose admiration he sought.

Despising his countrymen, admiring their achievements, forever an outcast in his own nation, subscribing to the Anglo-Indian mentality, his attitude toward the Islamic Orient was undoubtedly mixed. It was a confused mixture of domination, and dehumanization, and of a sense of belonging in the Orient. Like the true "white sahib" from India he had a sense of superiority toward anything Eastern, but on the other hand, as an outsider in his country he felt more open to other norms and customs, and could mingle amongst the Orientals with ease.

His ability to mix with the natives wherever he went, took on an emotional content in Arabia because, unlike India, it was, as he says in his introduction to his translation of the *Arabian Nights* (1885) "the land of my predilection." Early in life, at Oxford, he had developed an interest in Arabic and had learnt it himself without a teacher. Burton never lost his interest in the language and peoples of Arabia to the end of his days. Towards the end of his career, when he was translating the *Arabian Nights*, he wrote that Arabia was "a region so familiar to my mind that even at first sight, it seemed a reminiscence of some by-gone metempsychic [presumably from metempsychosis, the transmigration of souls] life in the distant past" (introduction to translation of *Arabian Nights* viii). Burton thus felt not only disgust for his countrymen, but also a special affinity for the Arabs, and although he shared in the Orientalist thought of his country, he felt an outcast in that same country: an extremely complex frame of mind which can be seen clearly in the contradictory attitudes toward the Orient which co-exist in his *Personal Narrative of a Pilgrimage to Al-Madinah and Meccah.*

Critical Works on the *Pilgrimage*

Critical studies of his major travel book, the *Pilgrimage*, are few and far between, but are of an interesting and illuminating nature. The varied responses reveal the complexity of Burton's attitude toward the Orient, and indicate the need for an analysis of the tension underlying his representations of it. Both nineteenth and twentieth century responses to this travel book indicate great differences of opinion that need to be explored.

In the nineteenth century the work was very popular and went into four editions, three during Burton's own lifetime. The *Athenaeum* of 1855 admired both the scholarship and the lively style of this narrative. The reviewer writes:

> the last terrors are now vanishing from the mysterious East. Here we have from Mr. Burton fresh from the most sacred of Arabia's sacred places, — from the place of the Prophet's tomb, — from spots where the foot of the giaour is pollution, and where on being discovered he is liable to be quietly put out of the way, or at least unpleasantly made to conform to certain ancient customs of the country! Having done so much, Mr. Burton has a claim to no ordinary attention when he writes. The first requisite to an Odyssey is an Ulysses. Most of our Oriental travellers perform a route fast becoming as hackneyed as that from London to Brighton. They do nothing new, and naturally can write nothing new. But in the case of Mr. Burton, experience, backed by knowledge, gives value and interest to his page. He has produced a book which unites characteristics hardly thought compatible, — the solid old Oriental knowledge, — the lively familiarity of a contemporary of Eothen, — and a wild adventurousness like that of Mr. Gordon Cumming. He will please the Geographical Society, and please the circulating libraries (865).

According to the *Athenaeum*, Burton had done a service to the Geographical Society and to the world at large, the Western world, by destroying the almost mythic terrors of the East. The reviewer is clearly enthusiastic and excited by Burton's daring escape, as was the rest of London society, and had Burton been in England at this time he would have received the attention and adulation he craved.

The *Edinburgh Review*, however, feels some misgivings about Burton's exploit and the type of Oriental knowledge he conveyed. Burton went on this pilgrimage as a "true believer," a native born Muslim, and the *Edinburgh Review*, 1856, feels that he went a bit too far in his act. This act, the reviewer suspects, became a reality:

> And although there are few sacrifices which it is possible to make in the cause of knowledge that would not command our warmest sympathy, yet we must say, that even information so novel and so difficult of attainment as all that concerns the sacred cities of Arabia must necessarily be, is in our judgement too dearly purchased at the price into which Mr. Burton's zeal for science has betrayed him. . . . Sharing, and perhaps, exaggerating their [the pilgrims] miserable exhibitions of reverence; quaffing cups of holy water from the consecrated well; repeating their prayers; joining in their litanies; reciting the 'Fat-hah' with them; copying their gesticulations; one time performing the *sujdah*, or single prostration, another time going as far as the *dua*, or double one; turning his face to Mecca; placing his right shoulder opposite the right pillar of the Prophet's Tomb; in a word, accommodating himself — not alone passively and by negative participation, but by acts, by words, and even by the simulation of devotional feeling — to every detail of their public and private worship. All this Mr. Burton professes to have done, and more. In order the more effectually to carry out his assumed character, he added to his own prescribed devotional exercises as a Haji, certain supererogatory and even vicarious prayers and visitations at the Prophet's Tomb, in the name and for the spiritual benefit of friends who had requested this good office at his hands! (200)

The reviewer is not accusing Burton, in so many words, of having adopted the Islamic faith (as many others did), but of having identified himself too wholeheartedly with the other pilgrims, and actively and spontaneously participated in their actions. The article insinuates that Burton abandoned his country by throwing himself with a "strange facility" into the assumed position. The *Edinburgh Review* also has reservations about the nature of Burton's discoveries of the sacred cities. The reviewer finds the ceremonies of Meccah and Madinah complicated and tedious, and remarks that "with all its minuteness Mr. Burton's account of the religious life of the Moslems is purely exoterical. . . . He never goes below the surface; he fails or he avoids to touch what may be called the inner life of Islam . . . " (*Edinburgh Review* 204). The information Burton provides is regarded as lifeless, and thus reflective of the "intellectual immobility of the system."

These two reviews demonstrate the two poles of the assessment of Burton's exploit and his contribution to knowledge. On the one hand, his feat is considered fascinating and heroic, while on the other hand it is viewed as an act of identification with the Arabs; the information provided in the *Pilgrimage* is perceived as both a great service to the world and as a barren piece of exoterical knowledge. Burton's approach to the Orient, as we shall see, was both a public act and a private pilgrimage into Arab life for although he detached himself from Orientals he also, to some extent, participated in their lives. And while his study of the sacred rites did reduce Islam to a meaningless list of facts (reflecting the Western opinion that it was intellectually immobile), at a personal level he involved himself in the lives of the pilgrims with a "strange facility."

Twentieth century criticism too is divided along similar lines. On the one hand, there are those who feel that Burton truly understood and identified with the Orientals, and perceived them from their own point of view, while others see him as one who kept a constant distance between himself and the Orient. Modern scholars are not shocked but instead, delighted with Burton's assimilation with the Orientals. Those twentieth century scholars who believe that he truly understood the Orientals, and became one with them, are by and large, the same critics who romanticize Burton, and regard him as some kind of lonely, neglected, heroic wanderer. With the notable exception of Thomas J. Assad, in *Three Victorian Travellers*, romanticization and belief in Burton's Oriental nature go hand in hand.

Although there is truth in the claim that Burton identified himself with the Orientals, particularly the Arabs, romanticizers like Achmed Abdullah and T. Compton Pakenham, in *Dreamers of Empire*, 1929, and Fairfax Downey, in *Burton: Arabian Nights Adventurer*, 1931, undermine their statements by their extravagance, and the absence of textual analysis. Abdullah and Pakenham, for example, write

> Such is the riddle of the Arab. Many have tried to solve it. Only one has succeeded. . . .
> What he has felt. . . .
> It is that which counts — more than minute observations and academic digging — when one wants to solve the riddle of the Arab: the feeling, the instinctive, almost psychic reaction and perception. And there was one man, England's greatest traveller and linguist, who had this quality.
> Sir Richard Burton. Who else? . . .
> He saw eye to eye with the Arab. He needed no lancets or scalpels or bone-scrapers of psychological vivisection to comprehend the immemorial unbending haughtiness of a man who prefers material poverty to spiritual poverty and, by the same token, prefers spiritual riches to material riches (Abdullah and Parkenham 1929: 57–58).

Abdullah and Parkenham have romanticized not only Burton, but also the Arabs — one could say that they Orientalized Burton because they identified him with the Orientals. Their account of Burton is clearly built on the legend of Burton rather than on a study of his personality or works. However, they are correct in observing the instinctive nature of Burton's relationship with the Orient, for Burton was not just an objective scientist in the Orient, but often a participant in its way of life.

In *Burton: Arabian Nights Adventurer*, Fairfax Downey too remarks on Burton's identification with the disguise he adopted. Burton departed from England as a Persian, Mirza Abdullah, and consequently, Downey writes, Richard Burton's identity was buried while

> Down to his henna stained skin, the Mirza was Moslem. The man had had himself circumcised at the age of thirty-two, since that

commandment which the Prophet gave the Faithful had not been performed in his infancy. Only dogs of infidels neglect it, and into Abdullah's eyes, as he watched the European passengers, crept a tinge of fierce contempt. Burton was beginning to exercise his extraordinary power to make his masquerade mental as well as physical (Downey 1931: 64).

Again, this is a very romanticized picture, and although this particular incident is not even mentioned in Burton's narrative of his journey from England to Alexandria, it is not necessarily an incorrect depiction of Burton. In the *Pilgrimage*, Burton did begin to perceive the Orient from a non-Western perspective, and even critiqued the Western sense of racial and moral superiority in the way an Oriental would. Burton's disguise led him to make a personal and private pilgrimage into himself, which resulted in the expression of an anti-Orientalist perspective.

Assad, in *Three Victorian Travellers*, is the only one of these critics who has, without romanticizing, observed Burton's understanding of the Orientals through a close study of the text. Unfortunately, Assad's work deals largely with Burton's translation of the *Arabian Nights* rather than the *Pilgrimage*. Assad analyzes the manner in which Burton commented on the Arabs, and notes that while he made sweeping generalizations, he could also be discriminating enough to realize that there were different types of Arabs, with both good and bad personality traits (unlike Morier who glosses over the good Persian characters and highlights the bad ones). It is these discriminations, says Assad, "and countless other pronouncements [that] show him as an objective observer of Eastern life" (Assad 1964: 19).

Assad also observes the tension in Burton between an advocacy of imperialism and an understanding of the Arabs whom he lived with. He observes that while Burton admired the Arab spirit of independence, he appreciates it only "when it agitates against Turkish rule in the Middle East. . . . It must be submissive to British superiority and rule, else it is a spirit of independence which is less than noble" (ibid., 22). However, Assad has not explored the text of the *Pilgrimage* as thoroughly as Burton's translation of *Arabian Nights*, nor examined the various literary techniques by which Burton represents what he perceives to be the inferiority of the Orientals.

Assad is the only critic so far who has observed the tension in Burton's attitude toward the Orient. Jonathan Bishop, in his article "The Identities of Sir Richard Burton: The Explorer as Actor," 1957, and Kathleen Zane, in her dissertation on "Paradigms of Place in Travel Literature: The Oriental Voyages of Nerval, Burton, Kinglake, and Chateaubriand," 1984, go to the other extreme from the romanticizers, and examine only the domination of and distance from the Orient that Burton expresses.

Jonathan Bishop views Burton as an actor, constantly playing different roles: the role of "Ruffian Dick" who loves to shock his countrymen; and the role of the injured, under-appreciated scholar and explorer. In the *Pilgrimage*, Bishop argues, Burton is just playing with these roles, identifying himself seriously with Muslim religious rituals and beliefs (to startle the English reading public), and at the same time disassociating himself from them. The problem with Bishop's analysis is that he himself, it seems, is offended by the fact that Burton identified himself with the Orientals and consequently twists the interpretation of Burton's statements in the light of his own prejudices to prove that Burton distanced himself from Orientals and asserted his English identity. Bishop's prejudice is evident in his interpretation of Burton's response to Meccah. Moved by the sight of Meccah, Burton says "I may truly say that, of all the worshippers who clung weeping to the curtain, or who pressed their beating hearts to the stone, none felt for the moment a deeper emotion than did the Haji from the far-north" (Burton 1893: 2, 160–61). According to Bishop, Burton only "flirts for a moment with feelings that may at the time have included the range from which he here disassociates himself: 'But, to confess humbling truth, theirs was the high feeling of religious enthusiasm, mine was the ecstasy of gratified pride.' The truth, if it is the truth, is not humbling. Why should he affect at such a moment to think himself the moral inferior of the dirty fanatics around him?" (Bishop 1957: 130). "Dirty fanatics"? Bishop is imposing his own prejudices on the author, claiming that Burton is only affecting humility and thus indicating to the reader, "jauntily", that his English self is very much present. Bishop is not even considering the personal nature of Burton's involvement in the lives of these so-called fanatics, nor the desire for identification with them that Burton's wistful tone suggests. Bishop has observed the two "selves" in Burton, but has weakened his analysis considerably by other such biased statements.

Kathleen Zane's study is free of Bishop's Orientalist perceptions, and presents an excellent analysis of Burton's representations of the Orient. Her study centers around the concept of "place" as that which defines individuals and is in turn given significance as "home" by these individuals. If an individual recognizes the uniqueness of his place, she argues, he would accept the difference, and uniqueness of "other" places. However, if this does not happen, the traveler, failing to acknowledge differences, would impose his world view, his own nationalistic sense of place on the "other", thus metaphorically appropriating it. Burton, she continues, is one such traveler, and his "systematic and orderly scientific attitude . . . is used as a pretext and a tool for [his] domination of place"; his "version [of the Orient] suggests the maintenance of order and codified distance as the essence of English place" (Zane 1984: 49–50). Zane proceeds to analyze Burton's ordering technique in his account of the pilgrimage and his tableaux style of presentation of group scenes to demonstrate Burton's distance from, and imaginative possession of, the Orient.

Burton's sense of place was, however, as we have seen, not very strong, and this uncertainty manifested itself in his work, particularly in his portrayal of Orientals. The techniques he uses to portray them depict his uneasy sense of identity and his doubts about his own culture's norms. Following in Assad's footsteps, the aim of this study is to examine the strange and contradictory nature of Burton's response to the Orient and, consequently, toward his own culture too. Burton was a reserved personality (he never mentioned his family life, except in his very private journals), not given to expressing the identity crisis he experienced as an Englishman in Arabia, the land of his predilection. It is only from his mixed pronouncements on Orientals, and his partial understanding of their feelings, that one can observe the conflicting demands his sense of self underwent on the pilgrimage.[1]

Objectification and Participation

Edward Said argued convincingly that "[n]o one has ever devised a method for detaching the scholar from the circumstances of life, from the fact of his involvement (conscious or unconscious) with a class, a set of beliefs, a social position, or from the mere activity of being a member of society. These continue to bear on what he does professionally, even though naturally enough his research and its fruits do attempt to reach a level of relative freedom from the inhibitions and restrictions of brute, everyday reality" (Said 1979: 10). In Richard Burton's vision of the Orient we see the pressure of the Orientalist environment affecting his attitude toward Orientals, but we also note the struggle to free himself from his position as an Englishman and a westerner. While on the one hand, he regards Orientals as static, inferior types, almost like animals, he also, at times, views his surroundings in the Orient from a native inhabitant's perspective, making himself so much at home with his comrades that one forgets he is a westerner.

Right from the start we come to know that Burton undertook the Hajj for both personal and national reasons. The journey represented to him both a personal and physical challenge, and also an achievement that would contribute to, and underscore his nation's glory. He

> offered [his] services to the Royal Geographical Society of London, for the purpose of removing that opprobrium to modern adventure, the huge white blot which in our maps still notes the Eastern and central regions of Arabia. . . . What remained for me but to prove, by trial, that what might be perilous to other travellers was safe to me? (Burton 1893: 1, 1–2).

His daring exploration will also redound to the credit of his nation because he will in addition make scientific and commercial observations on the people, the geography, and the horses of Arabia, and thus give meaning to that "white blot." In political terms too, he is aware that since Britain possesses the largest Muslim empire in the world, any information about Muslims would be very useful. Burton is a scholar working within the political power structure, gathering information that would be useful to the colonizers. To be an Orientalist, as Said argues, "means being aware, however dimly, that one belongs to a power with definite interests in the Orient" (ibid., 11). Burton, however, has a personal side that rebels against the nationalistic, patriotic, aspect of his personality, and he makes the pilgrimage partly to demonstrate his uniqueness as an individual who dares to do what no man has done before. This mixture of patriotism and a strong sense of his personal worth reveals itself in his perspective of Orientals which both echoes and defies the traditional Western attitude.

At one level, Burton regards the Oriental as a distinct type of personality, functioning in one consistent manner, regardless of time, place, or circumstance. Like other Orientalists he tried to "reduce the Orient to a kind of human flatness, which exposed its characteristics easily to scrutiny and removed from it its complicating humanity" (ibid., 150). Since the Oriental, from Burton's point of view, has no inner individual life, the narrative is rife with generalizations that assume the Orient to be one static, isolated type. The *Pilgrimage* is full of phrases like "Oriental barbarism", "Oriental mind", "lying to the Oriental is meat and drink," all statements which reflect his conception of the Orient as some kind of fixed quantity.

Burton also makes derogatory generalizations about British temperament but these do not represent a static externalized perception of the British. He views the British as capable of changing once they are aware of the necessity of doing so. After observing the poor conditions of the Indian Muslims on the pilgrimage, he realizes that to preserve its image the British empire should instruct the Vice-Consul at Jeddah to assist the pilgrims, and should, in addition, establish a Muslim agent in Meccah to help them. The narrative consists of numerous such observations, analyzes, and advice, clearly indicative of his belief in the British intellect as of a highly developed and developing order, not an eternally inferior, unchanging type.

The Oriental mind, however, he regards to be truly as ahistorical as the static generalizations he uses to typify it. "The Turks," he argues, "require the old statocracy," not " '[t]he solid rule of civil government' [which] has done wonders for the race that nurtured and brought to perfection an idea spontaneous to their organization" (Burton 1893: 1, 259). That changing political circumstances might make the "solid rule of civil government" natural to the Turks is completely ignored. As far as Burton is concerned, the "childish East" is permanently trapped in time, and his generalizations of what he considers to be Oriental "prepossessions" reflect his static concept of it. As Said would say "[t]he very possibility of development, transformation, human movement . . . is denied the Orient and the Oriental" (ibid., 208).

Burton's labeling of Orientals as types is not the result of lack of knowledge, but is, in fact, the application of a Western popular science to vindicate his notions of cultural superiority. Describing his Alexandrian Shaykh, he argues that

> my brother had shifting eyes (symptoms of fickleness), close together (indices of cunning); a flat-crowned head, and large ill-fitting lips; signs which led me to think lightly of his honesty, firmness and courage. Phrenology and physiology, be it observed, disappoint you often amongst civilised people, the proper action of whose brain upon the features is impeded by the external pressure of education, accident, example, habit, and necessity. But they are tolerably safe guides when groping your way through the mind of man in his so-called natural state, a being of impulse, in that chrysalis condition of mental development which is rather instinct than reason (Burton 1893: 1, 17).

Burton's typification of Orientals evidently is the result of a belief in their primitivity, and proceeds from the "scientific" theory that people in that condition possess a physiology that can be categorized and pigeon-holed, and a psychology that can be apprehended merely by externals. Phrenology was very popular in early nineteenth century England and was "applied to the reform of education and the criminal, as well as to the hiring of servants," as Roger Cooter explains in *Phrenology in the British Isles: An Annotated Historical Bibliography and Index* (viii); but Burton restricts its use to the study of Orientals, thus giving added weight to the flat, reductive conception of them.

Burton's use of animal metaphors for Orientals, and his juxta-position of descriptions of animals with those of Orientals also represents his belief in their primitive state of development. His descriptions of the different Arab tribes sounds as though he were discussing animals, objects of commercial value, which are prized for their physical traits. The Anzah and Nijidi families are repre-sented as "purely Caucasian, and [show] a highly nervous tempera-ment, together with those signs of 'blood' which distinguish even the lower animals, the horse and the camel, the greyhound and the goat of Arabia" (Burton 1893: 2, 78). The "even" suggests that the Arab is not very different or better than the animals, and by discussing the "blood" he treats them like animals, racehorses, for example, which are bred for their bloodlines. Burton's descriptions are so physical that they sound like presentations of animals or slaves (who were treated like animals) for sale: "The neck is sinewy, the chest broad, the flank thin, and the stomach in-drawn; the legs, though fleshless, are well made. . . . The shins do not bend . . . (ibid., 83). A good piece of human meat, not a thinking, feeling human being, has been displayed here.

Burton moves easily from a description of Arabs to a description of animals, as if there were no difference between the two. In volume two, page fourteen, of he writes "[t]he temperament of the Madani is not purely nervous, like that of the Badawi, but admits a large admixture of the bilious, and, though rarely, the lymphatic. The cheeks are fuller, the jaws project more than in the pure race, the lips are more fleshly, more sensual and ill-fitting; the features are broader, and the limbs are stouter and more bony"; and three pages later he proceeds to describe their sheep in a similar manner, stating that "[b]oth [breeds of sheep] are the common Arab species, of a tawny colour, with a long fat tail. Occasionally, one meets with what at Aden is called the Berberah sheep, a totally different beast — white, with a black broad face, a dew-lap, and a short fat tail." Given his style of description, it is hard to tell what he is describing, animals or humans. He moves rapidly and indis-criminately from a description of the temperament and physical attributes of the Madani to a presentation of their animals, and then to a portrayal of the manners of the Madani! By running these so-called scientific reports together, he is placing Orientals and animals in the same category.

By viewing Orientals as primitive, uncivilized beings, Burton maintains the popular Western image of a romantically simple, but inferior, Orient. In fact, Burton shies away from, and is threatened by any sign of intellectualism in the Orient. He is soon tired of staying at Khudabaksh's home because "my patience was thoroughly exhausted. My host had become a civilised man, who sat on chairs, who ate with a fork, who talked European politics, and who had learned to admire, if not to understand, liberty — liberal ideas! and was I not flying from such things?" (Burton 1893: 1, 35). Any sign of change in the East that parallels the Western nations is to be avoided, and Burton deliberately leaves Khudabaksh's house to live in the dirty Wakalah (rest-house) which "would disgrace a civilized prison" (ibid., 42). Burton clearly wants to live in the uncivilized portion of the Orient and at the same time be contemptuous of its inferiority as compared to the West! The Orient is clearly damned if it attempts to change, and damned if it does not. It is not judged by the same standards that are applied to the West, but is instead judged by the Western desire to maintain its image of it.

To some extent perhaps Burton is restless at Khudabaksh's home because for personal reasons he himself is disgusted with the West and with "European politics," but it seems that there are powerful nationalistic, patriotic causes underlying his behavior. As an Indian official Burton feels strongly the need to maintain the image of the Orient as a backward place because it affects his right to rule the country. Any sign of intellectual change in India is a threat to his conception of it and translates into a physical menace to the Empire for "[i]f the Indian has been a European traveller, so much the worse for you . . . and for aught you know, republicanism may have become his idol. He has lost all fear of the white face, and having been accustomed to unburden his mind in 'The land where, girt by friend or foe, / A man may say the thing he will,' he pursues the same course in other lands where it is exceedingly misplaced. His doctrines of liberty and equality he applies to you personally and practically . . . " (ibid., 38–39). As an officer in the Indian army, he obviously had such confrontations in India, and now as a pilgrim in Arabia he avoids any situation that constitutes a threat to his imaginative domination of the Orient. People like Khudabaksh and talk of civil government in the Otto-man empire are deliberately dismissed by Burton.

So far we have explored only one aspect of Burton's approach to the Orient, but his "legacy is more complex" as Said explains, for "in his writing we can find exemplified the struggle between individualism and a strong feeling of national identification with Europe (specifically England) as an imperial power in the East. . . . So what we read in his prose is the history of a consciousness negotiating its way through an alien culture by virtue of having successfully absorbed its systems of information and behaviour. Burton's freedom was in having shaken himself loose of his Euro-pean origins enough to be able to live as an Oriental" (Said 1979: 195). It is this individualism, this non-Orientalist perspective of the East, that needs to be investigated since Said has been unable to apply his assessment of Burton to his works. Said gets caught up in a circular, contradictory argument, claiming that Burton's knowledge of Oriental society is accessible only to a European and hence Burton's understanding of that society is actually a form of cultural domination. Since Burton identified himself so strongly with Arabs, a less biased reading of his rejection of the traditional Western vision of the Orient is clearly necessary.

Early on in the *Pilgrimage* it is evident that in spite of his strongly Western approach to the Orient, Burton deliberately chose to participate in the lives of Orientals by adopting the guise of a true believer. For both personal and practical reasons, he preferred to pass off as a "true believer" rather than a convert. To have gone as a convert would have prevented him from the freedom from observation of the true believer, but, more importantly, the role of a convert would have laid him open to the contempt of other Orientals, as he believed, and would thus have affected his pride: "My spirit could not bend to own myself a *Burma*, a renegade — to be pointed at and shunned and catechised, an object of suspicion to the many and of contempt to all" (Burton 1893: vol. 1, 23). Burton craved acceptance in Oriental society, not just for practical, but also for emotional reasons, and it is this disguise, and this yearning for acceptance underlying it, that leads to another picture of the Orientals. On the one hand, Burton views them as ahistorical, stereotypical, physical entities, but, on the other hand, as we shall see, he also views them as individuals existing under unique socio-economic conditions.

According to Kathleen Zane, in "Paradigms of Place in Travel Literature," Burton's adoption of a disguise is indicative of his consciousness of his British identity. "Burton's personal need to disguise his identity reflects his reluctance or refusal to assimilate," she argues, "as well as his membership in a culture [British culture] which is itself filled with disassociations [as opposed to a communal lifestyle]" (Zane 1984: 122). Instead of assimilation she believes that the disguise led to detachment from Oriental life because "Burton's measures at disguise . . . focuses upon his being out of place and permit him to regard himself as another, in the third person, and from a distance." Zane maintains that Burton's concealment of "his real place and identity leads to a covert and intensified identification with England. On the sixth of July 1853, while setting sail from Egypt, Burton says he 'could not help casting one wistful look upon the British flag floating over the Consulate' " (ibid., 136–37).

While it is true that Burton often maintains a scientific detachment from his object, and refers to himself, in the Oriental guise, in the third person, we should bear in mind that Burton did generally speak of himself in the third person. Even during his trip to the Mormon settlement in Utah (*The City of the Saints and Across the Rocky Mountains to California*, 1861) when he was not in disguise, he referred to himself in the third person or in the plural. It was not lack of identification, but a scientific bent of mind (or perhaps his arrogance) that resulted in this style. In the foreword to her *Life*, Isabel Burton writes "I always thought and told him that he destroyed much of the interest of his works by hardly ever alluding to himself, and now that I mention it, people may remark it, that in writing he seldom uses the pronoun *I*. . . . In his works he would generally speak of himself as the Ensign, the Traveller, the Explorer, the Consul, and so on . . ." (*Life* 1: vii).

Burton did cast a "wistful look upon the British flag" as he left Egypt, but then, he also looked back with sorrow at departing from his Oriental friends in Cairo: "Outside the gate my friends took a final leave of me, and I will not deny having felt a tightening heart as their honest faces and forms faded in the distance" (Burton 1893: vol. 1, 143). For Burton, the outcast from his native land, the disguise worked both ways: either it made him conscious of the home he left behind, or it gave him the freedom to assimilate, to find another home in a new place. And Burton assimilated to his new home to such an extent that he differentiated himself from other Western travelers:

> Nothing more delightful to the ear than the warbling of the small birds, that sweet familiar sound; the splashing of tiny cascades from the wells into the wooden troughs, and the musical song of the water-wheels. Travellers . . . in the East talk of the 'dismal grating,' the 'mournful monotony,' and the 'melancholy creaking of these dismal machines.' To the veteran wanderer [himself] their sound is delightful from association, reminding him of fields and water-courses, and hospitable villages, and plentiful crops (ibid., 400).

Although the act of taking on a disguise symbolizes, to a point, Burton's awareness of his British identity, it also symbolizes, to him, a new-found homeland, and permits him to participate in it.

Burton feels so much at home in his new environment that he even absorbs the prejudices and attitudes of the people he has chosen to identify with. He initially started on his journey as a Persian dervish, but soon changed his nationality to that of an Afghan because he realized that the Persians were regarded as despicable heretics by other Muslims. So completely does he iden-tify himself with his new role and new companions that, like them, he too becomes very aggressive towards the Persians. On the island of Tur, en route to Madinah, he takes offense at the presence of Persians:

> Amongst the large vessels was one freighted with Persian pilgrims, a most disagreeable race of men on a journey or a voyage. They would not land at first, because they feared the Badawin. They would not take water from the town people, because some of these

were Christians. Moreover, they insisted upon making their own call to prayer, which heretical proceeding — it admits five extra words — our party, orthodox Moslems, would rather have died than have permitted. When their crier, a small wizen-faced man, began the Azan . . . we received it with a shout of derision, and some hastily snatching up their weapons, offered him an opportunity of martyrdom. . . . These Persians accompanied us to the end of our voyage. As they approached the Holy Land, visions of the 'Nabbut' [wooden staves] caused a change for the better in their manners. At Mahar they meekly endured a variety of insults, and at Yambu they cringed to us like dogs (ibid., 205–6).

Burton has evidently imbibed the feeling of his companions, and has in fact, in the process, developed a real animosity for the Persians. Far from detaching himself from his group, he participates in the Persian baiting: "the Persians, who fearing to come on shore, had kept to their conveyance, appeared proper butts for the wit of some of our party: one of us stood up and pronounced the orthodox call to prayer . . . " (ibid., 1, 221). Burton does not describe the group as "the party," or the speaker as "one of the orthodox party," but instead uses the collective and plural pronouns of "our", and "us", clearly identifying himself with the others.

Burton may not have converted to Islam, but he did feel so much at home with his companions that instead of always being on guard about appropriate "Oriental" behavior, he could make popular jokes about some religious injunctions. Within the environs of Meccah, he, and the other pilgrims, are aware that not a tree should be injured by them, but Burton is sufficiently at ease to ask his camelman "Shaykh Mas'ud to break off a twig, which he did heedlessly. The act was witnessed by our party with a roar of laughter; and the astounded Shaykh was warned that he had become subject to an atoning sacrifice. Of course he denounced me as the instigator, and I could not fairly refuse assistance" (ibid., vol. 2, 149). Burton is not making fun of Islam, or of the orthodoxy of his party; he shares their feelings, and can play religious pranks very naturally.

Burton's depiction of the people that constituted "our party" is interesting. His portrayal of his group members is indicative of his

assimilation and understanding of them, and also of his consciousness of the traditional Orientalist techniques of depicting Orientals. One finds that even as he categorizes them as "Orientals", he
understands the circumstances of their lives, and describes them
in their various different roles as friend, father, husband, uncle, and
son.

Burton's description of his group of comrades is a fascinating
example of the tension between his Western approach to the
Orient, and his own trans-cultural relationship with his fellow
pilgrims. Salih Shakkar, a man of the party, who was much disliked
by Burton, is "a Turk on the father's side, and an Arab on the
mother's side, born at Al-Madinah. This lanky youth may be
sixteen-years-old, but he has the ideas of forty-six; he is thoroughly
greedy, selfish, and ungenerous . . ." (ibid., vol. 1, 164). So far we
have been presented only with Salih Shakkar's genealogy, and
certain personality traits that depict him as a youth who has grown
old and cynical before his time. Then swiftly, and momentarily,
Burton uses the genealogy to typify Salih as half-Turk and half-
Arab: "coldly supercilious as a Turk, and energetically avaricious
as an Arab." As the description progresses, however, we are informed why, and when, Salih Shakkar is supercilious: "his light
yellow complexion makes people consider him a 'superior person'.
We were intimate enough on the road. . . . But at Al-Madinah he
cut me pitilessly, as a 'town man' does a continental acquaintance
accidentally met in Hyde Park . . ." (ibid.). Salih Shakkar's pride
is viewed as a result of his elevated social status, owing to his
complexion and his Madanite origin. The Turk in him is no longer
regarded as the source of his superciliousness, rather his social and
racial circumstances are seen as the cause of such behavior.

The description of Omar Effendi reveals a similar combination
of distance-cum-assimilation. Omar Effendi, the son of a rich
Shaykh at Madinah, has run away from home to live the life of a
student: "His manners are those of a student; he dresses respectably,
prays regularly, hates the fair sex, like an Arab, whose affections
and aversion are always in extremes . . ." (ibid., 161). Omar Effendi,
however, we learn, has personal, and not "Arab" reasons for hating
the fair sex. His parents have been pressuring him to marry, whereas

he wants to be a student, and has had a major confrontation with his parents over this issue: "His parents have urged him to marry, and he . . . has informed his father that he is 'a person of great age, but little sense'. . . . he fled the paternal domicile, and entered himself a pauper Talib 'ilm (student) in the Azhar Mosque" (ibid.). On the one hand, the description is based on "Oriental" characteristics, as perceived by the West, on the other hand, on the socio-economic circumstances of his life.

As a fellow pilgrim, Burton is able to see others as individuals, rather than "Orientals", and although he continues to describe their behaviour as "Oriental", (often in a very condescending manner), he also learns to understand them in terms of their social circumstances. Shaykh Hamid, for example, is perceived in the universal role of husband and family man when Burton resides at his home in Madinah: "The Shaykh has preceded us early that morning, in order to prepare an apartment for his guests, and to receive the first loud congratulations and embraces of his mother and the 'daughter of his uncle [his wife]' " (ibid., 288). Like a true family man and host, the Shaykh's manners have also changed "from the vulgar and boisterous to a certain staid courtesy," protective of his guest, Abdullah [Burton], rescuing him from the nursery scamps, making him comfortable in his home, and only then returning to his family to distribute gifts. Through this depiction of Shaykh Hamid's actions and manners, Burton has succeeded in conveying a more genuinely multi-faceted portrait of a human being than Morier who wrote about the Orient in the form of a novel, a form that gave him much more scope for character portrayal. Burton not only presents these little touches of ordinary home life, he also understands the dynamics of this life, and avoids making generalizing comments. For example, Shaykh Hamid's method of distributing presents, which could easily invite some sweeping comment about Oriental miserliness, is instead regarded as natural and reasonable, given the circumstances of his situation:

> During the forenoon, in the presence of the visitors, one of Hamid's uncles had urged him, half jocularly, to bring out the Sahharah. The Shaykh did not care to do anything of the kind.

> Every time a new box is opened in this part of the world, the owner's generosity is appealed to by those whom a refusal offends, and he must allow himself to be plundered with the best possible grace. Hamid therefore prudently suffered all to depart before exhibiting his spoils; which, to judge by the exclamations of delight which they elicited from feminine lips, proved highly satisfactory to those most concerned (ibid., 294).

This type of depiction and understanding of Shaykh Hamid as an individual, and not an Oriental, is the result of Burton's identification of himself with "our party."

Burton's ability to perceive the Oriental as a growing, developing, multi-faceted, individual is particularly interesting in his depiction of Mohammed al-Basyúni, his servant and companion throughout the pilgrimage. Mohammed is an adolescent boy, journeying metaphorically from irresponsible, mischievous, childish behavior, from his home in Meccah to transform into a mature man of the house. Unlike Morier's Hajji Baba, or Kinglake's Dthemetri, Mohammed's personality changes and progresses. Initially he is depicted as the spoilt "youngest son of a widow, whose doting fondness had moulded his disposition; he was selfish and affectionate as spoiled children usually are" and a delightful, impulsive, youthful troublemaker, who, according to the amused Burton, "improved every opportunity of making mischief." Like other boys of his age, he considers himself a man, and feels frustrated at not getting the attention he thinks he deserves from women:

> The Persian's wife was rather a pretty woman, and she excited the youth's fierce indignation, by not veiling her face when he gazed at her — thereby showing, that as his beard was not grown, she considered him a mere boy.
>
> 'I will ask her to marry me,' said Mohammed, 'and thereby rouse her shame!'
>
> He did so, but, unhappy youth! the fair Persian never even ceased fanning herself.
>
> The boy Mohammed was for once confounded (ibid., 303).

This spoilt, mischievous, and trying young man undergoes a change with his circumstances. At Meccah, his home, he assumes the responsibilities of the man of the house and his manners change "from a boisterous and jaunty demeanour to one of grave and attentive courtesy," and he becomes a host to Burton. He proceeds to efficiently order the servants of the house, manage the other children, and finally even settle down to starting a little business.

The last time we see him is when he accidentally guesses Burton's true identity. Instead of going into a rage, or voicing indignation at the deception, he behaves like an adult, departing "with a coolness" which Burton cannot understand since he is unaware that his disguise is now exposed (ibid., vol. 2, 271). By the end of the tale Mohammed is truly a much wiser individual than the prankster at the start of the pilgrimage. He has matured over the course of the long journey, and Burton has recognized the changes that have taken place.

The dual aspects of Burton's identity, symbolized by his disguise — his consciousness of his Westernness, and his easy adaptation into Arab society — are so intertwined in his narrative, that it is difficult to sort them out and present them tidily. The tension between Orientalism, and his own independent perceptions was great, and manifested itself constantly. Such a situation arose partly because he possessed the knowledge that allowed him to assimilate himself in another culture, but also because he was instinctively, to some extent, in rebellion against British culture.

A Divided Loyalty: Possession and Exploitation

So far we have discussed the Western perspective of the East as static and inferior that Burton brought to bear on the Orientals, and also his participation in the life of the Orientals who accompanied him on the Hajj. In addition to his notion of superiority toward the Orientals, Burton also felt a sense of possession and domination toward the Islamic Orient, its sacred places and its rituals. He seems desirous to control them by categorizing, measuring and structuring them. But at the same time, in his role as an Oriental he meets with this kind of exploitation at the hands of other westerners and as a result he speaks out against Western domination, even critiquing the West for its assumption of natural superiority.

As Zane has observed, Burton possesses the Orient by his method of describing and categorizing it: he "'conquer[s]' it by scientific measures." Zane observes the scientific order Burton imposes on Meccah and Madinah, and brings to our attention the rigid structure used in his technique of place description:

> The structures of these two volumes show parallels that indicate Burton's sense of place as endowed with the following characteristics: a) prospect of the town from outside and above its boundaries; b) passage from exterior of town to the place of lodging . . . ; c) the arrival at the distinct goal of pilgrimage; measurement, classification of this place — its history, physical properties, customs; d) customs and spectacle of the larger town; f) the subsidiary places of visitation, subsequently described according to the structures of description of the main place, as in c) (Zane 1984: 105).

Just as Burton, following the Orientalist tradition, labels Orientals as if they had no individual inner life, so does he appropriate their places of worship by fitting them within a set system as if there was nothing more to them. In Zane's own words, Burton conquers these places imaginatively because he does not have "any doubt that some mysterious and essential quality of the place may have been missed" (ibid., 103).

While it is conceivable that any traveler to a new or unexplored region would describe it in a similar systematic pattern, in Burton's case it does seem that this is an act of control that stems from personal and cultural causes. At the first sight of Madinah, Burton says:

> I now understood the full value of a phrase in the Moslem ritual, 'And when his' (the pilgrim's) 'eyes shall *fall upon the Trees of Al-Madinah*, let him raise his Voice and bless the Apostle with the choicest of Blessings.' In all the fair view before us nothing was more striking, after the desolation through which we had passed, than the gardens and orchards about the town. It was impossible not to enter into the spirit of my companions, and truly I believe that for some minutes my enthusiasm rose as high as theirs. But presently when we remounted, the traveller returned strong upon me: I made a rough sketch of the town, put questions

about the principal buildings, and in fact collected materials for the next chapter (Burton 1893: 1, 280).

As the representative of his culture, as a person from another land, Burton feels the need to overcome his intimate personal response to the place. And when he views the Ka'abah at Meccah we realize that he needs to exercise this control simply because his passion is too strong:

> I may truly say that, of all the worshippers who clung weeping to the curtain, or who pressed their beating hearts to the stone, none felt for the moment a deeper emotion than the Haji from the far-north. It was as if the poetical legends of the Arabs spoke the truth, and that the waving wings of angels, not the sweet breeze of morning, were agitating and swelling the black covering of the shrine. But, to confess humbling truth, theirs was the high feeling of religious enthusiasm, mine was the ecstasy of gratified pride (Burton 1893: 2, 161).

These lines express a sense of ecstatic attraction toward Meccah and also a painful feeling of isolation. The rigidly structured description that follows (as Zane has already outlined for us) is in such contrast to this emotion that one feels Burton is deliberately controlling and dominating Meccah to discipline his own feelings toward it.

Burton's dry descriptions of the activities in the sacred cities also reduce Islam (perhaps unconsciously) to a sterile and meaningless ritual, for instead of dwelling on the philosophy or the passion of a symbolic ritual he emphasizes the mere act itself. His description of the first visit to the innermost shrine of the House of Allah reveals the aridity of his account:

> We then advanced toward the Eastern angle of the Ka'abah, in which is inserted the Black Stone; and standing about ten yards from it repeated with upraised hands, . . . [recites prayer]. After which we approached as close as we could to the stone. A crowd of pilgrims preventing our touching it that time, we raised our hands to our ears, in the first position of prayer, and then lowering them, exclaimed, . . . [recites prayer]. After which, as we were still

unable to reach the stone, we raised our hands to our ears, the palms facing the stone, as if touching it, recited the various religious formulae, the Takbir, the Tahlil, and the Hamdilah, blessed the Prophet, and kissed the finger-tips of the right hand. The Prophet used to weep when he touched the Black Stone, and said that it was the place for the pouring forth of tears. According to most authors, the second Caliph also used to kiss it. For this reason most Moslems, except the Shafe'i school, must touch the stone with both hands and apply their lips to it, or touch it with their fingers, which should be kissed, or rub the palms upon it, and afterwards draw them down the face. Under circumstances of difficulty, it is sufficient to stand before the stone, but the Prophet's Sunnat, or practice, was to touch it. Lucian mentions adoration of the sun by kissing the hand.

Then commenced the ceremony of *Tawaf*, or circumambulation, our route being the *Mataf* — the low oval of polished granite immediately surrounding the Ka'abah. I repeated, after my Mutawwif, or cicerone, ... [recites prayer]. Turning the west corner, or the Rukn al-Shami, we exclaimed, . . . [recites prayer].

Thus finished a Shaut, or single course round the house. Of these we performed the first three at the pace called Harwalah, very similar to the French *pas gymnastique*, or Tarammul, that is to say, 'moving the shoulders as if walking in sand.' The four latter are performed in Ta'ammul, slowly and leisurely; the reverse of the Sai, or running. These seven Ashwat, or courses, are called collectively one Usbu. The Moslem origin of this custom is too well known to require mention. After each Taufah or circuit, we, being unable to kiss or even to touch the Black Stone, fronted toward it, raised our hands to our ears, exclaimed, . . . [recites prayer] kissed our fingers, and resumed the ceremony of circumambulation as before, with 'Allah, in Thy Belief,' &c. (Burton 1893: 2, 164–67).

This quote comprises four pages, and although tediously long, is necessary to demonstrate Burton's descriptive style where ritual and ceremony are concerned. It is a highly technical presentation of each detail of the ceremony for an ignorant Western audience; the verbal communication, however, is not so important for what it literally states, but for the attitude it conveys. Burton does not appear to respond to the intensity that motivates the ritual as though he does not want to be drawn in. As a result, his description seems to convey the feeling that Islam is a rigid, stratified, religion which does not adapt or develop, and that, consequently, its followers themselves are equally limited: individuals weep at the Ka'abah, or kiss it, only because it was done by their religious predecessors.

One gets a better feel for the passion and emotion of the religion from Joseph Pitts' untutored, unscholarly response of his journey to Meccah (approximately AD 1690) recounted in *A Faithful Account of the Religion and Manners of the Mahometans*, and which Burton himself cites in Appendix V of the Pilgrimage. Describing the ceremonies at Mount Arafat, Pitts writes

> It was a Sight, indeed, able to pierce one's Heart, to behold so many Thousands in their Garments of *Humility* and *Mortification*, with their *naked Heads*, and *Cheeks watered with Tears*; and to hear their grievous *Sighs* and *Sobs*, begging earnestly for the *Remission of their Sins*, promising *Newness of Life*, using a Form of *penitential Expressions*; and thus continuing for the Space of four or five Hours, *viz.* until the Time of *Acsham-nomas*, which is to be performed about half an Hour after Sun-set (Pitts 1738: 138).

Instead of merely reciting prayers Pitts gives us the essence of the worship and the emotion that underlies it. And with one little anecdote he effectively portrays the depth of feeling that motivates the pilgrims:

> E'er I leave *Mecca*, I shall acquaint you with a Passage of a *Turk* to me in the *Temple Cloister*, in the Night-time, between *Acsham Nomas*, and *Gega Nomas*, i.e. between the Evening and the Night *Services*. The *Hagges* do usually spend that time, or good part of it (which is about an Hour and half) at *Towoaf*, and then sit down on the Mats, and rest themselves. This I did, and after I had sat a while, and for my more ease at last was lying on my Back, with my Feet towards the *Beat*, but at a distance, as many others did; a *Turk* which sat by me, ask'd me what Countryman I was: A Mogrebee (said I) i.e. one of the *West*. Pray, quoth he, *how far* West *did you come?* I told him from *Gazair*, i.e. *Algier*. Ah! replied

he, *have you taken so much Pains, and been at so much Cost, and now be guilty of this* irreverent Posture *before the* Beat-Allah? [the House of God which encloses the Ka'abah] (ibid., 144).

Pitts was a staunch Christian but that did not keep him from understanding and acknowledging the symbolism of Islam or what its rituals and shrines meant to the Moslems. His descriptions give expression to these emotions rather than suppress and control them as does Burton's arid, detached style.

Burton's style is instead like that of our old friend from Ispahan, Hajji Baba, and the similarity between his and Hajji's style of description of Muslim rituals reveals to what extent Burton was controlled by a Western voice. Hajji returned home just in time for his father's death, and in his prolix style presents us with an account of his funeral:

'In the name of Allah, arise,' said the old mollah to him; 'we are now writing your will.' He endeavoured to raise my father's head, but to no purpose: life had entirely fled.

Cotton steeped in water was then squeezed into his mouth, his feet were carefully placed towards the kebleh, and as soon as it was ascertained that no further hope was left, the priest at his bed-head began to read the Koran in a loud and sing-song emphasis. A handkerchief was then placed under his chin, fastened over his head, and his two great toes were also tied together. All the company then pronounced the *Kelemeh Schehâdet* (the profession of faith), a ceremony which was supposed to send him out of this world a pure and well-authenticated Mussulman; and during this interval a cup of water was placed on his head.

All these preliminaries having been duly performed, the whole company, composed of what were supposed to be his friends and relations, gathered close round the corpse, and uttered loud and doleful cries. This was a signal to the two mollahs (whom I before mentioned), who had mounted on the house-top, and they then began to chant out in a sonorous cadence portions of the Koran, or verses used on such occasions, and which are intended as a public notification of the death of a true believer.

The noise of wailing and lamentation now became general, for it soon was communicated to the women, who, collected in a

separate apartment, gave vent to their grief after the most approved
forms (Morier 1897: 384–85).

Hajji, according to himself, maintained an account of his adventures for the benefit of his countrymen, not for a Western audience,
but he described the rituals in the same manner as Burton: an
emotionless list of details. The detachment that such a style suggests is even more evident in Hajji's case because it jars with the
context, with the fact that it is his father's funeral. And the belittling
of the passion underlying such rituals that takes place in a description concerned only with externals is highlighted by the expressions
that Hajji uses. Phrases like "well-authenticated Mussulman," and
"most approved forms," are very sarcastic, and clearly suggest that
Hajji, or rather Morier, regards these ceremonies as ridiculous,
empty gestures. Morier's approach to the Orient was more aggres-
sively and rigidly Western than Burton's, perhaps because he was
only writing under the guise of an Oriental, whereas Burton was
living the life of one.

Burton's Oriental disguise places him in some very complex
situations. By virtue of his disguise he becomes one of the possessions of the British and is forced to see the position of the Orient
from the point of view of a subject of the British empire. As a
Pathan on the Hajj, he travels in a sphere over which the British
have considerable influence, and he has to face the domination
that is meted out to Orientals. Such a situation, combined with
his identification, and participation in the life of the Islamic Orient,
is bound to create a certain amount of resentment against the
British and their notions of superiority.

In his role as Oriental, Burton came to know too much about
the truth of British domination to make any statements about the
"White Man's burden" as other Orientalists were wont to do. In
spite of his Orientalist tendencies, he also came to see the Orient,
and the Oriental, as victims of British power. Arranging for his
trip to Cairo, as a native, he confronted the problems of being
subject to Western arrogance:

> The next step was to find out when the local steamer would start
> for Cairo, and accordingly I betook myself to the Transit Office.

No vessel was advertised; I was directed to call every evening until satisfied. At last the fortunate event took place: a 'weekly departure,' which, by the by, occurred once every fortnight or so, was in orders for the next day. I hurried to the office, but did not reach it till past noon — the hour of idleness. A little dark gentleman — Mr. Green — so formed and dressed as exactly to resemble a liver-and-tan bull-terrier, who with his heels on the table was dosing [*sic*], cigar in mouth, over the last 'Galignani,' positively refused, after a time — for at first he would not speak at all — to let me take my passage till three in the afternoon. I inquired when the boat started, upon which he referred me to the advertisement. I pleaded inability to read or write, whereupon he testily cried *Alle nove! alle nove!* — at nine! at nine! Still appearing uncertain, I drove him out of his chair, when he rose with a curse and read 8 a.m. An unhappy Eastern, depending on what he said, would have been precisely one hour too late. . . .

How many complaints of similar treatment have I heard in different parts of the Eastern world! and how little can one realise them without having actually experienced the evil! For the future I shall never see a 'nigger' squatting away half a dozen mortal hours in a broiling sun patiently waiting for something or for someone, without a lively remembrance of my own cooling of the *calces* at the custom-house of Alexandria (Burton 1893: vol. 1, 27–28).

Burton believed in the political necessity of ruling Egypt, and in the he predicted that the day was not far off when such a need would arise; but he was not blind to the exploitation and oppression it would lead to. He also knew that the tendency of the ruling class was to blame the "nigger" for laziness and slovenliness, whereas that behavior was the result of British domination. Placed in the position of the Oriental, he questions Western assumptions about the "nigger", and gives voice to the feelings of the subject peoples. As an imperialist, he is able to view Egypt as "the most tempting prize which the East holds out to the ambition of Europe"; at the same time, he could perceive, and feel, the sense of oppression and hatred the Oriental feels, a "repugnance to and contempt for Europeans," particularly the British who are regarded as "Shaytans".

Although Burton himself made sweeping generalizations about Orientals, he was himself aware of the imaginative domination of the Orient by the Western world, and realized the limitations of this kind of knowledge. Remarking on the kindness of the pilgrims to each other, he says,

> It would be well for those who sweepingly accuse Easterns for want of gallantry, to contrast this trait of character with the savage scenes of civilization that take place among the 'Overlands' at Cairo and Suez. No foreigner could be present for the first time without bearing away the lasting impression that the sons of Great Britain are model barbarians (ibid., 210).

Burton sounds as if he were rewriting history from the viewpoint of the object, the Orient. And unlike Morier, who glossed over the presentation of good Persian characters, and divided the world along good–bad, Western–Oriental, Christian–Islamic lines, Burton frequently breaks free from such cultural stereotypes.

Burton even goes so far as to critique the Western world for arrogating the right to set the standards by which they judge the Orient, and the assumption of superiority it implies. Burton's attitude toward slavery demonstrates his independence of thought and action in his assessment of the West and the East. He is aware that slaves in "the generality of Oriental countries," are treated well, and fare "far better than the servant, or indeed than the poorer orders of freemen." At the same time, he does not like the concept of slavery, and investigates the issue to see if he can find any way of putting an end to the slave trade. But while he plans to reorganize the Orient on his own principles, he is not convinced of his nation's claim to moral superiority on the same issue. He critiques the English social system that trains its women to hunt for the right master to buy them: in the "rosy lips", he writes, is "an implied, if not an expressed, 'why don't you buy me?' or, worse still, 'why *can't* you buy me?' " (ibid., 60). These words remind one of Edith in Charles Dickens' *Dombey and Son*, who is trained to display her wares to the highest bidder. Burton, however, is not just being a social critic, but also challenging the Orientalist assumptions that rest on the notion of Western moral superiority.

It is impossible to determine with certainty if Burton was writing in this manner merely to shock British society, or if he really meant what he was saying. However, given the extent to which Burton participated in the lives and attitudes of his fellow pilgrims, and his warmth of feeling for them that no amount of plain description can do justice to, it does seem as if here he is genuinely identifying himself with his companions and sharing their skepticism about Western perceptions of itself in relation to the Orient.

Burton's response to the Orient was a complex mixture of a consciousness of British power and prestige, of his dislike for English society, and his sense of identification with the Orientals. He echoed traditional Orientalist conceptions, and yet, in his very behavior, often contradicted them. Political and economic power alone, it seems, is not the only determinant of geographical attitudes. The individual's response to his culture, as in Burton's case, can exist in tension with received opinion.

Burton did not express his divided sensibilities in so many words, but it is evident in his many conflicting statements and points of view in the . Like T.E. Lawrence (Lawrence of Arabia), the other famous Englishman who assumed the Arab garb, he became "the man who could see things through the veils at once of two customs, two educations, two environments," and he had "dropped one form [the English] and not taken on the other, and was become like Mohammed's coffin in our legend [believed to be suspended in mid-air], with a resultant feeling of intense loneliness in life" (Lawrence 1935: 32). Burton's journey was a metaphoric pilgrimage into himself, revealing a state of homelessness, a condition in which he was neither completely Western nor completely Eastern in his conception of the Orient.

Notes

1. The pilgrimage carries great social and religious significance for Muslims. According to the 1985 edition of the *Encyclopaedia Britannica*

During the earliest decades after the death of the Prophet, certain basic features of the religio-social organization of Islam were singled out to serve as anchoring points of the community's life and formulated as the 'Pillars of Islam.' . . . The fifth pillar is the annual pilgrimage (*hajj*) to Mecca prescribed for every Muslim once in a lifetime — 'provided one can afford it' and provided a person has enough provisions to leave for his family in his absence. The pilgrimage rite begins every year on the 7th and ends on the 10th of the month of Dhu al-Hijjah (last month of the Muslim year). When the pilgrim is about six miles (ten kilometres) from the Holy City, he enters upon the state of *ihram*: he wears two seamless garments, and neither shaves nor cuts his hair or nails until the ceremony ends. The principal activities consist of walking seven times around the Ka'abah, a shrine within the Sacred Mosque; the kissing and touching of the Black Stone . . . ; and the ascent of and running between Mt. Safa and Mt. Marwah . . . seven times. At the second stage of the ritual, the pilgrim proceeds from Mecca to Mina, a few miles away; from there he goes to Arafat, where it is essential to hear a sermon and to spend one afternoon. The last rites consist of spending the night at Muzdalifah (between Arafat and Mina) and offering sacrifice on the last day of *ihram*, which is the *id* ('festival') of sacrifice.

At other times in the year it is considered meritorious to perform the lesser pilgrimage (*umrah*), which is not, however, a substitute for the Hajj pilgrimage (12–14).

It is not possible to supply the exact dates of the Hajj since the Arabian calendar is lunar and therefore does not correspond with the Gregorian calendar. When Burton undertook the Hajj the seventh day of Dhu al-Hijjah coincided with Sunday, eleventh September. Like all other pilgrimages the Hajj symbolizes man's journey through life. It is also, in this case, an act of self-purification and reaffirmation of one's relationship with God. The "haji", as the pilgrim is officially known, is forgiven all his past sins by this act and is bound not to sin again because each subsequent transgression would now be multiplied seventy times. The pilgrimage is also an occasion for both social and religious bonding of Muslims for to journey to Meccah is to journey to the centre of the Islamic world, the point at which all of them simultaneously turn toward from all corners of the world to pray.

Chapter 5

Gertrude Bell: The Romantic

A knowledgeable, politically-aware traveler in the East at the turn of the century would find it hard to cling to Western stereotypes of it. The romantically dangerous Orient was fast disappearing and being replaced as a tourist spot; and the backward, immobile East was moving at a fast and aggressive pace. The threat that such a situation posed to the Western traveler's preconceptions could lead to both defensive self-assertion and/or to an understanding of the people and the country he was traveling in.

Since 1869, the year of the opening of the Suez Canal (and of the Prince of Wales' visit to Egypt) the Orient had become a vacation spot. Thomas Cook's travel agency conducted organized tours in the Middle East, tours which anyone "with four weeks and couple of hundred pounds to spare" could afford.[1] In *The Desert and the Sown* Gertrude Bell remarks on the presence of tourists even in remote desert towns, bargaining for imitation Bedouin knives, and she observes that the native servant had become so "accustomed to feeding Cook's tourists on sardines and tinned beef [that he] thinks it beneath the dignity of a European" to eat delicacies like "salted pistachios, sugared apricots and Damascus cakes."

During the late nineteenth century the East not only became more accessible, it rapidly underwent changes which both questioned Western notions about it and threatened Western power over it. The year 1876 witnessed the rise of the nationalist Young Turk movement, a revolution which finally culminated in the rise of Kemal Ataturk in 1919, the foundation of modern Turkey, and the elimination of European military and economic power in the new nation. In 1882, Egypt experienced a nationalist, anti-foreign agitation, a movement which was suppressed by the British and led to their occupation of it. And a few years later, in 1906, Persia underwent a constitutional revolution. This development was praised by the British government, but discouraged in practice because just as the new government was establishing itself, Russia and Britain signed a treaty which divided Persia into spheres of interest between themselves. Without consulting the Persians they thus determined their trade monopolies over different parts of the country.[2]

During these times of upheaval Gertrude Bell was a frequent traveler in the East, visiting and exploring Persia, Mesopotamia, Syria, and the Arabian peninsula. She visited the Orient on numerous occasions from 1892 to 1916; and from 1916 till her death in 1926 she resided in Baghdad and Basra, occasionally visiting England. She was an exceptionally talented traveler: both a scholar and a politician. She studied history at Oxford and later worked and published with the well-known archaeologist and classical scholar Sir William Ramsay (1851–1939). Her interest in the Orient led her to master Persian and Arabic until, like Burton, she was completely at ease in these languages.

Born into a wealthy and powerful industrial family, she mingled with politicians her whole life, and world affairs consequently became a personal matter for her. So influential was her family that when her mother died in 1871 a Royal Navy warship was made available to speed Bell's uncle and aunt from Italy to Britain. Gertrude Bell mingled with senior government officials, diplomats, and future viceroys early in life and the European rivalries that led to the outbreak of the First World War were brought to her notice as something that perturbed her uncle, Sir Frank Lascelles. She writes from Berlin in 1897:

> Uncle Frank is in a great jig about Crete. He thinks there is going to be red war and an intervention of the Powers and all sorts of

fine things. I wonder. . . . We had a most exciting evening at the play yesterday [Henry IV]. We were all sent for in the entr'acte. We had a very agreeable tea party with the Emperor and Empress [of Germany] and her sister. . . . It was like an act out of another historical drama — but a modern one. A sheaf of telegrams were handed to the Emperor as we sat at tea. He and uncle fell into an excited conversation in low voices; we talked on to the Empress trying to pretend we heard nothing but catching scraps of the Emperor's remarks 'Crete . . . Bulgaria . . . mobilizing' and so forth. The Empress kept looking up at him anxiously — she is terribly perturbed about it all and no wonder for he is persuaded that we are all on the brink of war (Bell 1927: vol. 1, 45–46).

As a young woman she was acquainted with political issues first hand through her family members and their friends' involvement in them. Her early travels were in fact facilitated by her Uncle Frank when he was British minister at Tehran in 1892, and Dr. Friedrich Rosen (husband of her parent's friend, Nina Roche) while he was German minister at Tehran (1892) and German consul in Jerusalem in 1899. Even during her trek across the Syrian desert in 1905 she was conscious of the respect she gained through such connections:

This evening there appeared two high officials, sent up by the Kaimaikan of Drekish, where I go tomorrow, to welcome me and to put the whole of the forces of the Kaimaikamlik at my disposal. The Turkish government has decided that I am a great swell, and nothing will persuade them to the contrary. Next time I travel here I shall tell the officials that all my relatives are pork butchers. Perhaps that will discourage the Mohammedan mind. As it is, they all ask me about my uncle the ambassador. . . . I never thought to have regretted Uncle Frank's existence, bless him! but I could wish that he were an obscurer person (Burgoyne 1958: 206).

The attention she received as a result of her connections was perhaps a bit overwhelming!

Politics was the spice of her life, and she endeavored to keep track of all major events in between desert journeys and discussed them at length in her letters to her father. Finally, in 1916 she joined the government as an intelligence officer in the Basra (initially she was a part of the Cairo branch) division of the Arab Bureau and worked alongside T.E. Lawrence and David Hogarth (archaeologist and pupil of Dr. Ramsay) for the creation of the state of Iraq.

Not only did Bell's scholarship and exposure to politics make her more aware of events in the Middle East than the average traveler, her own personality also made her responsive to the Orient and its changing political climate. Her background reveals her as an individual who consented to the norms of her society but also felt restless under them. She never rejected her society but she obviously questioned it and sought to escape from it. In spite of the deep love that she expresses in her letters for her family, and in spite of her adherence to restrictive social norms, the fact remains that she chose to live out of England most of her life.

Although Bell's parents took the unusual step of educating her at a boarding school and then sending her to Oxford, they placed considerable restraints on her. Even Bell's younger sister, Elsa, admitted that their mother (step-mother to Gertrude Bell) was old-fashioned in many ways. Gertrude Bell's early letters, which have been published by Elsa, reveal that she received a considerable amount of disciplining on social matters: she must not be seen with men (even her cousin) without a chaperone, she must not read novels without parental approval, nor must she visit friends or be seen in the poorer districts of London. At school or college, she was constantly lectured and chastised by her mother. Bell was conscious that she had to defer to her parents' wishes on even the most trivial matters. She writes to her mother from school, in 1885,

> I hope you are not cross with me for taking it as a matter of course that you would not mind my going with Maude David [for supper with her school-friend Maude's family]. . . . Nellie Porter has written to ask me to be her bridesmaid. I suppose I may, I have told her I will if you'll let me. I'm sorry you're cross with me about the David business. It was pure ignorance on my part (Richmond 1937: 38–39).

She accepted the rules her parents laid down even as an undergraduate at Oxford, and if she broke a rule it was only with the consent of some person in authority. Writing from Oxford in 1887 she describes a meeting with her cousin Horace:

> Coming back from the Cathedral I met Horace with whom I strolled round the parks and subsequently on to Merton street. I hope you don't mind. Miss Wordsworth [principal of Lady Margaret Hall] says he may take me for little discreet walks every now and then. Please say you don't mind (ibid., 136).

Even when she was twenty-two years old, in 1891, she obediently accepted her mother's wishes:

> Of course send back the Disciple [*The Disciple* by Paul Bourget]. I asked for it a long time ago, I can't remember at this moment why I didn't consult you first, but naturally I should have asked you about it before I read it (ibid., 227).

Bell, it seems, was far too disciplined, and was more obedient than others of her age because at this point her sister inserts a note commenting that "Gertrude at that time was 22 and had had a winter season at Bucharest as well as two years at Oxford, but she still was not allowed to choose what book she might read" (ibid., 227–28). Gertrude, as her sister explains, was brought up in an "atmosphere of deference and convention" and "never dreamt of questioning any of the many regulations that were in force in her day" (ibid., 97–99). Elsa's explanation of her sister's upbringing explains why Bell regarded debates on women's suffrage during her Oxford days as 'amusing', and also explains to some extent why she was the Founder Member of the Women's Anti-Suffrage League in 1908.[3]

The extent to which Bell was steeped in a sense of obedience to her parents and adherence to convention is evident from the absence of bitterness or resentment towards her parents when they broke her engagement to Henry Cadogan, a young diplomat whom she met in Tehran in 1892. Instead, in her sorrow, she turned to her parents for consolation. To her mother she writes, "I wish I could go on and on writing to you, it's so consoling and I hate coming away from you and back to this place which is so full of memories and of things which are past, past.... Oh mother, mother."

After meeting her mother in London she writes to her father, "Dearest, dearest I did not think we could ever be closer to one another than we were, and yet this seems to have brought us closer. . . . What it is to be back and to have my mother again! I don't feel really to want anybody but her, except you" (ibid., 340–41). Henry Cadogan died nine months later, but although Bell felt the loss deeply she never reproached her parents for their interference.

However, under this calm acceptance of authority lay a restless personality impatient of social conventions and rules. Her letters and her actions both reveal a sense of frustration and a desire for liberty. While she did not criticize her society in so many words, she felt uneasy under it and broke many of its conventions. As a young lady in England she accepted chaperoning but felt restricted by it, often wishing she were a boy. While at school she could only complain about restrictions on her freedom:

> I'm so yearning to see some good pictures, old ones. I wish I could go to the National [National Gallery], but you see there is no one to take me. If I were a boy, I should go to that incomparable place every week, but being a girl to see lovely things is denied to me! (ibid., 66)

[and]

> I haven't heard any thing more about the German plan. . . . I don't think you must count upon its coming to anything. What a bore I am! I do wish I could be sent promiscuously like a boy to find my way! (ibid., 85)

The future adventurer is obviously chafing under these restrictions, and probably travel became a means for her to escape them. After graduating from Oxford, Bell traveled constantly: Bucharest, Persia, Switzerland, Algiers, Italy, Greece, Jerusalem, Paris, Gibraltar, Spain, Turkey, Syria, and the list goes on and on. She even became a renowned Alpine climber; one peak was named after her in honor of her ascent of the Englehorner group: Gertrude's Peak. Travel gave her the freedom she craved for so much. She gained the liberty to wander wherever she wished and with whomever (mostly men) she wanted to. Perhaps her parents did not object to her ways because she was out of England, and Bell clearly did not anticipate any objections either. She even once mentioned in a letter (August 1900) that she would be dining with a young man, a mountaineer, whom she had "picked up . . . casual in Paris."

Her travel in the East not only gave her personal liberty but also escape from Western civilization. While exploring the desert around Jerusalem in 1900 she asks her father for permission to stay longer because she would "rather do this than be in London." And even as she prepares to return to England she writes, "but you know, dearest Father, I shall be back here before long! One doesn't keep away from the East when one has got into it this far" (Bell 1927: vol. 1, 120). In *Desert and the Sown* she was more explicit as she observed the tourists near Jericho: "I sat and listened to their vulgar futile talk — it was the last I was to hear of European tongues for several weeks, but I found no cause to regret the civilization I was leaving" (Bell 1908: 10). Many years later in 1914 she wrote to her good friend Sir Valentine Chirol ("Domnul"), the foreign correspondent of *The Times*: "whether I can bear with England — come back to the same things and do them all over again — that is what I sometimes wonder" (Burgoyne 1958: 305). The East had finally become her home, and she was to live the rest of her life in Baghdad.

The fascinating part of Gertrude Bell's life is her constant vacillation between acceptance of and resistance to her cultural codes. Even as she climbed mountains and crossed deserts she always bore in mind that she was an English lady. Before returning to her hotel after an alpine climb, frost-bitten and frozen, she made it a point to change into a skirt in her tent; and like a good daughter she always maintained the habit of writing to her parents for permission before she ventured into the desert. Vita Sackville-West, a twentieth century traveler who met Bell in Baghdad, wrote that she traversed deserts "with all the evening dresses and cutlery and napery that she insisted on taking with her on her wanderings" (Sackville-West 1927: 58). Whether out of habit or a need for security, Bell could never shake off the influence of her culture. This tension between her own self-expression and her culture is reflected in her attitude toward the Orient and toward her country's imperial ambitions in the East.

Bell's first book on the East, *Persian Pictures*, consists of a series of short essays spanning her experiences in Persia as well as Constantinople. The collection reveals her intense yearning for liberty from her culture and, unconsciously and ironically, her identification with her culture as a result of her romanticization of the East as an escape world. But her essays also reveal her ability to transcend her society and to understand individuals and social events of another culture.

Reflecting on the need to be a wanderer Bell writes that "there are moments when the cabined spirit longs for liberty. . . . For one brief moment he shakes off the traditions of a lifetime, swept away by the mighty current which silently, darkly, goes watering the roots of his race. He, too, is a wanderer like his remote forefathers; his heart beats time with the hearts long stilled that dwelt in their bosoms, who came sweeping out of the mysterious East, pressing over resistlessly onward till the grim waste of Atlantic waters bade them stay" (Bell 1928: 69–70). The poetic metaphors and the mysteriousness attributed to the East suggest that in the process of trying to shake off the shackles of her civilization she is expressing the romantic desires of her culture. The East is not so much a geographical place or a civilization but a subconscious of the Western mind, a "dark current." It is also a romantic object, necessary to fulfil her cabined spirit's craving for a less prosaic, convention-ridden existence.

Bell is both attracted and revolted by this mysterious East; as a westerner she both desires this forbidden, sensuous world, but as a westerner she also judges it by her cultural norms. The mysterious East, she writes,

> [is] full of secrets . . . [and] its essential charm is of more subtle quality. As it listeth, it comes and goes; it flashes upon you through the open doorway of some blank, windowless house you pass in the East . . . then the East sweeps aside her curtains, flashes a facet of her jewels into your dazzled eyes, and disappears again with a mocking little laugh at your bewilderment . . . (ibid., 34–35).

But then, as if she is forbidden to enjoy such delights, she views the East as "misty", "unreal", and creating only "an impression" of "vague picturesqueness":

> a life into which no European can penetrate, whose standards, whose canons, are so different from his own that the whole existence they rule seems to him misty and unreal, incomprehensible, . . . ; a life so monotonous, so unvaried from age to age that it does not present any feature marked enough to create an impression other than that of vague picturesqueness, of dulness inexpressible, of repose which has turned to lethargy, and tranquility carried beyond the point of virtue (ibid., 41–42).

Like Burton who desires to see the East in its uncivilized form and also condemns it for being so, Bell takes pleasure in a romantic conception of the East and in identifying what she views as the limitations of that self-created Orient. She clearly reduces the Orient to a type which conforms to her personal, psychological, and cultural needs.

The text, however, breaks down often as Bell's vision of the East shifts away from her Orientalist attempt to regenerate herself through the Orient. As we will see, her romantic desire for liberty also finds expression in her freedom from dogmatic Orientalist perceptions of the East. Analyzing the nature of European travelers, she realizes that most of them do nothing but echo the conventions of their culture and merely regard the East as an interesting specimen. These, she argues, "are not travellers in the true sense of the word; they might as well have stayed at home and read a geography-book, or turned over a volume of photographs, and engaged a succession of cooks of different nationalities . . . " (ibid., 188). She herself, on the other hand, desires to meet people and to understand their "fine flavour of character" till you feel "as intimate as if you had shared the same slice of bread-and-butter in your nursery, and the same bottle of claret in your college hall" (ibid., 189). Like Burton she can present the many sides of individual characters, and her descriptive skill brings them to life on the page. Sheikh Hassan, her teacher, is her closest Persian acquaintance, and she portrays him as teacher, citizen, and husband as she describes their struggles with the poetry of Hafiz and Omar Khayyam. Her essay on the Sheikh contains an anecdote that demonstrates a student–teacher relationship that transcends all global East–West distinctions:

The Sheikh took a particular pleasure in the more philosophical verses. Over these I would puzzle for long hours, and in all innocence arrive at the conclusion that some anecdote of angels, or what not, appertaining doubtless, to the Mohammedan religion was related in them. The Sheikh would then proceed to annotate them in halting French, pointing out that a pun was contained in every rhyme, that half the words bore at the smallest computation two or three different meanings, and that therefore the lines might be done into several English versions, each with an entirely different significance, and with an equally truthful rendering of the Persian. At this my brain would begin to whirl. I was unable to deal with the confusion of difficulties among which the Sheikh Hassan was delightfully battling; it was enough for me if I could seize some of the beauty which lay like a sheath about the poems. . . . But this was wilful stupidity. If I had listened to the wisdom of Sheikh Hassan, I should have realized that we were in the midst of most sublime abstractions, and that the most rigid morality and the strictest abstinence were inculcated by those glowing lines (ibid., 102–3).

This is a very personal portrayal of the patient and enthusiastic teacher and the youthful, confused, student who is perhaps trying to get by with as little work as possible. In the very specificity of this description East–West distinctions melt away into a description of two individual personalities.

In his role as teacher the Sheikh even influences Bell's views on politics and European civilization: "his disbelief in the efficacy of European civilization [to solve the ills of Persia] was equally profound, and his pessimism struck me as being further sighted than the careless optimism of those who seek to pile one edifice upon another, a Western upon an Eastern world" (ibid., 98). Even though, as we have seen, she often brings a Western perception to bear on the East she also questions the assumptions of Western civilization concerning such issues as "progress", "march of civilization", "evolution of the race", and realizes that "they are not eternal, still less are they universal."

Bell's unease with Orientalist notions regarding the stereotypical nature of Easterners and the natural superiority of the West is evident as early as *Persian Pictures*. While Bell felt that she belonged to the more powerful and developed culture she is aware, to some extent, of the ethnocentric nature of her opinions; that she continued to feel this way can be seen in her next travel account, *The Desert and the Sown*.[4]

Bell's Vacillations in *Desert and the Sown*

Desert and the Sown consists of Bell's account of her 1905 journey on the fringes of the Syrian desert. She traveled for two months, starting from Jerusalem and stopping at numerous towns and villages like Tneib, Salkhad, El Barah and Salkin, and cities like Damascus, Aleppo, and Antioch. Although Bell traveled on further into Turkey she concluded her account at Alexandretta, on the shores of the Mediterranean, for she felt that her archaeological explorations in Asia Minor were out of place in a travel account. Bell was accompanied on her route by various different guides and escorts at different stages of the journey; her servant Mikhail was her only constant companion throughout her travels in Syria.

Desert and the Sown is more than just a travel itinerary, it is also a record of Bell's complex attitude toward the people and places she encountered. Early reviews of *Desert and the Sown* — *Athenaeum* 1907 and 1911, *The Dial* 1907, *The Fortnightly* 1911 — express an awareness of conflicts in Bell's attitude toward the Orient. These reviewers regard Bell both as a close and empathetic observer of the lives of the individuals whom she encounters, and also as a romantic "spectator" who makes sweeping generalizations about Orientals. Broadly speaking, reviewers felt that Bell's approach to the Orient was that of the romantic and the realist, the participant and the spectator, and that she fluctuated between imaginative and political domination of the Orient on the one hand, and participation and identification with it on the other hand. These varying responses indicate that the *Desert and the Sown* cannot be classified and dismissed easily as an Orientalist narrative.

In order to observe the tension in Bell's approach to the East we have to analyze both her character portrayal of Orientals and her romanticization of the East. While on the one hand we see her characters speak for themselves and tell a plain unvarnished tale of their lives, on the other hand it is also clear that considerable selection, if not shaping, has gone into their character portrayal. Morier selected and described Persian characters in a manner that portrayed them as inferior; Bell, as will soon be evident, manipulated her characters in a way that depicts them as subjects fit for British imperial domination. We also need to explore the images conveyed by the "ordinary" stories Bell recounts, for consciously or unconsciously these tales are enveloped in a romantic mist reflecting her own yearning for a simple, "uncivilized" existence.

Bell's vision of the Orient in the *Desert and the Sown* is not consistent, for she is both an insider and outsider with reference to the people and politics of Syria. Just as in her own life she fluctuated between rebellion against and submission to the voices of authority, her perception of the Orient too reveals itself to be a struggle between the reductive Orientalist approach toward it and her private involvement in and understanding of the Orientals she encounters. The interesting aspect of her Orientalism and non-Orientalism is that both of these attitudes are intertwined with each other. For example, as a young woman who feels restless within the constraints of her culture she treats the Orient as a romanticized object that will allow her spiritual and physical freedom; yet, on the other hand, precisely because she is dissatisfied with her environment she attempts to break away from her culture and its reductive perceptions of the Orient. We need to explore the manner in which she romanticizes the Orient and how in so doing she both dominates it at times and sometimes identifies with it. Similarly, we will also survey the way in which her intense awareness of political conditions in Europe and the Orient — when colored by her nationalism — leads her to dislike the imperialistic attitude per se but also to believe blindly in the goodness and rightness of British imperialism.

Edward Said expressed the opinion that westerners romanticized the Orient only to use it to regenerate themselves. While what he says is to an extent true, we need to explore the possibility that the westerner's regenerated self might feel the desire to express some attitudes contrary to the traditional Western approach to the East.

Glancing at the travel account of François-René Chateaubriand, Said writes that "what matters about the Orient is what it lets happen to Chateaubriand, what it allows his spirit to do, what it permits him to reveal about himself, his ideas, his expectations" (Said 1979: 172). However, in Bell's case we can add that as her spirit finds liberation from Western social norms it also attempts to question Western perceptions of the Orient. Orientalism, as Said has correctly argued, has to do with "our" world (the European), as opposed to the "other" (the Orient), and since Bell's "our" is not clearly defined we need to explore the ambivalence that this leads to in her vision of the Orient.

The Romance of the *Desert and the Sown*

Omar Khayyam "divides the desert from the sown," as Bell informs us, but does she herself in any way separate "the desert and the sown"? The title of her travel account suggests that she does differentiate between the two, but does she make any more than an artificial distinction, a separation that revolves only around the little "strip of herbage" that is planted in between? Are her images of the inhabited and the uninhabited essentially the same?

Gretchen Kidd Fallon, who feels that there is a marked distinction, has argued (in her 1981 dissertation "British Travel-Books from the Middle East, 1890–1914") that the structure of the narrative is a fairly regular movement from the sown to the desert, from the inhabited to the uninhabited, and that Bell constantly hankers to move into the desolate expanses of the desert. According to Fallon, Bell restlessly yearns to move on and "alternates chapters of 'on the road' (the desert) with chapters set 'in town' (the sown)":

> After a week at this settled village of Bedouin sheep-herders and corn-growers, the weather is still bad; but 'I resolved to go,' says Bell in the opening of Chapter Three. 'The days spent at Tneib had not been wasted. An opportunity of watching hour after hour the life of one of these outlying farms comes seldom, but my thoughts had travelled forward, and I longed to follow the path they had taken.' And so Bell and her companions 'set our faces

toward the open desert' riding north east across an empty plain bound for the Jebel Druze (Fallon 1981: 130).

Fallon bases the distinction between the two areas on Bell's desire to wander into the romantic desert away from the ordinary towns:

> The plotted design of Bell's book, and the author's imaginative forms, are indicated by the title — the elevated, ennobled spirit of the desert compared to the more ordinary, even mundane, concerns of the 'sown' or cultivated areas, . . . And the see-sawing movement so apparent in *The Desert and the Sown*, its dipping now into realism, now into romance as modes of presentation (ibid., 129).

The romance of the desert, she goes on to argue, lies in Bell's perception of it as a changeless zone where for centuries there has been a continuity in the landscape and in the lifestyle of the nomads.

However, it could be argued that Bell's perception of the desert is essentially the same as that of the town and that there is no sharp distinction between romance and realism in her account. A comparison between her approach to the two, reveals that they both represent to her freedom from the West and Western social complications, and a freedom from the force of time. Although the language of the "town" descriptions is not elevated, it possesses the images of liberty, simplicity, and agelessness similar to the portrayal of the desert.

The narrative begins with an elaborate flourish as she prepares to start her march into the desert:

> To those bred under an elaborate social order few such moments of exhilaration can come as that which stand at the threshold of wild travel. The gates of the enclosed garden are thrown open, the chain at the entrance of the sanctuary is lowered, with a wary glance to right and left you step forth and behold! The immeasurable world. The world of adventure and of enterprise, dark with hurrying storms, glittering in raw sunlight, an unanswered question and an unanswerable doubt hidden in the fold of every hill. Into it you must go alone, stripped of the purple and fine linen

that impede the fighting arm, roofless, defenceless, without possessions (Bell 1908: 1).

Unlike Adam, Bell does not love her "enclosed garden" and she joyously escapes from it. As Fallon has observed, this "escape" imagery does not literally apply to Bell's trek across the desert: Bell never travels alone, is never roofless, never called on to fight, and as a woman she is naturally protected by the Arab code of honor. As is evident from this quotation, Bell is celebrating an escape from Western civilization, from life in England as she has experienced it. Bell goes on to proclaim that

> The voice of the wind shall be heard instead of the persuasive voices of counsellors, the touch of the rain and the prick of the frost shall be spurs sharper than praise or blame, and necessity shall speak with an authority unknown to that borrowed wisdom which men obey or discard at will (ibid.).

As she walks into the desert she is able to discard the authoritarian voices that she has heard her whole life at home, school and college, for the desert is one place where she can do as she pleases.

However, while the desert travel affords her a means of escape from civilization, her very act of going to the East indicates that the Orient itself serves as a reprieve from European society. In her preface to *Desert and the Sown* Bell observes that it is not "impossible to be on terms of friendship with dwellers in [Eastern] regions":

> In some respects it is even easier than in Europe. You will find in the East habits of intercourse less fettered by artificial chains, and a wider tolerance born of a greater diversity. Society is divided by caste and sect and tribe into an infinite number of groups, each one of which is following a law of its own, and however fantastic to our thinking, that law may be, to the Oriental it is an ample and a satisfactory explanation of all pecularities. A man may go about in public veiled up to the eyes or clad if he please only in a girdle: he will excite no remark. Why should he? Like everyone else he is merely obeying his law. So too the European may pass up and down the wildest places, encountering little curiosity and

of criticism even less. The news he brings will be heard with interest, his opinions will be listened to with attention, but he will not be thought odd or mad, nor even mistaken, because his practices and the ways of his thought are at variance with those of the people among whom he find himself. 'Adat-hu' it is his custom (ibid., x).

In the East, Bell finds a physical release from the fetters of European society. At the same time, as an outsider in the East her foreignness is tolerated by the easterners and she is accepted as she is. She thus finds freedom from the norms of both European and Oriental society in the East, a liberty that is evident from her behavior in the "sown" areas.

While at home she was not allowed to be with men unchaperoned, in the East she traveled only with men, ignoring the women even when she had the chance to interact with them. Since Oriental women were generally secluded and little involved in politics or travel, it is not unusual that Bell saw little of them. And yet when she meets them it almost seems as if she is trying to escape from her own sense of womanhood. In a narrative composed of a series of individual voices, the women are not heard or are barely audible. We are informed that Bell visited Hassan Beg Na'i's harem and that the women were "delighted to have a visitor" and that they "were as friendly as he was surly" (ibid., 185). Then the account passes on to a description of the architecture of the harem as though the women did not even exist.

Hassan Beg's women led very secluded lives and it is possible that they had neither interesting personalities nor important events to narrate, but the quick dismissal of Musa's sister, Wardeh, seems unnatural in view of the fact that she is as strong-minded an individual as Bell. Just as Bell's actions are often in conflict with her parent's wishes, so is Wardeh's behavior a source of trouble to her family for, as Musa complains, "[s]he has declared that marriage is hateful to her, and that she will remain in our father's house, and we cannot move her. Yet she is a young maid and fair" (ibid., 295). Bell herself realizes that Wardeh is capable enough to "manage her own affairs" but in spite of her awareness of Wardeh's strength and determination she gives her no voice of her own. Instead, she merely dismisses her with a stereotypical remark on her "fair, and modest " looks.

As a European woman in the East, Bell gains the liberty to lead the life of a man: her childish wish to be a boy, which she gave expression to in some of her letters, has been finally fulfilled. Now she is neither constrained by the harem as an Oriental woman, nor is she obliged to follow the conventions of her society. Whether she is in the desert or in the sown areas of the East she is physically free from the norms of the society she has been bred in and the one she is traveling in.

Bell discovers a romantic, imaginative freedom in the East in addition to the literal and physical escape from European conventions. The sense of imaginative escape manifests itself in both the inhabited and uninhabited areas, and can be observed in her description of landscapes, events, and characters. By 'imaginative escape' I refer to the kind of feeling that Elizabeth Robins had upon reading *Desert and the Sown*. In her review of this travel account in *The Fortnightly*, she writes that she came away "with a sense of exhilaration so keen, bringing memories of adventure in the desert and Arabian Nights entertainment in Khans and Palaces" (Robins 1911: 470). She is describing an escape into a world of fantasy, of changeless old-world beauty, of romance and strange adventure. Robin's response describes Bell's own sense of entry into an exciting and wondrous past in the desert and the sown areas of Syria.

On the threshold of her desert adventure Bell's choice of words and rhythm convey her feeling of excitement and express her sense of entry into a glorious romantic era. As she prepares to leave Jerusalem she writes:

> It was a stormy morning, the 5th of February. The west wind swept up from the Mediterranean, hurried across the plain where the Canaanites waged war with the stubborn hill dwellers of Judea, and leapt the barrier of mountains to which the kings of Assyria and of Egypt had lain vain siege. It shouted the news of rain to Jerusalem and raced onwards down the barren eastern slopes, cleared the deep bed of Jordan with a bound, and vanished across

the hills of Moab into the desert. And all the hounds of the storm followed behind, a yelping pack, coursing eastward and rejoicing as they went (Bell 1908: 2).

Bell's sense of joy and excitement is evident in the elevated style and the bounding rhythm of these lines; equally obvious is the sense of entry into a stirring past, away from the ordinary 5th of February. The easy transition from the 5th of February, 1905, to the Biblical past generates the sense of a fantasy never-never land in which the power of time does not exist. Time is no longer the inexorable force of change in this land where past and present co-exist; instead there is a sense of agelessness and continuity:

> Every line of it [the desert] took on significance, every stone was like the ghost of a hearth in which the warmth of Arab life was hardly cold, though the fire might have been extinguished this hundred years. It was a city of shadowy outlines visible one under the other, fleeting and changing, combining into new shapes elements that are as old as Time, the new indistinguishable from the old and the old from the new (ibid., 60).

A transference of attributes from inanimate to animate has taken place here. Not only does the desert constitute an unchanging landscape for her, but she describes the life of the Arabs too as that of an unvarying type. The romance of the desert lies in the fusion of past and present, and also in the sense of continuity of a simple and primitive way of life, as she perceives it to be, as the campfire (or hearth) of one generation succeeds that of an earlier generation.

The desert alone, however, does not represent the romantic world she is pursuing. The inhabited regions of the Orient too possess, from her point of view, the glamor of the older world that she craves for. The ordinary work of the settled Arabs appeals to her in the same way as does the desert. Even the buying and selling of corn in Tneib appears to her a process that has continued unchanged, picturesquely unchanged, for many centuries. The Orientalist perspective, as Said argued, reduced the Orient to one position on the time scale:

In no people more than in the Oriental Semites was it possible to see the present and the origin together. The Jews and the Muslims, as subjects of Orientalist study, were readily understandable in view of their primitive origins. . . . The Semites [were regarded as] an instance of arrested development, and functionally speaking this came to mean that for the Orientalists no modern Semite, however much he may have believed himself to be modern, could ever outdistance the organizing claims on him of his origins. This functional rule worked on the temporal and spatial levels together. No Semite advanced in time beyond the development of a 'classical' period; no Semite could ever shake loose the pastoral, desert environment of his tent and tribe. Every manifestation of actual 'Semitic' life could be . . . referred back to the primitive explanatory category of 'the Semitic' (Said 1979: 234).

We clearly see this reductiveness in Bell's attitude toward Orientals when she describes her host at Tneib, Namrud, selling corn to the Sherarat and comments that but for her "incongruous presence and the lapse of a few thousand years, they might have been the sons of Jacob come down into Egypt to bicker over the weight of the sacks with their brother Joseph" (Bell 1908: 40). The very words she chooses to convey their dialogue, like "thy", are archaic and poetic:

> *Namrud*: Upon thee! upon thee! oh boy! may thy dwelling be destroyed! may thy days come to harm! [for having accidentally mixed the sifted and unsifted corn]
> *Beni Sakhr*: By the face of the Prophet of God! may he be exalted!
> *Sherarat* (in suppressed chorus): God! and Muhammad the Prophet of God, upon Him be peace!
> *A party in bare legs and a sheepskin*: Cold, cold!wallah! rain and cold!
> *Namrud*: Silence, oh brother! descend into the well and draw corn. It is warm there (ibid., 41).

The direct translation of Arabic phrases lends a poetic tone to this conversation, and the dramatic quality turns it into an exotic spectacle instead of the simple haggling and cursing over the purity of the corn that it is. To translate phrases like "[b]y the face of the Prophet of God! may he be exalted!" and "God! and Muhammad the Prophet of God, upon him be peace!" is equivalent to the translation of common forms like "goodbye" and "good night" as "may God be with you" and "may God be with you tonight" for a non-English speaking audience. As Sarah Searight says in *The British in the Middle East*, Bell's Arabs speak "in that curious English conventionally supposed to *represent* Arabic" (Searight 1970: 133 [emphasis mine]).

Even when Bell is not recreating a drama she makes her Arabs speak in an archaic style, in a manner which in fact resembles the poetic style of a translation of pre-Mohammedan verse that she recites for us. Namrud's tales told over the kitchen fire (as narrated by Bell) use the same word choice as the English renderings of early Arabic poetry. Namrud's story recounts a night attack that took place a few years ago:

> In the days when I was a boy . . . you could not cross the Ghor in peace. But I had a mare who walked — wallah! how she walked! Between sunrise and sunset she walked me from Mezerib to Salt, and never broke her pace. . . . And one night in summer I had to go to Jerusalem — force upon me! I must ride. The waters of Jordan were low, and I crossed at the ford, for there was no bridge then. And as I reached the further bank I heard shouts and the snap of bullets. And I hid in the tamarisk bushes more than an hour till the moon was low, and then I rode forth softly. And at the entrance of the mud hills the mare started from the path, and I looked down and saw the body of a man. . . . [The murderers prepare to kill Namrud] And he came near and looked into my face, and it was dawn. And he said: 'It is Namrud! for he knew me and I had succoured him.' (Bell 1908: 41–42).

Compare Namrud's archaisms and poetic sentence structure with the translation (by one of Bell's friends) of an old Arabic poem that Bell recites:

> Oh come rider! Uthail, methinks, if thou speedest well shall lie before thee when breaks the fifth dawn o'er thy road.

> Take thou a word to a dead man there — and a greeting sure, but meet it is that the riders bring from friends afar —

> From me to him, yea and tears unstanched, in a flood they flow
> when he plies the well rope, and others choke me that stay behind
> (ibid., 62).

Namrud's words possess the same poetic qualities as this poem on desert warfare despite the lapse of centuries and the difference that normally exists between a literary and conversational style of speech. (It is not surprising that the *Athenaeum* reviewer of 1907 felt that there was a "sameness" in her character portrayal). Bell's transference of the romance of the desert onto the speech of the town suggests that the entire East, not the desert alone, appeals to her and gives scope to her imagination.

Bell's craving to wander in the desert is born of a desire to escape Western civilization, and although she always hankers to leave the sown areas for the desolate expanses of the desert this line of march does not mean that the desert areas alone satisfy her craving for the wild, untramelled life. Her images dissolve all distinctions between the two, and the "wild free spirit of the desert" sweeps over Druze settlements of Salkhad where she is encamped for the night. The sown areas provide her with the same kind of excitement that she anticipated in the desert at the start of the narrative:

> The moonlight fell on the dark faces [of the Druzes] and
> glittered on the quivering blades, the thrill of martial ardour passed
> from hand to hand, and earth cried to heaven: War! red War!
>
> And then one of the three saw me standing in the circle, and
> strode up and raised his sword above his head, as though nation
> saluted nation.
>
> 'Lady!' he said, 'the English and the Druze are one.'
>
> I said: 'Thank God! we, too, are a fighting race' (ibid., 91–92).

Inter-tribal warfare is a grave matter for her companion Gablan who would "have been forced to join in the fray," but for Bell this terrible preparation for war is simply the type of "primitive" excitement she yearns for. She "[runs] down the hill under the moon . . . holding hands" with the warriors until she suddenly realizes that her actions may arouse the suspicions of Milhem, the Turkish agent of the treasury. Abruptly she leaves the ceremonies and

becomes "a European again, bent on peaceful pursuits and unac-
quainted with the naked primitive passions of mankind" (ibid., 92).
Bell is clear in her mind what it means to be a European as opposed
to Oriental, and she views the desert and the sown areas as one
homogenous type equally representative of the wild, primitive,
timeless Orient.

It appears that Bell does not merely "self-consciously [con-
struct] a romance, and then casually [furnish] the heroic landscape
with ordinary people" as Fallon argues. The romance is present
even in the ordinary people, consciously or unconsciously, in their
diction and in their actions. The entire Orient, its peoples and its
desolate expanses, fulfil her desire for an environment in which
she can experience literal and imaginative freedom. Like Morier
who romanticized the young Oriental girl, or Burton who came
to the Orient to escape "civilization", Bell views the Orient as a
private fantasy land.

Romanticism and Orientalism

The romantic approach to the East not only reduces it to a useful
object for the westerner, it also goes hand in hand with the concept
of the innate inferiority of it vis-à-vis the West. The very aspects
of the Orient that the nineteenth century Western traveler delighted in (its "simple", "primitive" state) were also simultaneously
perceived pejoratively — perhaps because to praise them would be
to indirectly question Western assumptions about "superior" and
"inferior" qualities. However, at the same time that romanticism
reflects the Orientalist attitude toward the East, it can also lead to
a questioning of that very approach. After all, the romantic quest
for freedom is an act of self-assertion and a repudiation of one's
culture to some extent. So while such a quest is in a way merely a
repetition of other such pilgrimages to the East, it also denotes an
attempt at freedom from one's cultural assumptions. Both aspects
of romanticism — cultural power and individual self-assertion —
should be explored in the context of Bell's journey to the East.

The very freedom that Bell experiences in the East is a symbol
of the physical power of her nation. To some extent the freedom

is born of her sex because, as she well knows, no Arab would harm a woman, not even during war. She could, however, be harassed and restrained in other ways if it were not for the British presence in Egypt and their interference in Syrian politics. Bell's confident escape into Druze territory, a violation of Turkish laws, represents her awareness of the fact that no official retribution would be meted out to her — for, after all, the Egyptians lost their nation when they massacred the English.[5] She is not wary of meeting Milhem either (in Druze territory), perhaps because she knows that he will not dare arrest her. In fact, the Turks are afraid of her presence because they regard her as a British intelligence agent. Poor Milhem, we are informed, constantly telegraphs the Turkish authorities at Damascus to keep them informed of her movements. Bell is clearly not the endangered party.

The British political and military presence not only permits her to break Ottoman laws with impunity, it also gives her the power to move freely in Druze territory. The lone Turk is in an unsafe position among the Druze tribes who are the subjects of his empire, but the Englishman or woman is guaranteed safe-conduct because of English involvement in Ottoman politics: "I had the guarantee of my nationality, for the Druzes have not yet forgotten our interference on their behalf in 1860 . . . " (Bell 1908: 70). Bell's security is a direct result of British "divide and rule" policy among the various ethnic groups of the Ottoman empire.

The imaginative escape that the Orient provides her also reflects, to some extent, a sense of power over the Orient, an awareness of cultural superiority. The notion of a primitive, simple, unchanging Orient, reduces the East to an immobile, child-like state of existence. For example, there is both a wistful and a condescending tone to her description of an "Eastern holiday":

> The Marj ul 'Asi, the meadow of the Orontes, is a good type of the kind of place in which the Oriental, be he Turk or Syrian or Persian, delights to spend his leisure. 'Three things there are,' says an Arabic proverb, 'that ease the heart from sorrow: water, green grass and the beauty of women.' . . . The river turned a great Na'oura, a Persian wheel, which filled the air with its pleasant

rumbling. A coffee maker had set up his brazier by the edge of the road, a sweetmeat seller was spreading out his wares by the water-side, and on a broader stretch of grass a few gaily dressed youths galloped and wheeled Arab mares. The East made holiday in her simple and satisfactory manner, warmed by her own delicious sun (ibid., 186).

The air of languor and ease that this scene portrays seems to appeal to her, but at the same time she views it patronizingly as if the East was a child, or in its second childhood. "Simple and satisfactory" suggests the way one describes a child playing happily with a toy! Her description of "the Oriental" is particularly revealing of this condescension:

> The Oriental is like a very old child. He is unacquainted with the many branches of knowledge which we have come to regard as of elementary necessity; frequently, but not always, his mind is little preoccupied with the need of acquiring them, and he concerns himself scarcely at all with what we call practical utility. He is not practical in our acceptation of the word, any more than a child is practical, and his utility is not ours (ibid., ix).

Bell makes these claims about the Orient as if they were scientifically established facts. In her Western laboratory the Oriental mind takes on a static quality that can be labeled like an object; and the "analysis" of this unvarying object's "simplicity" indicates the symptoms of an undeveloped adult, of "arrested development" as Said would say.

The stirring romanticism of the Orient, the tribal warfare that she so delights and participates in, also takes on a bad type of heroism: to return to the land of feuds is both a source of joy and condescension for Bell. At the Jordan bridge she hears accounts of warfare and responds almost as if such stories gave her a sense of homecoming: "[S]o the tale ran on through the familiar stages of blood feud and camel lifting, the gossip of the desert — I could have wept for joy at listening to it again" (ibid., 15). But these tales are too "familiar" and lead her to make sweeping pronouncements on the unvarying unwisdom of the Arab:

in all the centuries the Arab has brought no wisdom from experience. He is never safe, and yet he behaves as though security
were his daily bread. He pitches his feeble little camps, ten or
fifteen tents together, over a wide stretch of indefensible country
(ibid., 66).

Bell makes these generalizations without pausing to consider the
factors that force these Arabs to lead such a life. Given the nature
of the country, an arid land with few arable areas, there is no choice
but to pitch one's tent in indefensible areas. All the Roman, Syrian,
and crusader fortresses that Bell studies are built in open flat land,
and Bell herself pitches her tent in exposed areas. However, out of
what one might call a cultural blindness, she ignores the facts to
typify the Arabs in this manner.

Bell's romantic "break" from the West represents a traditional
Western desire to "use" the Orient and therefore paradoxically is
a product and manifestation of the Orientalist approach toward
the East. But her desire to express her freedom from her culture
does at times free itself of this paradox and manifest itself in non-
Orientalist attitudes toward the East. In fact, she even shows an
awareness of, and also criticizes, the limitations of Western binary
discourse on the East.

There is an aspect of Bell's romanticism that transcends binary
distinctions and seeks to learn from experience rather than cultural
"wisdom." Studying the gorgeous Roman, Greek, European and
Arabic ruins, she goes beyond the Arabian Night's conception of
them to appreciate all the cultures that created them. And although
she romanticizes the characters through her speech "reproduction",
she also shows an understanding of them and even seeks to ingratiate herself with them.

The ruins scattered throughout the desert undoubtedly captured Bell's imagination. Page after page of her tale is illustrated
with her photographs of forbidding fortresses and close-ups of
exquisite carvings. They breathe on her imagination just as "Oriental magnificence which never breathed without effect on the
imagination of the West" (Bell 1908: 250). Instead of describing
all the castles, churches, tombs, temples, ancient doodles, towns

and road markers together in one chapter, she scatters them throughout the account describing them as she run across them. The total effect is that of a magical land — barren, wild land with magnificent structures rising out of nowhere. Her descriptions too lend a magical quality:

> As I copied the phrases they seemed like the murmur of faint voices from out the limbo of the forgotten past, and Orpheus with his lute could not have charmed the rocks to speak more clearly of the generations of the dead. All the Safa is full of these whisperings; shadows that are nothing but a name quiver in the quivering air above the stones, and call upon their God in divers tongues (ibid., 123).

These ruins provide her with the imaginative freedom she is seeking in the East, but her delight in these ruins also transcends East–West distinctions. The "scratches" which she reads are in diverse tongues, both Eastern and Western, but through the distance in time she can see them all melt into "whisperings". The East–West difference ceases to matter and she is more interested in the individual who made the marks, "who left his record and departed into the mists of time," and in the unknown "errand that brought him into the inhospitable Ghadir el Gharz" (ibid.).

Bell's appreciation of the ruins of Ba'albek in fact leads her to make some very strong remarks on Orientalist attitudes. The archaeologist, she argues, finds beauty in every product of the human imagination and

> is thus apt to be well satisfied with what he sees, and above all, he does not say: 'Alas, alas! these dogs of Syrians! Phidias could have done so and so;' for he is glad to mark a new attempt in the path of artistic endeavour, and a fresh breath moving the acanthus leaves and the vine scrolls on capital and frieze (ibid., 168).

East–West distinctions based on the superiority of the creative powers are comically refuted by her. Her approach is very different from Kinglake who even distorts historical facts by arguing that the Arabian Nights were written by the Greeks to support his assumption that "for creative purposes [the Oriental] is a thing dead and dry" (Kinglake 1845: 53).

Bell not only questions the West's notions of its superiority over the Orient, she even laughs at its exotic conception of the East. Although she herself is guilty of romanticizing the East, she does at times observe the contrast between the reality she encounters and her imaginative perception of the Orient. Describing her entrance into the castle built by the Hospitallers she writes:

> And so at sunset we came to the Dark Tower and rode through a splendid Arab gateway into a vaulted corridor, built over a winding stair. It was almost night within; few loopholes let in the grey dusk from outside and provided the veriest apology for daylight. At intervals we passed doorways leading into cavernous blackness. The stone steps were shallow and wide but much broken; the horses stumbled, and clanked over them as we rode up and up, turned corner after corner, and passed under gateway after gateway until the last brought us out into the courtyard into the centre of the keep. I felt as though I were riding with some knight of the Fairy Queen, and half expected to see written over the arches: 'Be bold!' 'Be bold!' 'Be not too bold!' (Bell 1908: 201)

And then, as if she were laughing at herself and other romanticizers she continues:

> But there was no magician in the heart of the castle — nothing but a crowd of villagers craning their necks to see us, and the Kaimakam [deputy governor], smiling and friendly, announcing that he could not think of letting me pitch a camp on such a wet and stormy night, and had prepared a lodging for me in the tower (ibid.).

The terrifying Dark Tower incongruously and comically becomes her bedroom for the night, and the danger and darkness it initially represented to her are replaced by the reality of the bustling life at the center of the castle.

Bell's vision of the East is evidently ambivalent, for on the one hand, as we have seen, she reduces the Orientals to romantic stereotypes but, on the other hand, she is also able to break away from the Western approach to the East and view the Orientals as individuals. Perhaps she is able to see beyond the Orientalist concept of the easterner because, like Burton, she seeks to identify herself with them emotionally. Undoubtedly, one can label a west-erner's desire for identification with alien, exotic, people as merely an expression of his emotional needs and not as a representation of an altered vision of the Orient, but it is possible for such a yearning to translate (as it does in this case) into genuine and respectful understanding of these people.

Bell's emotional need for acceptance by the Orientals can be seen in the satisfaction she derives from becoming a part of Ori-ental social life in Damascus where she encounters

> the sweetmeat seller at the door of the Great Mosque, who helped me twice through the mazes of the bazaars and called to me each time I passed him: 'Has your Excellency no need of your Dragoman today?'; or the dervishes of Sheikh Hassan's Tekyah, who invited me to attend the Friday prayers. Not least the red-bearded Persian who keeps a tea shop in the Corn Market and who is a member of the Beha'i sect among which I have many acquaintances. As I sat drinking glasses of delicious Persian tea at his table, I greeted him in his own tongue and whispered: 'I have been much honoured by the holy family at Acre.' He nodded his head and smiled and answered: 'Your excellency is known to us,' and when I rose to go and asked his charge he replied: 'For you there is never anything to pay.' I vow there is nothing that so warms the heart as to find yourself admitted into the secret circle of Oriental beneficence — and few things so rare (ibid., 149–50).

Unlike Burton, Bell is no outsider in English society, but she is restless within that society and craves to identify herself with Orientals. Just as Burton tries to get into Mohammed's mother's good books by flattering her son, Bell tries to ingratiate herself with her new-found Persian friend by referring to her other Persian acquaintances.

It is perhaps this desire to belong in the "secret circle" that leads her to adapt her behavior to her new friends even though she knows that her foreignness would not be resented by the Arabs and that they would accept her behavior as her "custom". We have already seen her participate in the Druze war preparations, but it is important to observe that she involves herself even in the everyday life of the Orientals. When she arrives at the Kal'at el Husn after a long hard march through wind and rain she does not retire into her bedroom as someone from a foreign culture would have done:

> I was wet through, but the obligations of good society had to be fulfilled and they demanded that we [Bell and the Kaimakam] should sit down on the divan and exchange polite phrases while I drank glasses of weak tea. . . . We kept up a disjointed chat for an hour while the damp soaked more and more completely through my coat and skirt, and it was not until long after the mules had arrived and their packs had been unloaded that the Kaimakam rose and took his departure, saying that would leave me to rest (ibid., 201).

Bell's mother had firmly educated her in "proper" behavior and so now, when Bell craves identification with the Orientals, she carries over her mother's lessons on good manners into another culture.[6] Instead of imposing her culture on the Orient she accommodates herself to it as if it was the most natural thing to do.

When Bell is unfamiliar with any societal norms she makes it a point to consult her companions before taking any action. After feasting with the Kurds she does not simply walk away or make them a large present; instead she takes Najib aside and asks him whether she might give money in return for her entertainment:

> He replied that on no account was it to be thought of, Kurds do not expect to be paid by their guests. All that was left me was to summon the children and distribute a handful of metaliks among them, an inexpensive form of generosity, and one that could not outrage the most susceptible feelings (ibid., 274).

Unlike Kinglake who even changes the timings of a desert march to suit his opinions on the best conditions for desert travel regardless of the physical agony of his Arab companions, Bell constantly tries to understand the feelings of the people whom she encounters. Bell not only adapts her manners to these foreign social norms, she also structures her account like a string of conversations and anecdotes of and by the people of this other culture. In her preface she explains that she

> desired to write not so much a book of travels as an account of the people whom [she] met or who accompanied [her] on [her] way, and to show what the world is like in which they live and how it appears to them. And since it was better that they should, as far as possible, tell their own tale [she has] strung their words upon the thread of the road, relating the stories with which . . . they beguiled the hours of the march, the talk that passed from lip to lip round the camp fire, in the black tent of the Arab and the guest chamber of the Druze, as well as the more cautious utterances of Turkish and Syrian officials (ibid., ix).

This is an unusual attempt at travel writing. At least in theory she aims at writing about other peoples' feelings, attitudes, lives, instead of her own opinions about them — and to some extent she succeeds.

Although no single character's conversation dominates the account, Bell's brief presentation of their opinions shows her insight into the social, economic, and personal forces that govern their lives. That is, she regards them as individuals in a given context, not as representative specimens of "the Oriental". The few tidbits of Mikhail's conversations she records reveal the many facets of his personality. Mikhail is a courageous traveler who has faced many adventures, but is not boastful about his many achievements. When Bell inquires into certain incidents of his past he replies: "We were as near death as a beggar to poverty, but your Excellency knows a man can die but once" (ibid., 4). Although not a religious man he is quite philosophical and even moralistic. He boldly speaks his mind on the merits of other people and even criticizes Bell to her face. Whereas Kinglake feels that to intimidate the natives to obtain provisions from them is the only practical course of action, Bell recounts her conversation with Mikhail to demonstrate his sense of outrage at such tactics: "Doubtless your Excellency thinks you were the guest of the Kaimakam. I will tell you of whom you were the guest. You see those fellahin of the Nosariyyeh, the miserable ones, who sold you anticas at the ruins this morning?

They were your hosts. Everything you had was taken from them without return" (ibid., 217). On another occasion Mikhail's sense of outrage at Reshid Agha's villany challenges Orientalist assumptions about the character of "Orientals". Upon their departure from the prosperous Agha of Salkin, Bell exclaims,

> oh Mikhail! . . . I have travelled much in your country and I have seen and known many people, and seldom have I met a poor man whom I would not choose for a friend nor a rich man whom I would not shun. Now how is this? Does wealth change the very heart in Syria? For, look you, in my country not all the powerful are virtuous, but neither are they all rogues. And you and the Druze of Kalb Lozeh and Musa the Kurd, would you too, if you had the means, become like Reshid Agha? (ibid., 318)

Bell's attitude assumes that Orientals succumb to the dangers of wealth whereas Occidentals (who perhaps possess greater moral strength) are not always corrupted by riches. Mikhail promptly crushes her by reminding her that it is not just innate values but also political conditions that influence a man's life:

> Oh lady . . . the heart is the same, but in your country the government is just and strong and every one of the English must obey it, even the rich; whereas with us there is no justice, but the big man eats the little, and the little man eats the less, and the government eats all alike (ibid., 319).

Mikhail concludes by stating that "at least I did not eat the bread of Reshid Agha," causing Bell and Najib to hang their heads in shame. By portraying Mikhail's moral convictions and admitting her weakness it seems as though Bell is indirectly questioning stereotypical East–West notions concerning the global distribution of 'good' and 'bad' character traits. Said had argued that "[w]hen a learned Orientalist traveled in the country of his specialization it was always with unshakeable abstract maxims about the 'civilization' he had studied; rarely were Orientalists interested in anything except proving the validity of these musty 'truths by applying them [to natives], without great success . . . " (Said 1979: 52). Bell is one of those rare Orientalists, whom Said pays little attention to, in that she is willing to modify her initial application of "abstract maxims" when challenged by a "native".

While Mikhail's opinions and character challenge her notions of "Oriental corruption", Mahmud's dispute with Sheikh Yunis of El Barah enlightens her about certain social conditions. Bell's depiction of the clash of these two personalities portrays her acknowledgement of the individual character traits and social forces that guide a person's actions even in the Orient. The conception of a unified Oriental personality dissolves in the face of Mahmud's outrage at Sheikh Yunis' appropriation of another man's wife. Yunis started the debate by explaining that his second wife cost him a great deal of money because he took her from her husband:

'I had to pay two thousand piastres to the husband and three thousand to the judge.'

This was too much for Hajj Mahmud's sense of the proprieties. 'You took her from her husband?' said he. 'Wallah! that was the deed of a Nosairi or an Ismaili. Does a Moslem take away a man's wife? It is forbidden.'

'He was my enemy,' explained Yunis. 'By God and the Prophet of God, there was enmity between us even unto death.'

'Had she children?' inquired Mahmud.

'Ey wallah!' assented the Sheikh, a little put about by Mahmud's disapproval. 'But I paid two thousand piastres to the husband and three thousand — '

'By the face of God!' exclaimed Mahmud, still more outraged, 'it was the deed of an infidel.'

And here I put an end to further discussion of the merits of the case by asking whether the woman had liked being carried off.

'Without doubt,' said Yunis. 'It was her wish.'

We may conclude therefore, that ethics did not have much to do with the matter though he indemnified so amply both the husband and the judge.

This episode led us to discuss the usual price paid for a wife.

'For such as we,' said Yunis, with an indescribable air of social pre-eminence, 'the girl will not be less than four thousand piastres, but a poor man who has no money will give the father a cow or a few sheep, and he will be content' (Bell 1908: 253).

The comic depiction of the scene universalizes the incident into the stuff of social drama. Stereotypical images of the licentious or fanatical Oriental are here replaced by a well-known social situation: a woman, probably unhappy in her marriage, chooses to escape from it; an outraged ex-husband suing for justice; the new husband trying to placate people like Mahmud. And, as Yunis' explanation reveals, paying the judge and the husband does not represent scheming Oriental tactics but the act of paying the bride price. It seems, from the conversation and the reference to indemnification, that Yunis' fines are compensation for the ex-husband's investment in his wife.

Edward Said's statement that "[to] look into Orientalism for a lively sense of an Oriental's human or even social reality — as a contemporary inhabitant of the modern world — is to look in vain" is not wholly applicable in Bell's case. In spite of her Orientalist approach she often expresses a keen perception of the lives of the people she encounters. Even in a passing mention of the various characters she runs into, Bell reveals a quick grasp of the life of the individual citizens of the Orient. Her understanding of these people is not merely that of a collector of Oriental specimens, for she feels the pathos and the comedy surrounding the characters she portrays. The ragged Arab who guides them on their way, and 'Awad, the Don Juan of the party, are minor characters but they play a role in demonstrating Bell's ability to enter into their lives.

At the beginning of the journey, just after crossing the Jordan bridge, she meets an Arab on his way home. Conversing with him she realizes that "he had gone down to join the Redifs [soldiers], having been bought as a substitute at the price of fifty napoleons by a well-to-do inhabitant of Salt. When he reached the bridge he found he was too late, his regiment having passed through two days before. He was sorry, he would have liked to march forth to the war (moreover I imagine the fifty liras would have to be returned), but his daughter would be glad, for she had wept to see him go" (Bell 1908: 16–17). It is a brief description but one which sharply conveys a moving picture of the exigencies of poverty and its disruption of private life.

Bell is also quick to recognize comic statements and to associate them with the speaker's personality and not the culture as a whole. When 'Awad, shivering in the cold morning air, jests by calling out "lady, lady! do you know why I am cold? It is because I have four wives in the house!" Bell instantly grasps the context of the statement. She realizes that since 'Awad is a bit of a Don Juan his money probably goes toward maintaining his harem rather than his wardrobe. She does not associate the joke merely with "Oriental customs" but with 'Awad's personality too. It is the individual in the culture that she often chooses to portray than the stereotype.

One wonders why Bell vacillated so much between her cultural stereotypes and her non-Orientalist approach to the Orient. To some extent this is a reflection of her personality, of her natural tendency to stand on the fence between "authority voice" and "individual voice." Or perhaps this fluctuation represents the limitations of the views and opinions that she forms about things. As she once said in a letter to her mother,

> one suddenly finds that one had formulated some view from which it is very difficult to back out . . . because the mere fact of fitting it with words engraves it upon one's mind. Then one is reduced to the disagreeable necessity of trying even involuntarily to make the facts of one's real life fit into it thereby involving oneself in a mist of half-truths and half-falsehoods which cling about one's mind do what one will to shake them off (Bell 1927: 16).

Bell's perception of the Orient is an attempt to fit the facts to received ideas, and since she does not succeed completely her picture of the Orient is in a "mist" of cultural conventions and specific, independent observations.

The Imperial Theme

The romantic and the imperial approach to the Orient go hand in hand in that they both reduce the Orient to a useful object. The one (sometimes) turns it into an imaginative convenience, the other reduces it to a political possession. These two concepts are also related in the sense that the romantic perception of the Orient justifies the physical domination of it by the West.

In 1882, the British crushed an anti-foreign movement in Egypt and under the guise of "temporary advisors" took over the administration of the country. Bell viewed British rule in Egypt as a resounding success, and her opinion on the continuing political unrest there demonstrates the clear relationship between romanticism and imperialism. The wild, uncivilized state of the Orient that she finds so exciting and exhilarating is also her justification for English occupation of Egypt:

> The present unrest in Egypt may seem to throw a doubt upon the truth of these observations [that the Syrians want to be ruled by the English], but I do not believe this to be the case. The Egyptians have forgotten the miseries from which our administration rescued them, the Syrians and the people of the desert are still labouring under them, and in their eyes the position of their neighbours is one of unalloyed and enviable ease. But when once the wolf is driven from the door, the restraints imposed by an immutable law eat into the temper of a restless, unstable population accustomed to reckon with misrule and to profit by the frequent laxity and the occasional opportunities of undeserved advancement which characterize it (Bell 1908: 58).

Bell's belief in the "White Man's burden" to rescue the Orientals from themselves is evident in these lines. The Orientals seem to possess a homogenous, unchanging personality that makes them innately incapable of ruling themselves, and while she enjoys participating in their restless roving lives she also regards it as natural that they require and desire British government. As far as Syria is concerned she is firmly convinced that "we [the English] are the people who could best have taken Syria in hand with the prospect of a success greater than that which might be achieved by a moderately reasonable Sultan" (ibid., xi). There is a paternal quality in her attitude toward Syria. It seems as if she is portraying the English government as the ideal authority figure to control the unruly child, Syria, and to take it firmly in hand.

Perhaps to some extent her personal need to romanticize the Orient as some primitive, wild area is also a reflection of her nation's imperial ambitions. English imperialism, like that of most conquering nations, was justified by the colonizers on the grounds that they were on a civilizing mission. As Marlow says in Joseph Conrad's *Heart of Darkness*, "[t]he conquest of the earth, which mostly means the taking it away from those who have a different complexion or slightly flatter noses than ourselves, is not a pretty thing when you look into it too much. What redeems it is the idea only. An idea at the back of it; not a sentimental pretence but an idea; and an unselfish belief in the idea — something you can set up and bow down before ... " (Conrad 1971: 7). Sir Evelyn Baring (Lord Cromer), British "advisor" to the Khedive of Egypt from 1883 to 1907 and a good friend of Gertrude Bell, best expressed the "idea" or the sense of imperial mission toward the so-called barbarians: "one of the first qualifications necessary in order to play the part of a saviour of society is that the saviour should believe in himself and in his mission. This the Englishman did. He was convinced that his mission was to save Egyptian society, and, moreover, that he was able to save it" (Cromer 1909: 2, 124).

Bell's own naïve belief in her country's imperial glory did not go unnoticed. The *Athenaeum* reviewer (1907) and Elizabeth Robins both observed that when a Syrian praises English rule before Bell it is highly probable that he did so as an act of courtesy toward his host. The *Athenaeum* reviewer maintains that "the praises of English rule in Egypt, which Miss Bell heard on all hands, might, were it not for the politeness of the East, be thought valuable as evidence ... " (159). Robins too writes that although Bell "in other matters critical beyond most can take a simple-minded delight in a Moslem's compliment to her race as though the Oriental, with his habit of courtesy, would not have turned a flattering phrase as easily for Teuton, Gaul, or Japanese" (*Fortnightly*, 492). As will be seen, Bell not only uncritically accepts compliments from Orientals, she even fails to observe that she has selected only pro-British people to express their feelings on British rule in Egypt.

Bell's "simple-minded" assurance of the achievements of British rule is at odds with her "critical" ability. While on the one hand she seems to be carefully portraying only those characters who will support her opinions, her awareness of the political games of European powers leads her to question the very notion of impe-rialism. In *Desert and the Sown* there is a strange mixture of lapses in elementary analysis and a shrewd knowledge of international power struggles.

Bell's character portrayal suggests her desire to present British rule as "good" as opposed to "Oriental" administration. As can be seen from her reproduction of the opinions of the people she encounters, she is selectively giving a voice to only those who would support her attitude toward British imperialism. All the people who praise English rule or express their desire to escape from the Ottoman empire are either Christians or Druzes. Namrud, her host and a Christian, praises British justice in Egypt which has replaced blood feuds by a strict legal system. As the host and a family friend he is obliged by tradition and politeness to make Bell as comfortable as possible. The treasurer of Kal'at el Husn who argues that even the Muslim population would rather be ruled by the English is not only a Christian but also, like Bell, a guest in a Christian household. Unconsciously or consciously, Bell does not notice the personal biases of her interlocutors. Oriental politeness aside, these two individuals have very good private reasons for applauding the British administration.

Like the Christians, the Druzes too support British rule and wish they could take refuge in Egypt. From the information Bell herself provides we can see that Druze opinion is highly prejudiced for political and religious reasons. Politically the Druzes know the value of friendship with the British and they have "not yet forgotten our [British] interference on their behalf in 1860." In matters of religion they hate the Turks and there exists an "unbridged gulf of hatred between them [the Druzes] and Islam." Basing her claims on this selective material Bell opines that "the moral is obvious," the Syrian "wishes that he were under the rule that has given wealth to Egypt" (Bell 1908: 58).

Bell not only seems oblivious to the fact that she is citing the opinions of Great Britain's allies (for religious and political reasons), she also seems to deliberately ignore the feelings of those who might not have a good word to say about the English colonial enterprise. Of course we cannot read the author's mind or presume to know exactly why she told her tale in a particular manner, but it does strike one as peculiar, at least, that important people who are not pro-British don't get a chance to air their views on Egypt. Yusef Effendi, the governor of the turbulent Druze area, and his treasurer Milhem Ilian are just a few such characters.

Yusef Effendi, as Bell informs us, is aware of the problems of ruling the Druze areas and is anxious about the presence of an Englishwoman there. He is so disturbed that every day he dispatches three telegrams to the Vali of Damascus to keep him informed of her movements and the Vali, we later hear, fell sick out of anxiety the moment he heard of a potential British spy in the Jebel Druze. Instead of reporting Yusef Effendi's opinions, Bell dwells on the Druze point of view and identifies herself with them.

Anxious about Bell's presence, Milhem even takes vigorous measures to oppose her. Again Bell is aware of this and is consequently cautious about her movements lest he doubt the "innocence of [her] journey." Milhem very cleverly gives her a letter of introduction to Sheikh Mohammad en Nassar, a letter that prevents her from pursuing her journey: "I have a shrewd suspicion that Milhem's letter, which had been handed to me sealed, so that I had not been able to read it, was of the nature of that given by Praetus to Bellerophon when he sent him to the King of Lycia, and that if Muhammad was not commanded to execute the bearer on arrival, he was strongly recommended to discourage her project" (ibid., 105). Ultimately, after Nassar deliberately suggested a style of exploration that would be too time consuming, Bell had to abandon some of her plans to survey the Safa.

To judge by Yusef Effendi and Milhem's behavior, their opinions would have been very disagreeable to Bell. We have already seen her justifying British rule in Egypt in spite of nationalist agitation there, and from a 1903 entry in her diary on India we can tell that she does not tolerate any criticism of British imperialism. While visiting India as the Viceroy's guest at the Delhi Durbar of 1903 Bell passed through Calcutta where she met

> a member of the Council, and an ardent politician; not an effete Bengali, but an educated member of the fighting races. . . . He is I should say, a dangerous man. He talked about English and the Indians. It's an awful problem, the relations with the natives who are receiving, through our good offices, an education which makes

them feel that they are in every respect the equal of the best of us. He talked most excitedly and eloquently, saying that we use the country for ourselves (Burgoyne 1958: 149).

Considering that Bell finds such opinions dangerous and absurd, and bearing in mind that she had prefaced the *Desert and the Sown* with the statement that the English "are the people who could best have taken Syria in hand," it is perhaps not too far-fetched to conjecture that she unconsciously suppressed some offensive opinions on English rule in Egypt.

Bell believed firmly that the West was superior to the Orient and that the Orient was better off when ruled by the British. Like Lord Curzon, viceroy of India and her close friend, she felt that the British empire was "good" for the Orientals. According to Lord Curzon, "wherever this Empire has extended its borders . . . there misery and oppression, anarchy and destitution, superstition and bigotry, have tended to disappear, and have been replaced by peace, justice, prosperity, humanity, and freedom of thought, speech and action."[7] In Bell's own words, the Eastward facing Sphinx of Antioch "still remembers that the Greek she knew marched up from Babylonia, and since even the Romans did not teach her that the living world lies westward, I could not enlighten her, and so left her watching for some new thing out of the East" (Bell 1908: 325–26). It seems as if she is suggesting that culture, law and order, comes from the West to the East, to the place that is dead and has been a corpse for many years.

Bell's attitude toward the East is not unique: "the White Man's burden" was the traditional justification for the empire. Her imperialism, however, is complicated by the fact that it is so thoroughly British. She is convinced of the rightfulness of the British empire alone and resents the imperialism of other nations. This leads her to critique the involvement of other European nations in the politics of the Ottoman empire and to take note of the devastation that foreign powers have wrought in Syria, and thus indirectly to question the assumption that all "good" comes out of the West.

Bell's awareness of the past glory of Aleppo leads her to analyze the causes of its present decay. She feels that "it has been caught between the jealousies of European concession hunters," namely the French and the German. From the "native sources in Aleppo" — the selection of which might well have been biased — she learns that the French and the Germans have constantly thwarted each other's attempts in providing a good railway system to facilitate the merchants of Aleppo. Between their rivalry for economic control of the area they have done it no service. While Bell would never admit that British economic control led to economic and political instability in Egypt, she is quick to observe the mistakes of other Western nations.

Bell lays part of the blame for Aleppo's decay on the Ottoman government itself, which has depleted the city's strength by constantly recruiting baggage camels for the Yemen War, yet at the same time she is aware that the Ottoman empire in turn has been destabilized by the European powers. When a Damascene informs her that Turkey has been restricted from functioning as it should because of the intervention of foreign nations, she heartily agrees. The Damascene, referring probably to the Greek War of Independence (the Greek rebellion from the Turkish point of view) and to the Russo–Turkish War of 1877–1888 after the famous "Bulgarian Atrocities" issue, argues that

> the evils under which we suffer are due to the foreign nations who refuse to allow the Turkish empire to move in any direction. When she fights they take the fruits of victory from her, as they did after the war with the Greeks. What good is it that we should conquer the rebellious Albanians? The Bulgarians alone would gain advantage ... (Bell 1908: 152).

While Bell assents to this she does not comment on Britain's role as one of those "foreign nations".

Although Bell does not question the efficacy of British imperialism she does seem to have some doubts about the nature of imperialism per se. Perhaps it was these early questionings that led her to declare in 1919 that Arabs should rule themselves. In 1918 Bell was certain that the Arabs should be ruled by the British, but in a year's time she turned around completely. It is interesting to note that the wording and sentiment of her 1918 and 1919 report on Mesopotamia (Iraq) echoes those found in the *Desert and the Sown*. In 1918 she wrote that "in Mesopotamia they want us [the English] and no one else, because they know that we'll govern in accordance with the custom of the country"; and in 1919 she wrote that if the Arab administration of Mesopotamia crumbles "its failure will be attributed, not to inherent defects, but to British indifference and French ambition. . . ." [8] The same vacillation that she expressed in 1907 now seems to have stabilized in one direction. In fact, her doubts about imperialism seem to have increased, for now she even holds Britain partially responsible for the problems in Iraq.

Bell's biographer, H.V.F. Winstone (in *Gertrude Bell*, 1978) calls her comments of 1919 an "inexplicable volte face," and Susan Goodman, another biographer (*Gertrude Bell*, 1985), feels that this sudden change could be attributed to her friendship with T.E. Lawrence. Although Sarah Graham-Brown (in her introduction to the 1985 edition of *Desert and the Sown*) does not attempt to analyze the causes motivating Bell's turnaround, she does mention that the horrors of the First World War shook Bell's faith in the world order she so trusted, suggesting that perhaps this might have been one of the reasons for her abrupt decision.

It is not appropriate to re-evaluate Bell's previous life and work on the basis of the change of opinion she expressed in later years for it is possible that the emotionally devastating experiences she underwent in her personal life from 1909 to 1914 caused her to question her society's norms and conventions. She fell passionately in love with a married man, Lieutenant-Colonel Charles Doughty-Wylie, who refused to defy social convention by divorcing his wife and marrying her. Absolutely wretched, Bell became self-destructive and planned a desert journey to Hail, in the heart of the Arabian peninsula, at a time when that area was torn apart by inter-tribal warfare. In her agony she wrote to Domnul, Sir Valentine Chirol, at the start of her journey in 1914:

> The world must get along without me for a bit. Anyhow, I shall be glad to go. I want to cut all links with the world, and this is the best and wisest thing to do. . . . Oh, Domnul, if you knew the

way I have paced backwards and forwards along the floor of hell for the last few months, you would think me right to try for any way out. I dont [*sic*] know that it is an ultimate way out, but its [*sic*] worth trying. (Dearden 1969–70: 471).

And a year later, when she feared that Dick (Doughty-Wylie) would die as he led the landing on the Gallipoli peninsula at the outbreak of the First World War (he did), she even suggested suicide:

Feb 26 [1915]. I can't sleep — I can't sleep. It's one in the morning of Sunday. I've tried to sleep, every night it becomes less and less possible. You, and you, and you are between me and my rest; but out of your arms there is no rest. Life, you called me, and fire. I flame and am consumed. Dick, it's not possible to live like this. When it's all over you must take your own. You must venture — is it I who must breathe courage into you, my soldier? Before all the world, claim me and hold me for ever and ever. . . . If it's honour you think of this is honour and the other dishonour. If it's faith you think of, this is faithfulness — keep faith with love. . . . Take this letter and lay it somewhere near your heart that the truth of it may bore its way into you through the long months of war. I've finished. If you love me, take me this way — if you desire me for an hour, then have that hour, and I will have it and meet the bill. . . . And if you die, wait for me — I'm not afraid of that other crossing; I will come to you (ibid., 486).

The painful memory of this relationship remained with her the rest of her life even though she tried to forget it by immersing herself in military work. The horrors of the war too raised doubts in her mind about Western civilization and in December 1914 and January 1915 she wrote to Domnul,

I hear that on Xmas Day there was almost the peace of God. Scarcely a shot was fired, the men came out of the trenches and mixed together, and at one place there was even a game of football between the enemies. Strange, isn't it? I expect many strange things happen at either end of the scale — amazing relapses into savagery and amazing returns to humanity. . . . Sometimes we recover lost ground and find all our wounded carefully bound up and laid in shelter; sometimes we find them all bayoneted — according to the regiment, or the temper of the moment, what do I know? But day by day it becomes a blacker weight upon the mind.

[and]

My work goes on — quite continuous, very absorbing, and so sad that at times I can scarcely bear it. . . . The waste, the sorrow of it all. . . . Here we sit, and lives run out like water with nothing done (Burgoyne 1961: 21–22).

To reassess Bell's entire life and work from the standpoint of her change in attitude toward the end of her life might very well be an unreliable enterprise. One can only go so far as to observe that it appears that the seeds of that change lay in her as early as 1907 in her constant vacillation between Orientalism and non-Orientalism, imperial virtue and imperial vice.

Though Bell was disheartened with the state of Western civilization and had begun having doubts about Britain's abilities to discharge its imperial duties, she never took a stance as radical as that of the anti-imperialist British diplomat, Wilfred Scawen Blunt (1840–1922). In a diary entry dated 9 January 1896, Blunt wrote,

We [England] have now managed in the last six months to quarrel violently with China, Turkey, Belgium, Ashanti, France, Venezuela, America, and Germany. This is a record performance, and if it does not break up the British Empire nothing will. For myself I am glad of it all, for the British Empire is the great [*sic*] engine of evil for the weak races now existing in the world — not that we are worse than the French or Italians or Americans — indeed, we are less actively destructive — but we do it over a far wider area and more successfully (Blunt 1921: 212).

Bell was as aware as Blunt of Britain's political games in Egypt and the Arabian peninsula, but she never expressed this degree of cynicism with Britain's imperial policies.

Bell's vision of the East as expressed in *Desert and the Sown* cannot be described in static terms since she constantly vacillated between an imaginative and imperial possession and domination of the Orient, and a sense of friendship and equality toward it. A

1905 letter to her mother, written while she was crossing the Syrian desert, reveals her belief in Western superiority and her awareness that Western power is subject to the inexorable force of time. Observing the sites of old ruined cities, she wonders if civilization truly marches on or if it can even be regarded as synonymous with Western culture:

> Race after race, one on top of the other, the whole land strewn with the mighty relics of them. We in Europe are accustomed to think that civilization is an advancing flood that has gone on steadily forward since the beginning of time. I believe we are wrong. It is a tide that ebbs and flows, reaches a high water mark and turns back again. Do you think that from age to age it rises higher than before? I wonder — and I doubt. But it is a fine world for those who are on the top of the world and a good world isn't it . . . (Bell 1927: 1, 209–10).

Although Bell is here suggesting typical East–West binary distinctions, she also knows that such differences are not based on Orientalist theories of innate superiority or inferiority. And while she feels on "top of the world" she also looks around her at older Oriental cultures and wonders whether European civilization is located at the highest position that has been attained.

As the memorials to Bell in England and Baghdad show, she, like Burton, existed in two cultures. The plaque at her home in England describes her as "scholar, historian, archaeologist, explorer, poet, mountaineer, gardener, distinguished servant of the state." She is seen as possessing the traits of the upper-class English lady, accomplished, educated and patriotic. In her other home, in Baghdad, she is remembered as "Gertrude Bell whose memory the Arabs will hold in reverence and affection." Not only did she belong to two cultures, but each one also claimed her as one of their own.

Notes

1. Edmund Swinglehurst, *The Romantic Journey: The Story of Thomas Cook and Victorian Travel* (1974): 76.
2. *The Cambridge History of British Foreign Policy, 1783–1919*, volume 3,

describes a very apt Punch cartoon on the Anglo–Russian agreement: "The Treaty was viewed with apprehension by the Persian nationalists, whose feelings were depicted in a cartoon in Punch, in which the British lion and the Russian bear are mauling a Persian cat. The lion remarks, 'You can play with his head, and I can play with his tail, and we can both stroke the small of his back.' The cat moans: 'I don't remember having been consulted about this' " (413).

3. That a woman like Bell belonged to such a League is certainly very strange. Bell's biographer, H.V.F. Winstone, feels that her alliance with the anti-suffrage movement in spite of her own liberated existence has to do with her conviction that she merited her own freedom as a result of her skills and achievements. However, Susan Goodman, another biographer, feels that the Anti-Suffrage League was Bell's natural home since it comprised all the well-to-do, upper-class, prominent women of London. To join the anti-suffrage movement was for Bell merely a matter of aligning herself with her "social fraternity".

4. A prolific author, Bell wrote numerous popular and scholarly accounts of her expeditions in the East: *Safer Nameh. Persian Pictures*, 1894, a collection of lively essays on her stay in Persia; *Poems from the Divan of Hafiz*, 1897, a translation of the works of the Persian poet Hafiz; *A Thousand and One Churches*, 1908, an archaeological study written in collaboration with Sir William Ramsay; *Amurath to Amurath*, 1911, a travel account; *Palace and Mosque at Ukhaidir*, 1914, an archaeological study. In addition to these books she published numerous scholarly articles and also wrote important official reports analyzing the political conditions of the Middle East.

5. In 1881–1882 Colonel Arabi Pasha of the Egyptian army led a nationalist anti-foreign movement in Egypt for the overthrow of European economic imperialism of his country. A number of British were killed during the riots that ensued in Alexandria and as a result the English government intervened militarily in 1882 and occupied Egypt.

6. In *Earlier Letters* Elsa Bell gives a comic account of her sister's careful attention to social propriety. "The atmosphere of deference to convention in which Gertrude had been brought up," she writes, "perhaps explains the first impression she made on Mrs. Hassal, the wife of her tutor Arthur Hassal. Mrs. Hassal thought her prim. I can quite understand it. I can see Gertrude sitting very upright, rather self-conscious, what we used to call affected, anxious to make a good impression, and I can imagine the effect was prim" (Richmond 1937: 99).

7. Lord Curzon, "The True Imperialism", *The Nineteenth Century* 63 (1908): 154.
8. Quoted in Susan Goodman's biography, *Gertrude Bell*, pages 94–95.

Chapter 6

Epilogue

As has been seen, nineteenth century British Orientalists were prone to make reductive generalizations and assertions about the Orient. Rather than view easterners or their cultures in their socio-political-historical context, they were apt to impose their own dogmatic views on the people and places of the Orient. It is easy, however, to fall into the same methodological trap when studying Orientalists. In his introduction to *Orientalism* Said has voiced his fears about the possibility of such distortions occurring in his analysis of Western perspectives of the Orient:

> And yet, one must repeatedly ask oneself whether what matters in Orientalism is the general group of ideas overriding the mass of material — about which who could deny that they were shot through with doctrines of European superiority, various kinds of racism, imperialism, and the like, dogmatic views of the 'Oriental' as a kind of ideal and unchanging abstraction? — or the much more varied work produced by almost uncountable individual writers whom one would take up as individual instances of author's dealing with the Orient. . . . Isn't there an obvious danger of distortion (of precisely the kind that academic Orientalism has always been prone to) if either too general or too specific a level of description is maintained systematically? (Said 1979: 8)

If one were to study a small sample of writers and use them to generalize about Western perceptions of the East, one would make the same mistakes as the nineteenth century Orientalists who perceived every Oriental to be, for example, barbaric, sensuous, or crooked simply because one of the Orientals whom they met was of that type. On the other hand, if one were to focus purely on the reductive notion of the Orient prevalent in the nineteenth century Western world and apply it to a study of a handful of writers one would be "Occidentalizing" them in the same way as the Orientalists who borrowed traditional opinions of the Orient and its people and used these ideas to stereotype Orientals as unchanging, non-developing types. I have tried to avoid such distortions by selecting popular and/or politically influential writers of nineteenth century England and observing their cultural and private views of the Orient.

Since the four writers I have studied were widely read by the general populace or, as in Bell's case, by policy makers, they can be regarded as representative of the general British view of the Orient; in spite of the fact that one is dealing with specific authors it would not be a distortion, in this case, to generalize somewhat from them about their culture's preconceptions of the Orient. While examining the representativeness of these writers I have also observed their restlessness with received opinion of the Orient and the independent views they formed of it on their travels. By so doing I have sought to escape the stereotyping tendencies which, as observed in earlier chapters, Said himself was prone to in spite of his intentions to the contrary. As a result of this study one comes to realize both the enduring power of Orientalist thought in nineteenth century England and also the possibility of resistance to that vision of the Orient. Orientalism emerges as a strong but not entirely unshakeable system of power over the East.

That Orientalist thought was deep-rooted in the four writers we have studied is beyond question. As a diplomat Morier was well aware of his country's power, and this feeling carried over into a sense of cultural superiority over the Orientals. Such notions of cultural power were so strong that even the civilian Kinglake behaved as though he represented England in the Orient and treated it as a place that he could conquer and dominate. The tenacity of Orientalist thought is particularly striking in Burton's inability to disregard his nation's political ambitions in the East or its cultural assumptions about the Oriental "other". Even as he traveled in the land of his predilection, as he called it, he carried within himself the "White Sahib" mentality toward Orientals and so great was his arrogance, both personal and national, that at times his descriptions reduced Orientals to the level of animals in his description of them. In Bell we saw not only this imaginative, cultural domination but also a strong conviction of the necessity of British political imperialism of the Orient. Like others of her day and age she used the notion of Oriental "inferiority" to justify the British right to rule over that territory.

The literary techniques of these writers were related to their attitudes in that the stylistic devices they used distanced them and their audience from their subject, the Orient. Characterization often became simply a case of imposing a label on the Orientals, a label that implicitly or explicitly defined the West and westerners as active, mobile, and "good", and the Orient and its people as static, "bad", and inferior. This style was particularly evident in Morier who, although writing about his experiences in Persia, carved up his characters in broad East–West divisions. While Kinglake did not make such explicit "good" versus "bad" statements, his imagery clearly suggested that he saw himself as the masculine westerner conquering the feminine East. Both Morier and Kinglake thus made it clear to the reader that they were outside and superior to the culture and people they were writing about.

Burton and Bell too were prone to sweeping, reductive generalizations of the Orient, thus indicating their superiority over it, but they also had far more subtle literary devices at their command. Burton often used an arid, scientific style to keep his objects at bay and to turn them into creatures and their practices into static, meaningless rituals. Bell's Orientalism, on the other hand, took the form of romanticization of the Orient and its inhabitants; a romanticization which in her hands became a convenient glass for regarding easterners as incompetent types that require British rule. Kinglake's imaginative conquest became, in her case, a genuine belief in British imperial glory.

However, in these very writers we also saw a resistance, with varying levels of intensity, to the reductive image of the Orient which they reflected and perpetuated. As creative writers they brought more than just their political and cultural notions to their travels; their works gave expression to their private feelings toward the Orient and as a result their vision of the East was contradictory and ambivalent: Morier developed an attachment for Hajji that transcended his static and generalized portrait of Orientals; Kinglake brought his natural skepticism to bear on the egoism of the English in the Orient; Burton went so far as to be as much at home in the Orient as in the West; and Bell developed an understanding and sensitivity for the individuals she met on her travels.

The stylistic devices used by these authors often involved their audiences in the life of the country in which they were traveling, in the concerns of the individuals that made up that magical term "the Orient". By their own understanding of characters, whether fictional or real, they destroyed the myths and stereotypes prevalent in the West with reference to the Orient. Morier, as we observed, maintained a clear difference between himself and his narrator, Hajji, but this distance broke down sometimes when he entered into the life of his central character's personal problems and confusions. As a result, his vision of the static, corrupt, decaying Orient was temporarily pushed aside and replaced by the universal image of a young man trying to make his way through life as best as possible. Unlike Morier, Kinglake knew very little about the Orient, too little even to communicate with anyone on his travels; but he had a keen eye and a sharp tongue for the antics of Englishmen in the Orient. Utilizing the persona of a devil-may-care, happy-go-lucky youth he gained the social sanction to step out of his culture and critique the self-image that Englishmen sought to impose on the Orient. He did not destroy the notion of Oriental "inferiority", but he did question the concept of Western "superiority".

Burton and Bell were far more involved in the life of the Orient than either Morier or Kinglake, and they were not only able to step out of their culture but also able to step into another culture with ease. Living the life of an Oriental on a pilgrimage, Burton's narrative often assumed the voice of an insider in Eastern society, thus drawing the reader into his point of view. His natural and homey participation in practical jokes, family disputes, and private concerns of individuals broke down the sense of an outsider observing another culture. Bell could not enter as completely as Burton into the lives of the people she encountered, but her style of recounting anecdotes and tales of and by the people she met on her travels gave the reader a sense of a multitude of individual voices rather than that of one Western voice describing the East.

Why did these writers continue to believe firmly in their culture's reductive, generalized, image of the Orient in spite of their openness to their personal experiences on their travels? Their lives spanned a century, and they lived through different phases of British political strength — and yet they all shared the same sense of belief in their cultural superiority. To some extent they must have inherited and internalized traditional Western ideas of the Orient that existed since the days of the rise of Islamic power: notions of inherent Oriental tendencies to sexual excess, lawlessness, disorder, deceit, and treachery. But could it be possible that they shared these notions of the Orient as "other" and "inferior" because they belonged to the upper class of their society? The four writers we have studied all belonged to the affluent section of British society: Morier's father was the Consul-General of the Levant Company in Constantinople and later His Brittanic Majesty's Consul; Kinglake's father was an established lawyer who could afford an Eastern holiday for him; Burton's unemployed father was sufficiently well off to send him to Oxford and to buy him a commission in the Indian army; and Bell's parents were among the wealthiest people in England. This is not to say that everyone from the upper class, from the group which possessed social power, would perceive Orientals in the same reductive light, but it is important to admit the possibility of a relationship between social status in England and Orientalism, and to explore the situation further.

What leads one to suspect that Orientalism in the nineteenth century is linked to social class is the fact that only the moneyed and powerful class could afford to travel to the Orient. And since these people naturally moved in the same social circle they would not face any challenge that would drastically modify their opinions. The social world of Oriental travelers was a very small one and even the four travelers we have studied shared not just similar social environments but even some common friends despite the fact that their lives, combined, spanned a century. For example, Morier was a friend of Thackeray who was also a good friend of Kinglake. Kinglake was a close friend of Monckton Milnes at whose home many literary friends like Thackeray and Richard Burton congregated. It was Monckton Milnes in fact who gave a party for the newly married Burtons (with Lord Palmerston as one of the guests) and launched them into London society when they had been snubbed by their respective families. Bell was a good friend of Thackeray's daughter, Anne Ritchie, and while on her travels in the Orient she visited with the descendants of Morier's father's in-laws, the van Lenneps. These writers were not personally acquainted with the other, and yet they shared a common type of society; not surprisingly they perpetuated the same sort of ideas toward the Orient, usually reductive and imperialistic, and sometimes humane.

Considering that Oriental travelers inhabited a very narrow social and intellectual world, it would be interesting and fruitful to look at the works of people who did not belong to the literary, social, or political elite. Individuals who traveled in the Orient as independent soldiers in the Ottoman army, or as one of Cook's clients, or purely by virtue of being born and brought up in the Orient should be studied to analyze the way social class affects their vision of the Orient. Whereas upper class Oriental travelers felt uneasy with the traditional Western vision of the East, perhaps the poorer travelers felt hostile toward the Orientalist vision.

Possible authors for such a study might be, for example, Charles Frederic Moberly Bell and William von Herbert. Bell, author of *From Pharaoh to Fellah* (1888), was born in Alexandria in 1847 to a man who was, according to Bell's daughter, E.H.C. Moberly Bell, "a partner in the firm of Peel and Co., . . . a man of integrity rather than of any brilliant intellectual attainment or business acumen. He never succeeded in making a fortune in Alexandria, nor even in leaving his family in a position of independence" (Bell 1927: 18). Upon the death of his mother in 1852, Moberly Bell was sent to England to be looked after by a widowed relative on his father's side, who herself was in financial difficulties. After his father died, his half-brother Cecil financed his schooling, but Bell realized that he would soon have to fend for himself. Unable to afford an education that would have led to a career in the Indian Civil Service he took a job as a clerk at Peel and Co. in Alexandria when only eighteen years old. By dint of hard work and perseverance he rose to become general manager of all but the cotton department of the firm in 1873. At the same time he worked as a journalist for different British newspapers until in 1890 he became manager of the London *Times*.

Pharaoh to Fellah, a book which Bell claimed he wrote around a few sketches of Egypt by a French artist for the sake of the money the publisher offered him, reveals his awareness of the Western perception of the Orient. He observed, as does Said, that the westerner often carried his own preconceived notions of the Orient and imposed it on the reality. Bell also realized that even when the Western traveler claimed to be academic and objective in his study of the Orient his methodological approach often distorted his vision of the Orient. The two main travelers (to Egypt) in the book are Scribbler, the Englishman, and Sketcher, the Frenchman. Scribbler is the academician, full of facts which, however, are very unreliable because he is not clear of their chronology. As Scribbler himself once says:

> It was the misfortune of my life . . . to acquire at an early age a considerable amount of desultory historical information, without any chronological sequence. By the time I was eighteen, I was deeply learned in various periods of history; my reading had ranged from Herodotus to Macaulay, or I should speak more correctly if I said from Macaulay to Herodotus, for I had the vaguest notion of what I will call the sequence of history. The longer I have lived the more convinced I am that half of even the educated world suffers from the same defect (Bell 1888: 50).

Self-knowledge, however, does not restrain Scribbler from attempting to educate the Turtle, a member of the British Parliament who firmly believed that he "individually represented a nation that ruled the waves." The information that the academic Orientalist, Scribbler, provides this maker of foreign policy is based on a very twisted methodological approach. Scribbler argues:

> Your Turk may be a brute, but he is not generally a contemptible one. He is probably a thief, but it is on a liberal scale. The Egyptian, as a governed animal possesses many excellent qualities; as a governing one, he is as a rule the incarnation of brutality, ignorance, servility, and corruption (ibid., 84).

Sketcher immediately observes the problems inherent in such sweeping generalizations and comments:

> That proposition . . . is peculiarly your own — one of good, general, uncompromising assertion; but before you thus condemn the whole race, is it not fair to remember that the Egyptian has been for thousands of years a subject race, while the Turk has been for as many hundreds a governing one; and that the vices you mention are only the natural consequence of the position they have occupied, not a vice of character (ibid.).

Scribbler misses the point of Sketcher's analysis and excitedly argues that Egyptians should be ruled by outsiders since they do not know how to rule themselves. "All which," comments Sketcher sarcastically, "is based on your assertion that the Egyptian can't rule."

But if Scribbler is quick to make assertions to prove that the Egyptians cannot rule themselves, Sketcher tends to form his opinions in an equally intellectually limited manner:

> The Sketcher was apt to form rapid judgments, and to evolve startling theories therefrom. Like the traveller who declared all women in Belgium to be ugly and red-haired, adding 'At least the one I saw was,' he was apt to argue from the particular to the general.
>
> 'That peculiar frame of mind,' he [Sketcher] said, . . . 'is due solely to the unit of coinage. You will find that every nationality corresponds to its monetary unit. In Egypt it is a piastre; and you will admit they are eminently a twopenny-halfpenny lot. In France it is the franc; and I confess we are trivial. In Germany it is the mark; not very much better. In England it is the sovereign; good,

solid, but heavy. In India it is the lakh; I don't know what a lakh is,' he added frankly 'but I believe it's a very large coin, in which the salaries of Anglo–Indian officials are paid, and it accounts for that supercilious air of superiority.'

But the Sketcher's judgment of character was not much more accurate than his knowledge of the Indian currency, and when he got to know the Nabob better, and had had the mysteries of the rupee explained to him, he squared his opinion with his theory, and found that the Anglo–Indian was, like his coin, inclined to undue self-depreciation (ibid., 78).

It is important to observe that Sketcher does not question his theory but merely forces his new opinion to somehow fit into it. Both Sketcher and Scribbler possess knowledge of some facts, but the way they use and apply them portrays a distorted view of the Orient and reduces people to accommodate their theories.

Finally all of them depart Egypt without having learned anything about the country. All they did was bring to it their own prejudices and guidebooks, and they leave with that same baggage:

> Nor did the party neglect the procession of the Mahmal, the orgies of the Mulid el Hossenayn, and that melancholy festival the Mulid el Nebbi. Are not they written in the book of Murray?
>
> And at last they felt that they had religiously performed their pilgrimage and 'done' Egypt. The Scribbler [the scholar] was going to shake from his feet the classic but unwholesome dust of the East. The Sketcher [the romantic] was mournfully regretting that he was not for ever able to bask in its sunshine ... while the Turtle [the member of parliament] felt that he had exhausted the Eastern Question, and for the future would be able to pose with increased authority as one who had studied Egypt upon the spot (ibid., 187).

Each one in his own way dominates the Orient, imposing his academic, romantic, and political preoccupations on Egypt, completely ignoring the country he is passing through. And finally when Sketcher and Scribbler compose a book on their travels they include "some facts," a few sketches to brighten it, and some "local colouring" in the form of a "preface at the end — that would be so excessively Egyptian, you know."

Thus in a comic style Bell identified the Western approach to the Orient through the opinions and attitudes of his little group of travelers. As early as 1888 he was well aware of the distortions that people bring to the Orient to satisfy their scholarly, imaginative, and political aspirations. While Bell's work critiqued the limitations of the Western approach toward the Orient, William von Herbert supplied an alternative vision of the Orient in his *Defence of Plevna*.

Very little is known of Herbert although he was the author of two books on the Russo–Turkish War and even a science-fiction novel. The little we know of his life is gathered from his statements about himself in *The Defence of Plevna*, 1895. He was of mixed German and English descent and brought up probably in a small town in England. From his account of the *Defence of Plevna* it appears that he had not been to London until after his experience of the Russo–Turkish war of 1877. At the age of eighteen he threw away a job in a merchant's office to join the War, aligning himself with the underdog, Turkey. He became a lieutenant in the Turkish army, and after the fall of Plevna was taken prisoner by the Russians, probably in December 1877. It seems he joined the British army after his release since he authored his book as *Captain* von Herbert. In 1895 he published the *Defence of Plevna*, a narration of the events of the War and of his personal experiences as a participant in it. Although the book was well-received by the *Athenaeum*, Herbert seems to have gained no personal prominence for he is not mentioned either in the *Dictionary of National Biography* or in any other similar index. He came from an obscure lineage and remained an unknown.

The Defence of Plevna is a powerful and moving narrative of the horrors of war which also evokes the lives and feelings of the individuals who participated in, and were victims of the Russo–Turkish war. As the Turkish army prepares for the siege he describes his last meeting with his seventeen-year-old girlfriend (a Turk) in the war-torn town of Plevna:

> We met at a corner of the garden, where there was a dogs' kennel, the inmates of which had died of starvation, and, unburied, were

sending forth a stench that attracted a crazy crew of carrion crows and croaking ravens. So ferocious were these birds in their disgusting greed that our approach did not disturb their ghastly labours. The girl had donned the garments usually worn by an old woman of her acquaintance to avoid detection. Some evergreen shrubs hid us from the soldiers who were continually passing in the street, with corpses bound up in scanty sacking — for there was no wood for coffins, and the raiment of the dead was always utilized — or with carts of arms or ammunition on their way to some redoubt. The sullen dawn of a winter day shed a ghastly light, that gave to all things a hideously unearthly aspect, and with the snow-laden roofs and trees made the surroundings appear as if they belonged to another world. . . . In the road, a shivering wretch in tatters was raking up a rubbish-heap in search of scraps of offal that might serve as food; two little outcast urchins, Bulgarians by their ragged garment, toddled through the slush, hand-in-hand, crying, but happy in the possession of a mud-begrimed crust, whilst a mangy cur followed them with hungry eyes and felonious intent; and a woman, with an evidently dying baby at a breast that refused to yield sustenance, stumbled along, bewildered in her indescribable misery (von Hebert 1895: 350–51).

In that nightmare vision the tragedy of the victims is paramount and their lives and sorrows take precedence over their "Oriental" nature. Throughout the tale we are informed not of "Orientals" but of the courage, or stupidity, or pride, or military and administrative abilities of the individuals who fought in the war or suffered through it as innocent bystanders. And the ultimate defeat of the Turks is not imputed to their "Oriental" incompetence but to the administrative and tactical problems they faced. Herbert deals with issues and people on their own merits, not through the mist of ethnic prejudices.

Herbert, in fact, vehemently refuses to make any East–West, Christian–Islam distinctions on questions of moral superiority or inferiority. He regards courage and patriotism as qualities that exist even in Turks and does not acknowledge brutality to be in any way an "Oriental" prerogative. Tracing the factors that led to the Russo–Turkish War Herbert writes

Meanwhile the insurrection of Bulgaria, planned and prepared by Russia, had broken out (June 1876). It was the Christian Bulgarians' war of annihilation against the Mahomedan minority. . . . Unmentionable horrors were committed in the name of the Saviour.

But the rebels had undervalued the Porte's vitality. The troops suppressed the revolt, paying the Christians back in their own coin with barbarism, incendiarism, outrages, slaughter, and wholesale executions.

Thus broke out the tenth Russo–Turkish War. It promised to be all the more bloody and barbaric from the fact that the rulers on both sides took care to stamp it as a 'holy' one.

A really grand patriotic movement made itself felt throughout the Turkish possessions. It was a question of existence (ibid., 3–5).

Of the ensuing brutalities of the war he argues that the

wounded prisoners were treated in exactly the same manner as their Turkish brethren. Isolated instances of barbarism will happen in every war and among the most civilised troops (*vide* the horrible occurrences in Bazeilles during the battle of Sedan), but it is a lie to say that maltreatment of the wounded or prisoners was habitual, or even frequent, with the Turks. The officers had strict orders — always obeyed and enforced, as I know from experience — to check excesses and bring offenders to book (ibid., 207).

In fact he feels the Turkish forces lost the war partly as a result of their commander Osman Pasha's compassion in sheltering some 500 families of Plevna: "What a hideous mockery it is that to obey the dictates of humanity should constitute an offence against an exact science (i.e. strategy) — which was undoubtedly the case in this instance; for had not the army been fettered by that cumbersome burden, it is quite possible that the sortie might have succeeded" (ibid., 347–48). All the so-called exclusively Western moral traits he applies to the Turks, thus breaking away from the stereotypes usually applied to them and regarding them as individuals and equals.

Herbert has transcended binary distinctions to such an extent that he neither Orientalizes nor Occidentalizes; instead he seeks to maintain an unprejudiced attitude towards both the East and the West, Christianity and Islam. Even under the most difficult circumstances, he tries to judge people as individuals, not types. After the fall of Plevna, the Russian soldiers took to drinking and looting, but Herbert was luckily rescued from them by Russian officers. He is full of praise for the officers and differentiates their conduct from that of their soldiers: "Their chivalry and courtesy, their magnanimous and unselfish hospitality, stand out in bold contrast to the disgraceful behaviour of the common soldiery."

His description of Oriental women is in striking contrast to the picture of the sexually dangerous Zeenab of *Hajji Baba*:

> On each occasion I was met in Plevna by my girlfriend, who did me many an important service. At midnight, at three in the morning, in the early dawn — whatever the hour — she was at the place of tryst, and always had something to give me — a cigarette, a drop of brandy, a loaf. It would lead too far to enumerate the extraordinary ruses she employed to deceive her father. She was cheerful, gentle, and a real comforter (ibid., 346).

The tryst and the escape from the father, activities that form the setting for a sexual encounter, are here merely means to get food to a tired soldier. And the girl is appreciated for her good nature rather than her sexual charm. Herbert goes on to say,

> It has been my lot to meet in Turkey two of the best specimens of womanhood — one a Jewess, the other a Mahomedan. I have known hundreds of Western Christian women, of all classes and many nationalities, but, outside my family circle, only one who could compare with these half-educated girls in heroism, patience, and sacrifice of self. True, there were never again opportunities for the display of the finest qualities of heart and head; . . . (ibid., 346–47).

Though Herbert is commenting on women from different cultural backgrounds and religions, there is no attempt at assessing their personalities on the basis of their background. Instead, he emphasizes the importance of context in drawing out an individual's heroic qualities.

Social class, however, cannot be the only influence on a traveler's perception of the Orient. Harford Jones, as the Envoy to Persia, must have moved among the upper classes of society, but his approach to the Orient ran counter to the dominant nineteenth century view of the East. Long residence in the Orient and his ability to mix freely with the Persians enabled him to transcend his Western perception of the Orient. His account of his stay in Persia and his criticism of *Hajji Baba* reveal his opposition to binary distinctions about "us" and "them" and his desire to understand the "other".

One particularly revealing passage shows the extent to which he had transcended binary distinctions. Commenting on the executions that take place in the Shah's court he says:

> If any of the King's sons are present, as some of them generally are, they all (. . .) stand by the side of the Shah. At this court, all presentations take place, all public honors are conferred, all promotions are declared, and, what may appear strange to us, all public executions take place, within twenty to thirty feet of the Shah. The present Shah, who is a very humane person, when he first came to the throne, whenever an execution took place, found himself obliged (. . .) to turn his head aside. Meerza Bozurg one day made a remark to me, which I think a very judicious one. He said, 'Our kings, speaking of them generally, are more careless about shedding blood than they otherwise would be, perhaps, from the circumstance of the frequent executions which take place before them; for depend upon it, the first sight of human blood, strikes all of us with more or less horror and remorse, but the oftener we see it shed, the lighter we esteem its value' (Jones 1834: 1, 421).

This passage challenges the myth of the blood-thirsty Oriental despot and places the Shah's behavior within a specific context which reveals how his personality has become what it is. Meerza Bozurg's remarks reveal that he is sensitive to Harford Jones' feelings and, by showing sensitivity, reveals that there is little difference between the feelings of easterners and westerners. Moreover, by valuing Meerza Bozurg's remarks, Jones shows his inclination to treat Orientals as friends and equals. In fact, throughout his account, Jones shows awareness of the traditional Western perception of the East and takes pains to distance himself from it.

One can only conjecture why some individuals were able to resist the dominant cultural view of the Orient more vigorously than others. Social class, experience, personality, knowledge, political climate, emotional need, and a host of other factors probably combined in some special way to give rise to a perception of the Orient that ran counter to the dominant Western view of the East. Travel accounts that opposed the traditional perception of the Orient were not as popular as *Hajji Baba* or *Eothen*, but their presence and the unease of popular writers with the official view of the Orient indicates that the Western world's perception of the East was neither homogenous nor static.

In Morier, Kinglake, Burton, and Bell we saw the continuity of the reductive Orientalist vision of the East but also their capacity to challenge it. Orientalism, as observed in the first chapter, has a long history in Western intellectual and political attitudes toward the East. But in nineteenth century Britain this approach to the Islamic Orient was, in spite of its dominance, most likely to be challenged, or at least questioned, since English interests in India often led Britain to ally itself with its traditional enemy, the Ottoman empire, against the other European colonial powers. And just as British policy toward the Islamic Orient vacillated between alliance and alienation, the English men and women in the East too, for political and personal reasons, fluctuated between Orientalism and non-Orientalism. Travelers like Morier, Kinglake, Burton, and Bell carried their awareness of national power to the Orient but were not completely blinded by their sense of imperial glory. Sometimes consciously, and often unconsciously, they had the independence of mind to critique the very Orientalism they espoused.

The threat to the traditional concept of the East was even more visible in the works of lesser known nineteenth century writers like Moberly Bell, William von Herbert, and Harford Jones. A study of these and other similar writers would probably reveal that Orientalist thought was not the only vision of the Orient that existed in nineteenth century England and that running parallel to the dominant vision of the Orient there existed a less known, less popular, counter-current that mocked and challenged it.

Bibliography

Abdel-Malek, Anouar. "Orientalism in Crisis". *Diogenes* 44 (1963): 103–40.

Abdullah, Achmed and T. Compton Pakenham. *Dreamers of Empire*. New York: Frederick A. Stokes Company, 1929.

Al-Azmeh, Aziz. "The Articulation of Orientalism". *Orientalism, Islam and Islamists*. Asaf Hussain, Robert Olson, and Jamil Qureshi, eds. U.S.A.: Amana Books, 1984.

Amelinckxi, Frans C. and Joyce N. Megay. *Travel, Quest and Pilgrimage as a Literary Theme: Studies in Honor of Raino Virtanen*. Ann Arbor: Society of Spanish and Spanish–American Studies, 1978.

Arberry, A.J. *Oriental Essays: Portraits of Seven Scholars*. New York: Macmillan, 1960.

Assad, Thomas J. *Three Victorian Travellers: Burton, Blunt, and Doughty*. London: Routledge and Kegan Paul, 1964.

Baker, Ernest A. *The Age of Dickens and Thackeray*. The History of the English Novel. 12 vols. New York: Barnes and Noble, 1936. Vol. 7.

Barker, Francis, Peter Hulme, Margaret Iversen and Diana Loxley, eds. *Europe and its Others*. Proceedings of the Essex Conference on the Sociology of Literature. 2 vols. Colchester, U.K.: University of Essex, 1985. Vol. 1.

Beckford, William. *Vathek*. Roger Lonsdale, ed. London: Oxford University Press, 1970.

Bell, C.F. Moberly. *From Pharaoh to Fellah*. London: Wells Gardner, Darton, and Co., 1888.

Bell, E.H.C. Moberly. *The Life and Letters of C.F. Moberly Bell*. London: Richards Press, 1927.

Bell, Gertrude Lowthian. *Syria: The Desert and the Sown*. London: William Heinemann, 1908.

——. *Persian Pictures*. First edition 1894. London: Ernest Benn, 1928.

Bell, Lady Florence. *The Letters of Gertrude Bell*. 2 vols. New York: Boni and Liveright, 1927.

Benaboud, M'hammad. "Orientalism and the Arab Elite". *The Islamic Quarterly* 26: i (1982): 3–15.

Bercovici, Alfred. *That Blackguard Burton!* New York: Bobbs-Merrill, 1962.

Bishop, Jonathan. "The Identities of Sir Richard Burton: The Explorer as Actor". *Victorian Studies* 1 (September 1957): 119–35.

Blake, Gerald, John Dewdnew and Jonathan Mitchell, eds. *The Cambridge Atlas of the Middle East and North Africa*. Cambridge; New York; Australia: Cambridge University Press, 1987.

Blunt, Wilfred Scawen. *My Diaries, Being a Personal Narrative of Events 1888–1914*. Vol. 1. New York: Alfred A. Knopf, 1921.

Brodie, Fawn M. *The Devil Drives: A Life of Sir Richard Burton*. New York: Norton, 1967.

Brown, Wallace Cable. "The Popularity of English Travel Books About the Near East, 1775–1825". *Philological Quarterly* 15: iv (1936): 70–80.

——. "Prose Fiction and English Interest in the Near East, 1775–1825". *Publications of the Modern Language Association of America* 53 (1938): 827–36.

Browne, Edward Granville. Introduction. *The Adventures of Hajji Baba of Ispahan*. By James Morier. London: Methuen and Co., 1895.

——. *A Year Amongst the Persians: Impressions as to the Life, Character, and Thought of the People of Persia Received During Twelve Months' Residence in That Country in the Years 1887–1888*. 3rd. ed. London: Adam and Charles Black, 1950.

Brydges, Sir Harford Jones. *The Persian Revolution of 1905–1909*. London: Frank Cass, 1910.

——. *An Account of the Transactions of His Majesty's Mission to the Court of Persia in the Years 1807–11. To Which is Appended a Brief History of the Wahauby*. 2 vols. London: John Bohn, 1834. Vol.1.

Burgoyne, Elizabeth. *Gertrude Bell: From Her Personal Papers 1889–1914*. London: Ernest Benn, 1958.

Burgoyne, Elizabeth. *Gertrude Bell: From Her Personal Papers 1914–1926*. London: Ernest Benn, 1961.

Burton, Isabel. *The Life of Sir Richard F. Burton*. 2 vols. London: Chapman and Hall, 1893.

Burton, Richard. *Personal Narrative of a Pilgrimage to Al-Madinah and Meccah*. Isabel Burton, ed. Memorial Edition. 2 vols. London: Tylston and Edwards, 1893.

———— (trans.) *The Book of the Thousand Nights and a Night*. 10 vols. Privately printed by the Burton Club, n. d. Vol. 1.

————. *The City of the Saints and Across the Rocky Mountains to California*. Fawn M. Brodie, ed. New York: Alfred A. Knopf, 1963.

Butor, Michel. "Travel and Writing". *Mosaic* 8.i (Fall 1974): 1–16.

Carroll, E. Malcolm. *French Public Opinion and Foreign Affairs 1870–1914*. New York; London: The Century Company, 1931.

Case, Lynn M. *French Opinion on War and Diplomacy During the Second Empire*. Philadelphia: University of Pennsylvania Press, 1954.

Chandler, Frank Wadleigh. *The Literature of Roguery*. 2 vols. Boston and New York: Houghton, Mifflin, 1907. Vol. 2.

Chew, Samuel C. *The Nineteenth Century and After*. A Literary History of England. Albert C. Baugh, ed. 4 vols. New York: Appleton-Century-Crofts, 1948. Vol. 4.

————. *The Crescent and the Rose: Islam and England During the Renaissance*. New York: Oxford University Press. 1937.

Clifford, James. Rev. of *Orientalism*, by Edward Said. *History and Theory* 19.i (1980): 204–23.

Coblentz, H.E. Rev. of *The Desert and the Sown*, by Gertrude Bell. *The Dial* 152 (January–June 1907): 371–74.

Conant, Martha Pike. *The Oriental Tale in England in the Eighteenth Century*. First edition 1908. New York: Octagon Books, 1966.

Conrad, Joseph. *Heart of Darkness*. Robert Kimbrough, ed. Norton Critical Edition. Rev. ed. New York: Norton and Co., 1971.

Cooter, Roger. *Phrenology in the British Isles: An Annotated Historical Bibliography and Index*. Metuchen, New Jersey; London: The Scarecrow Press, 1989.

Courtney, Janet E. *The Women of My Time*. London: Lovat Dickson, 1934.

————. *An Oxford Portrait Gallery*. London: Chapman and Hall, 1931.

Cowlin, Dorothy. *A Woman in the Desert: The Story of Gertrude Bell*. Britain: Frederick Muller, 1967.

Cromer, Lord. *Modern Egypt.* 2 vols. New York: Macmillan Company, 1909. Vol. 2.

Cunningham, Allen. "The Wrong Horse? — A Study of Anglo–Turkish Relations Before the First World War". *Middle Eastern Affairs Number 4.* Ed. Albert Hourani. St. Anthony's Papers Number 17. Great Britain: Oxford University Press, 1965.

Curtin, Philip D., ed. *Imperialism.* The Documentary History of Western Civilization. New York: Walker and Company, 1971.

Curzon, George N. *Persia and the Persian Question.* 2 vols. London: Longmans, Green and Co., 1892. Vol. 1.

———. Introduction. *The Adventures of Hajji Baba of Ispahan.* By James Morier. London: Macmillan, 1895.

———. "The True Imperialism". *The Nineteenth Century* 63 (January–June 1908): 151–65.

Daniel, Norman. *Islam Europe and Empire.* Edinburgh, U.K.: Edinburgh University Press, 1966.

Dearden, Seton. "Gertrude Bell: A Journey of the Heart". *Cornhill Magazine* 177 (1969–70): 457–510.

Dekker, Thomas. *The Non-Dramatic Works of Thomas Dekker.* Ed. Alexander B. Grosart. 5 vols. New York: Russell and Russell, 1963. Vol. 3.

Downey, Fairfax. *Burton: Arabian Nights Adventurer.* New York; London: Charles Scribner's Sons, 1931.

Dunlap, Benjamin. "Kinglake's *Eothen*". *Studies in the Literary Imagination* 8: ii (1975): 77-91.

Elton, Oliver. *A Survey of English Literature 1780–1880.* 4 vols. New York: Macmillan Company, 1920. Vol. 1.

Fallon, Gretchen Kidd. "British Travel-Books From the Middle East, 1870–1914: Conventions of the Genre and Three Unconventional Examples". Dissertation. University of Maryland, 1981.

Farwell, Byron. *Burton: A Biography of Sir Richard Francis Burton.* London: Longmans, 1963.

Fedden, Robin. *English Travellers in the Near East.* Writers and their Works 97. London: Longmans, Green and Co., 1958.

Foster, E.M. *Abinger Harvest.* 1936. New York: Meridian Books, 1955.

———. *A Passage to India.* 1924. England: Penguin Books, 1965.

Foucault, Michel. *The Archaelogy of Knowledge.* Trans. A.M. Sheridan Smith. New York: Pantheon Books, 1972.

Foucault, Michel. *The Order of Things: An Archaelogy of the Human Sciences.* 1966. New York: Vintage Books, 1973.

———. *Language, Counter-Memory, Practice.* Trans. Donald F. Bouchard and Sherry Simon. Ed. Donald F. Bouchard. New York: Cornell University Press, 1977.

Freeth, Zahra and H.V.F. Winstone. *Explorers of Arabia: From the Renaissance to the End of the Victorian Era.* London: George Allen and Unwin, 1978.

Gail, Marzieh. *Persia and the Victorians.* London: George Allen and Unwin, 1951.

Gaury, Gerald de. *Travelling Gent: The Life of Alexander Kinglake.* Boston: Routledge and Kegan Paul, 1972.

Gendron, Charisse. *"Eothen* Again". *Victorian Newsletter* 68 (Fall 1985): 11–14.

Gibbon, Edward. *Gibbon's Decline and Fall of the Roman Empire.* Ed. Oliphant Smeaton. Rev. ed. 6 vols. London: J.M. Dent and Sons, 1957. Vol. 5.

Gobineau, Joseph Arthur. *Romances of the East (Nouvelles Asiatiques).* Collection of Foreign Authors 6. 1878. New York: Arno Press, 1973.

Goffman, Erving. *Frame Analysis: An Essay on the Organization of Experience.* New York: Harper and Row, 1974.

Goodman, Susan. *Gertrude Bell.* Berg Women's Series. U.K.: Berg Publishers, 1985.

Gould, Stephen Jay. *The Mismeasure of Man.* New York: Norton, 1981.

Grabar, Terry Harris. "Hajji Baba of Ispahan: A Critical Study." Dissertation. University of Michigan, 1962.

———. "Fact and Fiction: Morier's Hajji Baba". *Texas Studies in Literature and Language* 11 (Spring 1969–Winter 1970): 1223–36.

Graham-Brown, Sarah. Introduction. *The Desert and the Sown.* By Gertrude Bell. Boston: Beacon Press, 1985. v–xviii.

Gray, Herbert Branston. *The Public Schools and the Empire.* London: Williams and Norgate, 1913.

Gregory, Augusta. " 'Eothen' and the Athenaeum Club". *Blackwood's Edinburgh Magazine* 962 (1895): 797–804.

Harris, Frank. *Contemporary Portraits.* New York: Mitchell Kennerley, 1915.

Harvey, Charles H. *The Biology of British Politics.* London: Swan Sonnenschein and Co., 1904.

Hayward, Abraham. *A Selection from the Correspondence of Abrahan Hayward, Q.C. from 1834 to 1884. With an Account of his Early Life*. Ed. Henry E. Carlisle. 2 vols. London: John Murray, 1886. Vol. 1.

Herbert, Frederick William von. *The Defence of Plevna, 1877 Written by One Who Took Part in it*. London: Longmans, Green, and Co., 1895.

Heseltine, J.E. " 'The Royame of Verse' ". *The Legacy of Persia*. Ed. A.J. Arberry. London: Oxford University Press, 1953.

Hourani, Albert. Rev. of *Orientalism*, by Edward Said. *The New York Review of Books*. 8 March 1979: 27.

Hugh of Saint Victor. *Didascalion*. Trans. Jerome Taylor. New York; London: Columbia University Press, 1961.

Hussain, Asaf, Robert Olson, and Jamil Qureshi. Introduction. *Orientalism, Islam and Islamists*. Ed. Hussain, Olson, and Qureshi. U.S.A.: Amana Books, 1984. 1–4.

Hussain, Asaf. "The Ideology of Orientalism". *Orientalism, Islam and Islamists*. Ed. Asaf Hussain, Robert Olson, and Jamil Qureshi. U.S.A.: Amana Books, 1984.

Ince, Richard B. *Calverly and some Cambridge Wits of the Nineteenth Century*. London: Richard and Toulmin, 1929.

Jack, Ian. "English Literature, 1815–1832". *The Oxford History of English Literature*. 12 vols. Oxford, U.K.: Clarendon Press, 1963. Vol. 10.

Javadi, Hasan. "James Morier and his Hajji Baba of Ispahan". *Iran Society Silver Jubilee Souvenir 1944–1969*. Calcutta: Iran Society, 1970.

Jennings, Richard. Introduction. *The Adventures of Hajji Baba of Ispahan*. London: The Cresset Press, 1949.

Jewett, Iran Banu Hassani. "Kinglake and the English Travelogue of the Nineteenth Century". Dissertation. University of Maryland, 1964.

———. *Alexander W. Kinglake*. TEAS 324. Boston: G.K. Hall, 1981.

Kamm, Josephine. *Gertrude Bell: Daughter of the Desert*. New York: Vanguard Press, 1956.

Kamshad, Hassan. "New Lights on the Translation of Hajji Baba Isfahani". *Persica* 1 (1963–64): 70–75.

Keegan, P.Q. "Gleanings From Anglo–Oriental Literature, Vathek-Anastasius-Hajji Baba". *New Monthly Magazine* 11 (1877): 674–87.

Kernan, Alvin B. *The Plot of Satire*. New Haven and London: Yale University Press, 1965.

Kidd, Benjamin. *Social Evolution*. 1894. New York and London: Macmillan, 1895.

Kiernan, R.H. *The Unveiling of Arabia: The Story of Arabian Travel and Discovery.* London: George G. Harrap, 1937.

Kiernan, V.G. *The Lords of Human Kind: Black Man, Yellow Man, and White Man in an Age of Empire.* Boston; Toronto: Little Brown and Company, 1969.

Kinglake, A.W. *Eothen or Traces of Travel Brought Home From the East.* Rev. ed. New York: Wiley and Putnam, 1845.

———. "The Rights of Women". *Quarterly Review* 75 (1844–1845): 95–125.

———. Rev. of *The Crescent and the Cross; or, Romance and Realities of Eastern Travel,* by Eliot Warburton. "The 'French Lake' " *Quarterly* 75 (1844–45): 532–69.

Knox, Robert. *The Races Of Men, A Fragment.* First edition 1850. Florida: Mnemosyne Publishing, 1969.

Kolmodin, Johannes. "The Rev. Dr. Fundgruben". *Le Monde Oriental* 25 (1931): 67–80.

Kolodny, Annette. "The Land as Woman: Literary Convention". *Women's Studies* 1.ii (1973): 167–82.

Kucich, John. "Narrative Theory as History: A Review of Problems in Victorian Fiction Studies". *Victorian Studies* 28 (1985): 657–75.

Lamartine, Alphonse de. *A Pilgrimage to the Holy Land.* First edition 1838. New York: Scribner's Facsimilies and Reprints, 1978.

Lane, E.W. *The Manners and Customs of Modern Egyptians.* Rev. ed. London: J.M. Dent and Sons, 1923.

Lawrence, Thomas Edward. *Seven Pillars of Wisdom.* First edition 1926. New York: Doubleday, 1935.

Lesage, Alain-Rene. *The Adventures of Gil Blas of Santillane.* Trans. Tobias Smollet. Oxford: Oxford University Press, 1937.

Lewis, Bernard. "The Question of Orientalism". *The New York Review of Books* 29 (June 24, 1982): 49–56.

Marchand, Leslie A. *Byron's Letters and Journals.* 12 vols. Cambridge, Massachusetts: Harvard University Press, 1974. Vol. 3.

Meester, Marie E. de. "Oriental Influences in the English Literature of the Nineteenth Century". *Anglistische Forschungen* 46 (1915): 1–80.

Miller, Stuart. *The Picaresque Novel.* Cleveland: Case Western Reserve University Press, 1967.

Montagu, Lady Mary Wortley. *The Letters and Works of Lady Mary Wortley Montagu.* Ed. Lord Wharncliffe. Rev. ed. 2 vols. London: Swan Sonnenschein, 1893. Vol. 1.

Monteser, Frederick. *The Picaresque Element in Western Literature*. Studies in the Humanities 5. Alabama: University of Alabama Press, 1975.

Moore, Thomas. *The Poetical Works of Thomas Moore*. Ed. A.D. Godley. London: Oxford University Press, 1910.

Morier, James. *A Journey Through Persia, Armenia and Asia Minor, to Constantinople, in the Years 1808 and 1809*. London: Longman, 1812.

——. *A Second Journey Through Persia, Armenia and Asia Minor, to Constantinople, in the Years 1810 and 1816. With a Journal of the Voyage By the Brazils and Bombay to the Persian Gulf. Together With An Account of the Proceedings of His Majesty's Embassy Under His Excellency Sir Gore Ouseley*. London: Longman, 1818.

——. *The Adventures of Hajji Baba of Ispahan in England*. New York: J. and J. Harper, 1828.

——. *The Adventures of Hajji Baba of Ispahan*. Ed. C.J. Wills. London: Lawrence and Bullen, 1897.

Moussa-Mahmoud, Fatma. "Orientals in Picaresque: A Chapter in the History of the Oriental Tale in England". *Cairo Studies in English* (1961–1962): 145–88.

"Muhammad and the Religion of Islam". *Encyclopaedia Britannica*, 1985 edition.

Muir, Sir William. *The Life of Mohammad from Original Sources*. Ed. T.H. Weir. Rev. Ed. Edinburgh: John Grant, 1912.

——. *The Mohammedan Controversy, Biographies of Mohammad, Sprenger on Tradition, the Indian Liturgy and the Psalter*. Edinburgh, T&T Clark, 1897.

Nerval, Gerard de. *Journey to the Orient*. Trans. Norman Glass. New York: New York, University Press, 1972.

Ockley, Simon. *The History of the Saracens; Comprising the Lives of Mohammed and his Successors, to the Death of Abdalmelik, the Eleventh Caliph*. 5th. ed. London: H.G. Bohn, 1848.

Ouida. "Richard Burton". *The Fortnightly Review*. 79 (January–June 1906): 1039–45.

Paston, George. *At John Murray's. Records of a Literary Circle 1843–1892*. London: John Murray, 1932.

Phillot, D.C. Introduction. *The Adventures of Hajji Baba of Ispahan*. By James Morier. Trans. Shaikh Ahmad-Ikirmani. Calcutta: Asiatic Society of Bengal, 1905.

Pitts, Joseph. *A Faithful Account of the Religion and Manners of the Mahometans*. 4th ed. London: T. Longman and R. Hett, 1738.

Pratt, Mary Louise. "Conventions of Representation: Where Discourse and Ideology Meet". *Georgetown University Round Table on Languages and Linguistics*. Washington D.C. (1982): 139–55.

Pritchett, V.S. "Kinglake's *Eothen*: A Nineteenth Century Travel Classic". *Prarie Schooner* 44 (1970–71): 11–18.

Pritchett, V.S. *The Tale Bearers: Literary Essays*. New York: Random House, 1980.

Pruett, Gordon E. "'Islam' and Orientalism". *Orientalism, Islam and Islamists*. Ed. Asaf Hussain, Robert Olson, and Jamil Quereshi. U.S.A.: Amana Books, 1984.

Quennel, Peter. *The Singular Preference: Portraits and Essays*. London: Collins, 1952.

Ramm, Agatha. *Sir Robert Morier, Envoy and Ambassador in the Age of Imperialism, 1876–1893*. Oxford: Clarendon Press, 1973.

Reid, T. Wemyss, ed. *The Life, Letters, and Friendships of Richard Monckton Milnes, First Lord Houghton*. 2 vols. New York: Cassell Publishing Company, 1891. Vol. 1: 347–48.

Review of *Amurath to Amurath*, by Gertrude Bell. *Athenaeum* (January–June 1911): 151–52.

Review of *Eothen*, by Alexander Kinglake. *Athenaeum* 880–881 (September 1844): 803–5, 823–25.

Review of *Eothen*, by Alexander Kinglake. *The Dial* 55 (1913): 482.

Review of *Lalla Rookh: an Oriental Romance*, by Thomas Moore. *British Review* 10 (1817): 30–54.

Review of *Personal Narrative of a Pilgrimage to Al-Madinah and Meccah*, by Richard Burton. *Athenaeum* 1448 (July 1855): 865–66.

Review of *Personal Narrative of a Pilgrimage to Al-Madinah and Meccah*, by Richard Burton. *Edinburgh Review* 103: ccxii (1856): 186–204.

Review of *The Adventures of Hajji Baba of Ispahan*, by James Morier. *Quarterly Review* 30 (1824): 199–216.

Review of *The Adventures of Hajji Baba of Ispahan*, by James Morier. *Blackwood's Edinburgh Magazine* 15 (1824): 51–57.

Review of *The Adventures of Hajji Baba of Ispahan*, by James Morier. *The Oriental Herald* 1 (1824): 451–66.

Review of *The Desert and the Sown*, by Gertrude Bell. *Athenaeum* 4137 (January–June 1907): 159–60.

Review of *Zohrab the Hostage*, by James Morier. *Athenaeum* 257 (September 29, 1832): 625–27.

Richmond, Elsa. Ed. *The Earlier Letters of Gertrude Bell*. By Gertrude Bell. New York: Liveright Publishing Corporation, 1937.

Robins, Elizabeth. Rev. of *The Desert and the Sown* and *Amurath to Amurath*, by Gertrude Bell. "A New Art of Travel". *The Fortnightly* 89 (January–June 1911): 470–92.

Sackville-West, Vita. *Passenger to Tehran*. New York: George H. Doran, 1927.

Said, Edward. *The World, the Text, and the Critic*. Cambridge, Massachusetts: Harvard University Press, 1983.

———. *Orientalism*. First edition 1978. New York: Vintage Books, 1979.

Sandison, Alan. *The Wheel of Empire: A Study of the Imperial Idea in Some Later Nineteenth and Early Twentieth-Century Fiction*. London: Macmillan; New York: St. Martin's Press, 1967.

Schwab, Raymond. *The Oriental Renaissance: Europe's Rediscovery of India and the East, 1680–1850*. Trans. Gene Patterson-Black and Victor Reinking. New York: Columbia University Press, 1984.

Searight, Sarah. *The British in the Middle East*. New York: Atheneum, 1970.

Shakespeare, William. *The Riverside Shakespeare*. Ed. G. Blakemore Evans. Boston: Houghton Mifflin Company, 1974.

Shepherd, William R. *Shepherd's Historical Atlas*. 9th. ed. Totowa. New Jersey: Barnes and Noble, 1964.

Smith, Byron Porter. *Islam in English Literature*. Beirut, Lebanon: American Press, 1939.

Steegmuller, Francis, ed., trans. *Flaubert in Egypt: A Sensibility on Tour*. Boston; Toronto: Little Brown and Company, 1972.

Swinglehurst, Edmund. *Romantic Journey: The Story of Thomas Cook and Victorian Travel*. London: Pica Editions, 1974.

Symons, Arthur. *Dramatis Personae*. Indianapolis: Bobbs-Merrill, 1923.

Tibble, Anne. *Gertrude Bell*. London: Adam and Charles Black, 1958.

Tregaskis, Hugh. *Beyond the Grand Tour: The Levant Lunatics*. London: Ascent Books, 1979.

Trevlyan, G.M. *British History in the Nineteenth Century (1782–1901)*. London: Longmans, 1922.

Tuckwell, William. Introduction. *Eothen*. By A.W. Kinglake. Ed. William Tuckwell. London: George Bell and Sons, 1898. 9–18.

———. *A.W. Kinglake: A Biographical and Literary Study*. London: George Bell and Sons, 1902.

Turner, Bryan S. "Orientalism and the Problem of Civil Society in Islam". *Orientalism, Islam and Islamists*. Eds Asaf Hussain, Robert Olson and Jamil Qureshi. Brattleboro, Vermont: Amana Books, 1984

Warburton, Eliot. Rev. of *Eothen, or Traces of Travel Brought Home from the East*, by Alexander Kinglake. *Quarterly 75* (1844–45): 54–76.

Ward, A.W. and G.P. Gooch, eds. *The Cambridge History of British Foreign Policy, 1783–1919*. New York: Octagon Books. Vol. 3: 413.

Weinberger, Ava Inez. "The Middle Eastern Writings of James Morier: Traveller, Novelist and Creator of Hajji Baba". Dissertation. University of Toronto, 1984.

Weitzman, Arthur J. "Who Was Hajji Baba?" *Notes and Queries* 215 (1970): 177–79.

Wemyss, Alice. "The Birth of Hajji Baba as Seen Through the Letters of James Morier". *Persica* 7 (1978): 165–72.

Wemyss, Rosslyn. *Memoirs and Letters of the Right Hon. Sir Robert Morier, G.C.B. From 1826–1876*. 2 vols. London: Edward Arnold, 1911. Vol. 1.

Wiener, Joel H., ed. *Great Britain: Foreign Policy and the Span of Empire 1689–1971, A Documentary History*. 4 vols. New York: Chelsea House and McGraw Hill, 1972. Vols. 1 and 3.

Winstone, H.V.F. *Gertrude Bell*. New York: Quartet Books, 1978.

Williams, Raymond. *The Long Revolution*. New York: Columbia University Press, 1961.

Woodward, Sir Llewllyn. *The Age of Reform 1815–1870*. The Oxford History of England. 14 vols. 2nd ed. London: Oxford University Press, 1962. Vol. 13.

Wright, Denis. *The English Amongst the Persians During the Qajar Period 1787–1921*. London: Heinemann, 1977.

Yapp, Malcolm E. *Strategies of British India, Britain, Iran and Afghanistan 1798–1850*. Oxford, U.K.: Clarendon Press, 1980.

Zane, Kathleen J.C. "Paradigms of Place in Travel Literature: The Oriental Voyages of Nerval, Burton, Kinglake, and Chateaubriand". Dissertation. City University of New York, 1984.

Index

For Product Safety Concerns and Information please contact our EU
representative GPSR@taylorandfrancis.com
Taylor & Francis Verlag GmbH, Kaufingerstraße 24, 80331 München, Germany

www.ingramcontent.com/pod-product-compliance
Lightning Source LLC
Chambersburg PA
CBHW071507110726
47908CB00003B/759